ALASKA BICYCLE
TOURING GUIDE

ALASKA BICYCLE TOURING GUIDE

Including Parts of the Yukon Territory and Northwest Territories

Alys Culhane

Pete Praetorius

THE DENALI PRESS

Denali, a Tanaina Indian word meaning "the great one," is the native name for Mount McKinley. Mount McKinley, at 20,320 feet, the highest mountain on the North American continent, is located in Denali National Park. The lowlands surrounding this majestic mountain provide a diverse wildlife habitat for a variety of animals including grizzly bears, wolves, caribou and moose.

Copyright © 1989 by Alys Culhane and Pete Praetorius
Cover design by Ron Berry
Designed and typeset by Janos Sturm

Published by The Denali Press
Post Office Box 021535
Juneau, Alaska USA 99802-1535

ISBN 0-938737-17-1

TABLE OF CONTENTS

Foreword

Steve Cowper
Governor, State of Alaska

The gold seekers on the beaches of Skagway, Alaska, during the gold rush of 1898 were amazed to see a few hardy souls roll off the gangway of the steamships on two wheels. At the time, the Territory of Alaska had no roads—and it was winter. The men fully intended to ride their bicycles over the 3,000-foot Chilkoot Pass, then on down the Yukon River to the goldfields of the Klondike and the Fortymile Rivers. Some of them made it. Some of them went on to the the Bering Sea coast and boomtown of Nome—more than 800 miles on the frozen Yukon, riding in the ruts left by the runners of the dog sleds.

As you can see, bicycling in Alaska has a long and adventurous history. But today, you don't have to mount a winter trip down the Yukon to find stunning scenery and real adventure.

Alaskans already know that we've got some of the best summer bicycling weather in North America. They're familiar with an extensive system of state and private campsites along the highways, and the unlimited possibilities for mountain bike camping in state and national parks. But even long-time Alaskans may be surprised to find the kind of detail on trips, facilities and terrain included in this guide.

If you've picked up this guide outside Alaska, you'll definitely be surprised at what you'll find.

If you start your summer trip to Mount McKinley from my hometown of Fairbanks, in Alaska's Interior, you will likely begin riding in dry, 75 degree, windless summer air. And of course, you don't have to plan your riding schedule around day and night, since the Interior enjoys nearly 24 hours of daylight in June.

If you've planned a mountain bike trip from Anchorage, you won't have to travel far from downtown. The trailheads of Chugach State Park—nearly half a million acres of mountains and alpine valleys—are less than 15 miles from the international airport. You'll find the weather a little cooler than the Interior—about 55 to 65 degrees—but it should make it a little more comfortable riding in the mountains.

Or perhaps you'd like to use the Alaska Marine Highway as a jumping off point. The Southcentral ferries connect Kodiak Island with the mainland port cities of Prince William Sound, Homer and Seward, all on the major road system out of Anchorage. The ferry system also provides access throughout Southeast Alaska from Juneau to British Columbia and Seattle. The road systems out of Ketchikan, Sitka, Petersburg, and Juneau aren't extensive, but you can put together a staged trip from the top to the bottom of North America's last true rain forest. You'll get wet, but you'll remember the eagles, whales, seals and brown bear long after your shoes have dried out.

This guide is the only one of its kind, and it will prove invaluable to you on your trip through Alaska and Canada's Yukon Territory. I think you'll find that the opportunities for bicycle travel in the North are limited only by your imagination. The miners who biked to the Klondike in '98 proved that a long time ago.

Steve Cowper
Governor

Introduction

Alaska and Western Canada are suited for all types of bicycle riding. For cyclists who want a leisurely trip, ferries travel between a number of diverse and interesting towns in Southeast Alaska. For those who want to travel long distances on pavement, the Richardson, Alaska, Parks, and Glenn Highways are ideal for conventional touring. For mountain bikers, there are plenty of sideroads which aren't heavily travelled by vehicles. And everywhere, including Southeast Alaska, there are thousands of miles of trails and mining and logging roads. In the *Alaska Bicycle Turing Guide*, we have tried to strike a balance. Information is given on all of Alaska's main and secondary roads and in British Columbia, the Yukon Territory and the Northwest Territories, on the Klondike, Alaska, Haines, Top of the World, and Dempster Highways. Since we didn't have the time to do as much off-road riding as we would have liked, we've provided the names of individuals who are familiar with area trails.

We enjoyed the sideroads as much as the main thoroughfares. Getting from one major point to another became less important as we explored the places in-between. When we decided to ride the Dempster, we had no idea that this would be the high point of our trip. After much deliberation, we decided to hitch a ride from the Klondike Lodge outside of Dawson City, Yukon Territory to Inuvik, Northwest Territories. When no opportunities presented themselves, we pedaled up the road, uncertain about how we'd get back. This turned out to be the most scenic, and ecologically diverse ride of the summer. And without much difficulty, we got a ride back to our starting point.

After the Dempster, we did sidetrips to Eagle, McCarthy, Nabesna, and Wonder Lake. There was minimal traffic on these roads, and the people, who weren't "touristed out," were very friendly. This is not to say that Alaska and Yukon's main roads weren't enjoyable. The Richardson, Haines, Seward, and the Top of the World Highways offer spectacular views of diverse landscapes. If there is a philosophy behind this book, it's that Alaska and parts of the Yukon Territory and Northwest Territories covered in this guide, are special places—the slower you go, the more you'll enjoy the tour.

VISITOR'S CENTERS

All the major towns and cities in Alaska, and many in Canada have staffed information desks and brochures on lodging, eating establishments, and adventure activities as well as historical information. For Alaska information write: Alaska Division of Tourism, Box E-301, Juneau, AK 99811 or phone 465-2010 (Juneau) or 563-2167 (Anchorage). For Yukon information write: Tourism Yukon, Box 2703, Department VG88, Whitehorse, Yukon Y1A 2C6. For Northwest

Territories information write: Tourism Industry Association of the NWT, Box 506, Yellowknife, NWT, X1A 2L9.

MAPS

Most Visitor's Centers as well the Alaska Public Lands Information Office (see Chapter 19) have maps. However, some of the best maps we've seen are produced by Alaska Road and Recreation Maps. The maps contain information on roads and trails, fishing spots, campgrounds, viewpoints, points of interest, and mileposts. All but the Parks Highway Map have contour lines. The Parks Highway map costs $2.75; the others, $2.95. The maps are available at sporting goods stores, and at Book Cache stores throughout Alaska. Write: Alaska Road and Recreation Maps, Box 102459, Anchorage, AK 99510.

ALTERNATIVE TRANSPORTATION

There are three ways to get to Alaska. One way is via the Inside Passage. The Alaska Marine Highway System (Ferry System) stops in all the major Southeast Alaska towns, and cyclists can ride to the Interior from either Haines or Skagway. In addition to the Inside Passage, the Alaska State Ferries operate in the Southwest and Southcentral areas of the state: Prince William Sound, the Kenai Peninsula and the Aleutians. Unfortunately, there is no connecting ferry service between Southeast and Southwest Alaska. Effective May, 1989 there is a fee ($4.00-$28.00) to transport bikes on the ferry. For more information write: Alaska Marine Highway System, Box R, Juneau, AK 99811, or phone (800) 551-7185 (within Alaska) or (800) 544-2251 (outside Alaska).

There are some two dozen major airlines that serve Alaska as well as an equal number of charter airlines and air taxis that provide service solely within Alaska. It is best to consult a travel agent for specific flight information.

Finally, cyclists can reach Alaska from the Lower 48 via Canada.

In the summer months, the Alaska Railroad, the northernmost U.S. railroad and Alaska's only operating railroad, runs 470 miles from Seward and Whittier to Anchorage, and on to Fairbanks. Service is daily between mid-May and mid-September. The ARR features flag stop service between Anchorage and Hurricane Gulch and runs summer express trains from Anchorage to Fairbanks and Denali National Park. The baggage fee for bicycles on the express train is $6.00. A one day excursion to Seward is provided weekly. Whittier is the connecting point of the Alaska Railroad and the Alaska Marine Highway System. Ferries depart Whittier for Cordova and Valdez, in Prince William Sound as well as the Kenai Peninsula and the Aleutian Chain. There is no charge for bicycles on the self-propelled rail diesel cars which run between Whittier and Anchorage, Seward and Anchorage, and Hurricane Gulch and Anchorage. On all trains, bicycles are taken only on a space-available basis.

For more information contact: The Alaska Railroad, Pouch 107500, Anchorage, AK 99510.

Alascon Express Motor Coaches run between Fairbanks, Whitehorse, Haines and Skagway and carry bicycles on a space available basis. Alascon Express makes roadside stops. For a current schedule phone (800) 544-2206.

LODGING/CAMPING

Cyclists may camp formally in private, state, or Federal campgrounds. Permission must be obtained prior to camping on privately owned land.

Most private campgrounds have showers, laundromats and running water. Unfortunately, the majority of privately owned campgrounds, such as the Bear Paw RV Park in Valdez, cater mainly to RVer's. Most of these campgrounds are expensive, and have open, hard gravel tent sites.

Most of Alaska's State campgrounds have water, level dirt campsites, fire pits, picnic tables, and outhouses. Wood isn't provided, but can be scrounged up. At many of the campgrounds, campground hosts have information on the facilities and surrounding areas. The nightly site fee at Alaska State Campgrounds is $5.00. There is a $10.00 per night fee at the Chena River and Eagle River Recreation Sites. $50.00 annual passes are also available. Passes may be purchased at any state park office or from state park rangers. To order a pass, write: Annual Camping Pass, Box 107001, Anchorage, AK 99510-7001 or phone 345-5014 (Anchorage). Public rental cabins are available in several state parks. Most rent for $15.00 a night. Regional park offices have information on cabin reservations. The Alaska Parks System also maintains state historical parks, state historical sites, trails, and wilderness parks.

The U.S. Forest Service maintains about 25 campgrounds in the Tongass and Chugach National Forests. All campgrounds are available on a first come, first serve basis. Length of stay is limited to 14 days. Campground fees range from $4.00 to $8.00 per night. Forest Service campgrounds have level dirt campsites, fire pits, picnic tables and water. For more information write: USFS, Box 1628, Juneau, AK 99802 or phone 279-5541 (Anchorage).

The Bureau of Land Management maintains about 25 campgrounds in Interior Alaska. BLM campgrounds are free. The BLM has six public use cabins in the White Mountain National Recreation area. A user fee of $15.00 per party per night (maximum stay three nights) is required for permits, which may be obtained at the BLM Fairbanks District Office. Brochures describing BLM campgrounds are also available. Write: BLM, District Office, 1150 University Avenue, Fairbanks, AK 99709, or phone 474-2200.

The U.S. Fish and Wildlife Service has several wildlife refuges open to campers, although most are not accessible by highway. The Kenai National Wildlife Refuge, however, has several free campgrounds accessible from the Sterling Highway.

Level dirt campsites, fire pits, picnic tables, water, outhouses, picnic shelters with cookstoves, and free firewood are provided in most of the 48 Yukon Government Campgrounds. The campgrounds are well maintained and secluded, and we highly recommend them. For non-residents, the nightly fee is $5.00. Seasonal $25.00 permits are available at the campgrounds. Write: Director, Parks, Resources and Regional Planning, Government of the Yukon, Box 2703, Whitehorse, YT Y1A 2C6. In general, the majority of the Yukon Government campgrounds have shelters, while the majority of the Alaska ones do not.

Alaska and the Yukon Territory have numerous roadside lodges and cabins for rent. Because prices change from season to season, costs aren't given in this book. In 1988, the average roadside lodge room was $35.00 per night, except for the Denali area, where, because of high demand, the average price of a single room exceeded $100.00.

Alaska's 13 American Youth Hostels (AYH) are located in Anchorage, Delta Junction, Fairbanks, Girdwood, Haines, Juneau, Ketchikan, Seward, Palmer, Sitka, Slana, Soldotna, and Tok. The price range for members is from $5.00 to $10.00 per night. Most hostels provide travellers with separate male/female sleeping accommodations, showers, laundry and cooking facilities, and a common room. In accordance with international hosteling customs, alcohol consumption is prohibited. Most hostels are open between 5 p.m. and 9 a.m. with registration until 11 p.m. The annual membership fee for those under 18 is $10.00; for those over 18 the fee is $20.00. For additional information write: AYH Alaska Council , Box 91461, Anchorage, AK 99509-1461 (276-3635).

Juneau, Fairbanks, Anchorage, Dawson, Whitehorse and many smaller towns have bed and breakfast accommodations. For about $35.00 a night, home owners provide sleeping quarters and breakfast *Bed and Breakfasts in Alaska: A Directory* (Glacier House Publications, Box 201901, Anchorage, AK 99520) includes names, addresses and phone numbers. The book also includes maps of several B&B referral associations and state maps showing the general location of mentioned establishments. For bed and breakfast referral associations contact: Box 110624, Anchorage, AK 99551 (345-4761) and Stay with a Friend, 3605 Arctic Blvd., No. 173, Anchorage, AK 99503 (344-4006).

ROAD CONDITIONS/TERRAIN

Road conditions in Alaska vary from the Richardson and Parks Highways, which are paved, and have an eight foot shoulder for almost their entire length, to the Nabesna Road, which has a gravel surface, and no shoulder. The same holds true of the terrain. Alaska and Western Canada have their share of hills and passes.

The major Alaska and Yukon roads have state mile or kilometer posts, but as a result of road improvements, are not always an accurate indication of actual highway mileage. Since no other identifying markers exist, information in this book is based on these posts.

In 1988, at one time, over 20 miles of the Taylor Highway was torn up. This is the rule rather than the exception in Alaska and the Yukon, because heavy road construction is usually done in the summer when the days are long and the weather is warm. In places, for insurance reasons, road crews prefer to carry cyclists and their bicycles in a pilot car.

In the *Alaska Bicycling Touring Guide*, under each highway, Road Condition/Terrain, Water, Camping, Food/Lodging and Roadside Sight information is given in 50 mile sections.

PROFILE INFORMATION

To illustrate the roads' overall elevation gains and losses, profiles are included for every given highway. The profiles have a vertical exaggeration of 100:1. For this reason the hills on paper look steeper than they actually are.

The english measurements of miles and feet are given for the Alaska roads. The metric measurements of meters and kilometers are provided for the Canadian roads.

Each profile represents up to 50 miles of road, with 10 mile divisions. In the metric system, the equivalent is 80 kilometers. Conversely, 10 miles equals 16 kilometers.

Elevations are given in 500 foot intervals. The metric equivalent is 152.4 meters. In Canada, elevations are given in 150 meter intervals.

It is hoped that by keeping the linear and elevation distances the same, those unfamiliar with system will find it easy to make the transitions.

GETTING IN SHAPE

A twenty mile ride in Alaska, because of hills, inclement weather, and a lack of roadside facilities, can be comparable to a forty mile ride in the Lower 48. For this reason, out of shape riders should not overextend themselves.

The inexperienced touring cyclist should do some reading before The Big Adventure. A list of books on the subject of touring is provided at the end of this book.

GROUP TOURS/ADDITIONAL TOUR INFORMATION

For those who wish to travel first class, with a group, Back Roads Bicycle Tours offers 7 1/2 day guided Alaskan tours. For more information write: Box 1626, San Leandro, California 94577 or phone (415) 895-1783. Another organization is Engle Expeditions which also provides bike tours in Alaska. Write: Box 90375, Anchorage, AK 99509. Telephone: (800) 462-BIKE.

Bikecentennial, a national organization promoting cycling, has maps, books and other cycling products. Their *North Star Notes* gives route information for a Missoula, Montana to Anchorage, Alaska tour. One of the booklets in this series describes the route from Boundary to Anchorage via Fairbanks. The cost of this booklet for members is $5.95, for non-members, $6.95. Bikecentennial also offers guided tours and leadership courses. A year's membership is $22.00 for an individual, $19.00 for a student and $25.00 for a family. This includes the *Cyclist's Yellow Pages*, which lists Alaska State campgrounds. Write: Bikecentennial, Box 8308, Missoula, MT 59807, or phone (406) 721-8719.

FOOD:

Food in Alaska, especially in restaurants, tends to be more expensive than in the Lower 48. This is partially because the tourist season is short, and many area business owners depend on the tourist trade for their livelihood. Prices are also high because the majority of goods are shipped from outside.

Alaska is best known for its seafood products. Fresh salmon, crab and halibut is plentiful in the Southeast and Kodiak. Most roadside lodges offer full breakfast, lunch and dinner menus, and serve pie and hamburgers. Many lodges maintain small or limited grocery stores; some lodges sell groceries directly from the kitchen.

BICYCLING/CLOTHING RECOMMENDATIONS

All of the major highways can easily be done on touring bicycles, where there is a smooth asphalt or chipseal (cobbly) surface. For gravel surface roads such as the Dalton, Dempster, Nabesna, Denali Park, and McCarthy Roads, a mountain bike is a better choice. That is not to say that these roads can't or haven't been tackled by travellers on light- weight frames with dropped handlebars. Its just more difficult.

Bicycle repair shops in Alaska and Western Canada are few and far between. For instance, there are no shops on the Parks Highway between Fairbanks and Anchorage, or on the Richardson Highway between Valdez and Fairbanks. While extra tires aren't necessary, its wise to bring along extra tubes, cables, housing and spokes. A repair kit should include applicable allen keys, wrenches, and screw drivers. A pump, and a chain lubricant should also be carried. In addition to extra nuts and bolts, duct tape and baling twine are other useful emergency items.

Alaska and the parts of Canada covered in this book are vast areas, and the weather in all parts is variable. Southeast cyclists should be prepared for rainy conditions. The Alaska/Yukon bicycling season is shorter than the Lower 48's. Often snow will fall at higher altitudes in mid-May or late August. Cyclists should carry a wool sweater, socks, hat, a nylon or Gore-Tex windbreaker, and overpants. Lining panniers and sleeping bag stuff sacks with plastic bags will protect cameras and keep clothes and sleeping bags dry. A good waterproof tent with no-seeum mosquito netting is a necessity.

In the interior, there is less rain, but in the summer it can be warm, and in some places, like the Top of the World Highway, which has a semi-arid desert climate, water is limited. Carry extra fluids if possible.

Because of long daylight hours, flashlights are not generally required in the interior for midsummer riding. In Alaska's more southerly latitudes, lights are needed at night.

If the unforeseen breakdown occurs, phone orders are one way to get needed parts. Bike Nashbar (4111 Simon Road, Youngstown, OH 44512-0449) carries a complete line of components and touring accessories and will ship to Alaska and Canada. Their 24-hour phone number is (800) 345-BIKE. Mountain Bike Specialists also offers similar components and prices. Write: 340 South Camino del Rio, Durango, CO 81301 or phone (800) 255-8377.

R.E.I. (Recreational Equipment Inc.) sells some componentry and touring equipment, plus other outdoor gear, including stoves, tents, and sleeping bags. R.E.I.'s membership fee is $10.00, though membership isn't required. R.E.I. has a store in Anchorage. (See Chapter 27 for more information.) For additional information write: Box 88125, Seattle WA 98138-0125. Phone: (800) 426-4840.

BEARS

Alaska has a large bear population. For this reason, it is best to take precautions, even near towns. Avoid camping on trails, or on the banks of rivers which contain spawning salmon. In known bear areas, carry a noisemaker, such as a bell, radio or can filled with pebbles. Never take food into your tent, and put garbage in the proper containers. Clean cooking utensils, sleep away from cooking areas, and hang your food in a tree. To do this, tie a rock to a rope, and attach the other end of the rope to the food bag or pannier. Toss the rock end of the rope over the branch of a tall tree. Then, pull the bag into the tree, and secure the rock end of the rope. Good quality rope works best, and birch or aspen trees work easier than spruce.

If you encounter a bear, don't run. Throw an object on the ground and then back away from it. If the bear advances, there is a good chance that it will stop to inspect the item, giving an indication of whether or not this is a bluff charge. Climb a tree if time allows, or take a "cannonball" pose if the bear becomes aggressive: kneel on the ground, put your hands over the back of your neck, bend over so that your forehead touches your kneecaps, and elbows touch the outside of your legs. Assuming this position will protect the vital body parts. A pack will offer additional protection. Hold this position until the bear leaves.

WATER

Many of Alaska's rivers and streams are clear in appearance, giving the impression that the water is pure and safe to drink. However, water clarity is not an indication of presence or absence of contaminants. Since stream conditions change daily, it isn't possible for Alaska's public health authorities to always know which streams have been contaminated with intestinal wastes from humans, animals or birds. The parasite *Giardia lamblia* is particularly harmful to humans. The symptoms of Giardiasis are abdominal bloating, cramps, excessive gas, diarrhea and a feeling of physical discomfort. The incubation period after ingestion of the cysts is one to four weeks with an average of 10 to 14 days. If a combination of the above symptoms lasts longer than seven days, consult a physician and mention the possibility of Giardiasis.

To reduce the possibility of Giardisis, treat lake, stream and river water before drinking. Water purification pumps, and water purification tablets are sold in most major Alaska towns. Purification tablets, however, do not always kill the parasite *Giardia lamblia*.

Water can be purified by bringing it to a full rolling boil for one minute. If the water tastes flat, pour it back and forth between clean containers two or three times. Water can be purified with chlorine. Add one drop of household bleach such as Clorox or Purex (containing 5.25% available chlorine) to each quart of water. If the water is cloudy, add three drops of the solution to each quart of water. After adding the chlorine solution, mix thoroughly and allow to stand 30 minutes before drinking.

MOSQUITOES

Mosquitoes are found just about everywhere in Alaska and Western Canada, but they tend to be more numerous in wet, swampy, closed areas. Repellents containing diethyltoluamide (DEET) are perhaps the most effective when used in roughly 50 percent concentrations of the active ingredient.When camping, pick a slightly breezy spot or light a small campfire. Wind or smoke will reduce the number of mosquitoes.

MEDICAL SERVICES

Towns which have health facilities are listed. However, its best to be prepared for emergencies: carry a first aid kit.

Although roads described in this book aren't as heavily trafficked as roads in the Lower 48, we suggest wearing a helmet and light colored clothing, particularly at dusk.

FIRES

Don't leave campground fires unattended, and extinguish your campfire before leaving it. Always light fires on a mineral surface rather than on peat or organic matter, because embers may smoulder and even a year later, ignite.

POST OFFICES

Most Alaska and Western Canada towns and all large cities have post offices where mail and parcels can be picked up or dropped off. Many of these post offices and their zip/postal codes are listed.

CUSTOMS

The points of entry into Canada are along the Haines, Klondike, Alaska and Top of the World Highways. To enter the U.S. from Canada, a passport, driver's license, birth certificate or other valid form of citizenship is needed. No specific amount of money is required to enter either Canada or the U.S. However, it is recommended that travellers either carry a credit card or have on hand enough cash to pay for food and lodging.

TELEPHONES

The area code for Alaska is 907. Western Canada area codes are: Yukon Territory (403); British Columbia (604); and the Northwest Territories (403).

CURRENCY

Please note that in the Canadian sections all financial references are to the Canadian dollar. As of March, 1989 the Canadian dollar is worth US $ 0.85. Though establishments in Canada will accept US dollars, it is recommended to use Canadian money while in Canada and avoid exchange and other problems.

UPDATED INFORMATION

Information on changes in food or lodging establishments, roadside sights, as well as road conditions and terrain should be sent to The Denali Press, Box 021535, Juneau, AK 99802.

ACKNOWLEDGEMENTS

This book would not have been possible without the help of many individuals, many of whom we've known for years, and others we met along the way.

Those who provided us with a place to stay include Deb Smith, Mike and Nancy King, Sean McQuire and Suzi Lozo, Physician Assistant Dennis Rogers, Vern Smith, Alan, Debra and Zeb Schorr, Glenda Choate, Forest Service interpreter Jim Case and Joanne Waterman.

Alaska Department of Transportation engineers John Ryer, Steve Powers, and Grant L. Lewis provided profile information. Nicole McCulloch of the Fairbanks North Star Borough Planning Department and Adrienne Lacy of Alaska Road and Recreation Maps provided map information.

Others who helped us include Marvin Pollard with computer support, Roger Hockings who drove us up the Dalton Highway, and Ellen Wood who proofread portions of the manuscript.

Campbells Sports gave us a discount on bicycling and touring equipment. Sherman Burton, Alaska Marine Highway System, was kind enough to assist with passage on the ferrries of Southeast Alaska.

Thanks also to the University of Alaska, Fairbanks Archives, the National Park Service, the Forest Service, the many community museums throughout the state, and the Dot Lake Service Clinic.

The *Alaska Bicycle Touring* Guide is for our parents.

Alys Culhane

Pete Praetorius

Fairbanks, Alaska

ALASKA AND WESTERN CANADA

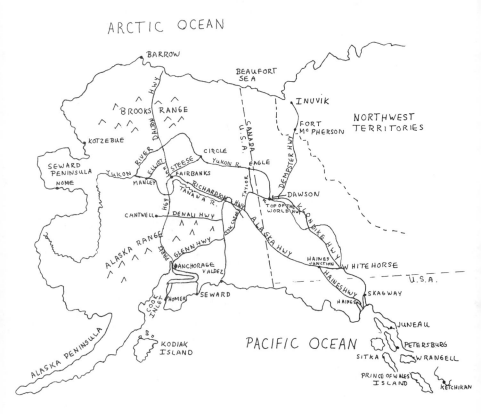

I: SOUTHEAST ALASKA

SOUTHEAST ALASKA

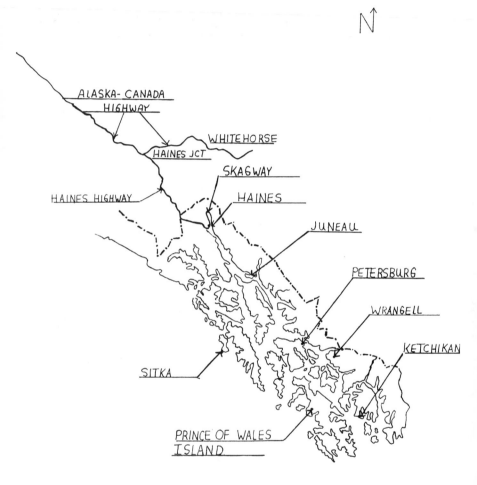

Chapter 1: Introduction

Location and Climate:

Southeast Alaska parallels Northern British Columbia. There are approximately 320 air miles between Skagway and Ketchikan. Southeast Alaska is considered to be a rain forest and the towns in the more southerly panhandle receive the most precipitation. Overcast skies and cool, moist temperatures are the norm. The average year-round temperature is 40° F, and July is both the driest and warmest month. The temperature in the summer months is usually between 55° F and 65° F. The prevailing winds are from the southeast.

Transportation:

The major Southeast Alaska towns can be reached by airplane or ship. The Alaska Marine Highway System began operations in 1963 when three mainline motor vessels, the *Malaspina*, the *Taku* and the *Matanuska* were placed in service. Since 1963 three smaller ferries, the *Aurora*, the *LeConte*, and the *Chilkat*, and one larger vessel, the *Columbia* have been added to the fleet.

The ferries depart from Seattle, Washington or Prince Rupert, British Columbia and travel as far north as Skagway. As of October, 1989 the ferries will depart from Bellingham, not Seattle. Passengers can disembark and board the vessels at any port. In addition to calling at the seven central towns of Ketchikan, Wrangell, Petersburg, Sitka, Juneau, Haines and Skagway, the ferries also travel to the communities of Prince of Wales Island, Metlakatla, Kake, Angoon, Tenakee, Hoonah and Pelican.

Ketchikan is a day and a half run from Seattle. In 1989 the one way adult fare is $138.00 with an additional cabin charge of $123.00-$216.00.

The ferries have observation lounges, bars, cafeterias and staterooms. The food is not inexpensive, and cyclists may wish to bring their own. However, cooking is not permitted on board any of the vessels.

Stateroom reservations should be made well in advance of the trip. Most hardy individuals prefer to stay in the solariums: open, partially enclosed areas in the rear of the ferry. The solariums are heated, and have lounge chairs. The solariums also offer plenty of fresh air, companionship, and are free! (The MV *Chilkat* is the only ferry without a solarium.)

Showers are free. As of May, 1989 there is a small charge to transport bicycles. For example, the charge from Seattle to Ketchikan is $20. In the summer foot passengers needn't make reservations, but those with cars should. For reservation or scheduling information write: Alaska Marine Highway System, Box R, Juneau, AK 99811. Telephone: (907) 465-3941 or (800) 642-0066.

The British Columbia Ferry System offers passenger and vehicle service between Prince Rupert and Port Hardy on the northern tip of Vancouver Island and from Prince Rupert to the Queen Charlotte Islands. Stops are made at points in between. A small fee is charged for bicycles. For additional information contact: BC Ferry System, 1112 Fort Street, Victoria, BC V8V 4V2. Telephone: (206) 445-6865. Travel agents can provide information on the numerous cruise ships that travel the Inside Passage.

Alaska Airlines (800-426-0333) and Delta Airlines (800-221-1212) are the only two scheduled airlines providing service between the Lower 48 and Southeast Alaska. Check with a travel agent for information on the numerous charter and air taxi operators in Southeast Alaska.

Southeast Alaska, which contains the Tongass National Forest, (the largest forest in the U.S.) is inhabited by many species of wildlife. Throughout all Southeast there are numerous birds, including bald eagles, ravens, jays, and geese. Land mammals include black and brown bear, Sitka black tail deer, wolves, and mountain goats. Marine mammals include sea otters, sea lions, porpoises, and humpback, grey, killer, and Minke whales.

There are spruce forests at the southern, and mountainous glacial terrain at the northern ends. In between there is the Sergius Narrows, a narrow treacherous body of water. The ferries must time their passage to coincide with its high and low tides. U.S. Forest Service interpreters give talks, answer questions and provide maps and reference materials in the summer.

THINGS TO DO:

Kayaking, fishing, hiking, glacier trekking, and river rafting are popular activities in Southeast Alaska. Walking tours, maps and visitor guides are available in the Visitor Centers and Ferry Terminals of major Southeast towns.

The Southeast area has a rich cultural heritage. Southeast museums, bookstores and libraries have information on the Native Haidas and Tlingits as well as the early explorers.

SAFETY CONSIDERATIONS:

Medical facilities are readily available in Southeast Alaska.

Travellers should be aware of paralytic shellfish poisoning. PSP is caused when massive blooms of dinoflagellates cause "red tides." These organisms produce neuromuscular toxins which accumulate to lethal levels in the meat of clams. Alaska clams may be poisonous unless they've been harvested from an approved beach.

When toxins are present, symptoms may appear shortly after the clams are eaten. Signs of PSP are a tingling numbness of the lips and tongue followed by the same in the fingers and toes. Dizziness, weakness, drowsiness, incoherence, and/or loss of muscle coordination may follow. Death from respiratory paralysis may occur three to twelve hours after the clams are consumed. Anyone with these symptoms should seek immediate medical attention. Artificial respiration may be helpful if breathing becomes difficult or ceases. Leftover clams should be saved for laboratory tests.

Hypothermia, *Giardia lamblia* and bears can be as much a problem here as elsewhere in Alaska. See the Introduction for more information on these subjects.

WHAT TO WEAR:

Southeast Alaska is often wet and even in the summer months can be cold. A wool hat, gloves, socks, and sweater are essential for warmth, as are a waterproof raincoat and rainpants for dryness. Long underwear is a must. Rubbers or overbooties are a good investment. A Polarguard sleeping bag is better than a down one, because when wet, Polarguard will still insulate. Tents should be seam sealed so that they are water tight.

BICYCLE AND ADDITIONAL GEAR RECOMMENDATIONS:

Most areas in Southeast Alaska are suited for both touring and mountain biking. The main roads are paved and towns are generally close to the ferries. However, there are numerous trails and logging roads that would be easier to ride on a mountain bike.

Only Ketchikan, Juneau, Sitka, Haines and Skagway have repair shops, so it's best to pack a repair kit with at least one spare tube. (It's hard to patch a tube in the rain.) It's also a good idea to line your panniers and stuff sacks with plastic bags. A day pack for hiking and a pair of binoculars are worth the extra weight.

U.S. FOREST SERVICE CABIN RENTAL INFORMATION:

Forest Service recreation cabins are located on lakes, rivers, streams, or on salt water beaches. Most cabins are accessible only by float plane or boat, although a few, like the Control Lake Cabin on Prince of Wales Island, may be reached by foot. Reservations are required. Forest Service cabins may be reserved up to six months in advance by obtaining a permit and paying the nightly $15.00 fee. The maximum length of stay is seven days and the fees are used for cabin maintenance. All FS cabins sleep at least four and include tables, benches, bunks, stoves, and outhouses. Boats are furnished at lakefront cabins. Reservations can be made at the listed addresses.

CHAPTER 2: KETCHIKAN

BACKGROUND

Ketchikan, (pop.7,311) built on a steep slope along the Tongass Narrows on Revillagigedo Island, is the first large community north of Dixon Entrance.

Ketchikan has been called "The Salmon Fishing Capital of the World," and "The Rain Capital of Alaska," since the city's main industry is salmon fishing and it receives an average of 162 inches of rain a year. Ketchikan's average July temperature is 58° F. The average July rainfall is eight inches.

Much of the town is built on pilings over the water or on the adjoining hillsides. At present Ketchikan's main road extends approximately 20 miles north and 14 miles south of town.

In 1883 a small salmon saltery was built at the mouth of Ketchikan Creek. Two years later, canneries were established in the nearby communities of Quadra on the mainland and Loring on Revillagigedo Island. In 1887 the Quadra cannery was moved to Ketchikan and the town was settled.

The name Ketchikan may have come from a Tlingit Indian word once meaning "the salmon creek that flows through town," or "the thundering wings of an eagle." As local legend has it, before white people arrived, a Tlingit Indian named Kitsch established a summer fishing camp near Ketchikan Creek. Thus the creek was called Kitschkin or Kitsch's stream, the Tlingit word "hin" meaning stream. The name, maybe because it was difficult to pronounce, was shortened to Kitskan which became Ketchikan.

After the Klondike Gold Rush ended, fishing became the town's central industry. The prostitutes clustered near the harbor where the fishing fleet was moored. The red light district became so famous that it was called "Alaska's Tenderloin," and "The Barbary Coast of the North," by Alaska Judge James Wickersham. The red light district was closed in 1953. It is estimated that at this time there were about 18 "Bawdy" houses.

VISITORS INFORMATION

VISITOR'S CENTER:

The Ketchikan Visitor's Information Center is located on the dock at 131 Front Street. The center has town maps and information on walking tours, lodging, restaurants, kayak, and flightseeing trips. The Visitor's Center is open daily during business hours. Write: 131 Front Street, Ketchikan, AK 99901. Phone: 225-6166.

FERRY TERMINAL:

The Ketchikan Ferry Terminal is located about two miles northwest of the town center on Tongass Avenue. There are no baggage lockers in the terminal. Information is available at the front desk and in the terminal information rack. Phone: 225-6181.

FOREST SERVICE INFORMATION:

The Ketchikan Area Ranger Station, on the ground floor of the Federal Building at 629 Dock Street, has films, historical and cultural displays, free handouts, maps and information on Forest Service cabins. The office is open from 8 a.m. to 5 p.m. Monday through Saturday. 16 FS cabins are available for rent. For cabin reservations write: Forest Supervisor, Tongass National Forest, Federal Building, Ketchikan, AK 99901.

TRAVELLER'S NEEDS

MEDICAL SERVICES:

Ketchikan General Hospital is at 3100 Tongass Avenue. Phone: 225-5171.

GROCERIES:

Super Value Supermarket is located across the street from the Ferry Terminal at 2485 Tongass Avenue. Hours: 9 a.m. to 8 p.m. Monday through Saturday and 10 a.m. to 6 p.m. Sunday.

BICYCLING/OUTDOOR STORES:

"I won't let people be disappointed with what they are getting," says Larry Humberg, the owner of People Power, Ketchikan's only bicycle store. Humberg, a former bicycle racer, says he learned a lot about cycling the hard way. Now he's eager to talk to others about training, bicycle selection, and maintenance. Humberg believes that the bicycle should fit the rider, and stocks quality equipment. He has a complete line of Shimano, Suntour and Campagnolo parts and carries Araya rims. Humberg has limited touring gear but has accounts with Madden, Rhode Gear and Eclipse. People Power is located at 1920 Tongass Avenue, adjacent to his house. Phone: 225-2488.

LODGING/CAMPING:

The Ketchikan Youth Hostel is located in the Methodist Church at Grant and Main Streets, downtown Ketchikan. The 35-bed hostel has separate sleeping facilities for men and women, showers, and a conversation, reading and games area. The nightly fee is $5.00 for AYH members and $7.00 for non-members. The hostel is open from 7 p.m. to 8:30 a.m. only. Doors are locked at 11 p.m. and each hosteller is expected to do a chore. No smoking, alcohol or illegal drugs are permitted on the premises. Reservations not accepted. For additional information write: Box 8515, Ketchikan, AK 99901. Phone: 225-3319.

There are no campgrounds in town. See Road Information for out of town campgrounds.

POST OFFICE:

The Ketchikan Post Office is located next to the Ferry Terminal on Tongass Avenue. Zip Code: 99901.

LAUNDRY/SHOWERS:

Suds and Duds Laundry is located at 325 Bawden Avenue, three blocks from the harbor. The laundry is open from 8 a.m. to 9 p.m. daily.

ALTERNATIVE TRANSPORTATION:

The Ketchikan Airport is on Gravina Island, across the narrows from the ferry dock. A round trip ferry ticket costs $1.75.

ENTERTAINMENT AND RECREATION

TRAILS:

Most of the trails around Ketchikan are unsuitable for riding. However, the Blue Lake, Ward Lake, Deer Mountain, Twin Peaks and Perseverance Lake Trails are popular short day hikes. The Forest Service has trail information.

MUSEUMS/HISTORICAL SITES:

The Tongass Historical Museum has early mining and Southeastern Indian artifacts. A permanent exhibit, "From Catch to Can in Ketchikan," provides a historical overview of the southern Southeast fishing industry. The museum is located in the Centennial Building on Dock Street, adjacent to the library.

The 25 poles at the Saxman Totem Park were relocated here from abandoned villages on Tongass Island, Pennock Island, and from the old Cape Fox Village at Kirk Point under a U.S. Forest Service and Civilian Conservation Corps project in the 1930's.

In addition to the pole carving, verbal legends were collected. Dr. Viola Garfield of the Department of Anthropology at the University of Washington travelled around Southeast Alaska and collected the Indian folklore stories of the totems. Linn Forest, the regional architect in charge of the project, also collected stories. Linn and Garfield's collaborative book, *The Wolf and the Raven* (University of Washington Press, 1962) contains information about the Saxman totem poles, as well as the poles in Totem Bight and in the Klawock Totem Park.

In addition to the Saxman Park Totem Poles, there are over 30 original, unrestored totem poles at the Totem Heritage Center. These poles are from the deserted Tlingit communities of Tongass and Village Islands and the Haida village of Old Kasaan. Traditional woodcarving tools, artifacts, and art are on display and Native craft workshops are held here. The Totem Heritage Center is located at 601 Deermount Street.

Dolly's House at 24 Creek Street has been preserved as a museum. The green house with the red front door was the home of "sporting woman," Dolly Arthur for more than 50 years. Dolly bought her place in 1919 and left it in 1974 when she moved into a nursing home. She died in 1975 at age 85. Dolly's dishes, furniture, clothes, needlework, and cash box are on display in her former home. Hours: 9 a.m. to 5 p.m. Admission: $2.00.

St. John's is one of Ketchikan's oldest churches. Located on Mission Street, it was built in 1903, as part of an Episcopal complex of hospital, mission, and church. The inside paneling is original native cedar cut in the Native operated sawmill in Saxman.

The Deer Mountain Hatchery was started by the Ketchikan Chamber of Commerce about 30 years ago in an attempt to improve the depleted king and coho salmon runs. The facility is now operated by the Alaska Department of Fish and Game. The hatchery is located across the footbridge near the Totem Heritage Center.

The Ketchikan Creek Falls and Fish Ladder can be viewed from the Park Street Bridge, where in season several species of salmon can be seen jumping from the falls or using the fish ladder. The king salmon on the bank was carved by master carver Jones Yeltazie.

BOOKSTORES:

Parnassus, at 28 Creek Street, is a new and used bookstore. The store has an excellent selection of travel literature and a good number of books by women authors. Espresso is sold for $1.00 a cup, and says Miss Lillian, the store owner, "it's quite all right to sit and read unless you're drinking a moca and looking at something expensive." Postcards and classical music tapes are also for sale. The Voyageur Bookstore is located at 405 Dock Street. Waldenbooks is located in the Plaza Port Mall.

GIFT SHOPS:

The Once in a Blue Moose gift shop sells jewelry, wood carvings, and cards. Ketchikan artist Ray Troll's T-shirts are on sale here. Some of his more popular works are entitled "Spawn Until you Die," "There's no Nookie like Chinookie," and "Humpies from Hell." The gift shop is located at 407 Stedman Street.

SIDE TRIPS:

Misty Fjords National Monument is a remote wilderness area 50 miles east of Ketchikan, and is only accessible by plane or boat. The park, 118 miles long and 50 miles wide, contains 2.3 million acres. Misty Fjords is a major source of all species of Pacific salmon, and shellfish are plentiful. There are 15 Forest Service recreation cabins on freshwater lakes and three on saltwater as well as three shelters and 15 miles of trail in the Walker Cove and Rudyerd Bay areas.

Southeast Exposure and Kayak Alaska, both located on Stedman Street, offer kayak lessons, day trips, and expeditions.

PUBLIC RECREATION:

The Ketchikan High School Pool is open from 5 a.m. to 7:30 a.m. and 10 a.m. to 8 p.m. daily. The charge for a sauna and shower is $2.50.The school is located at 308 Grant Street.

ROAD INFORMATION:

There are two main roads in Ketchikan. They both begin in front of the Federal Building on Mill and Stedman Streets and run in opposite directions. Stedman Street becomes South Tongass Highway. Mill Street becomes North Tongass Highway. Together they form one road, approximately 30 miles in length.

NORTH TONGASS HIGHWAY

ROAD CONDITIONS/TERRAIN:

The road, 17.2 miles in length, is paved and mostly flat for the first 10 miles. Wide shoulder to Mile 10.4, narrow shoulder to Mile 13.2. At Mile 15 the road becomes gravel.

JUNCTIONS:

Mile 2.3., Ketchikan Ferry Terminal. Mile 5.5., Ward Lake Road.

WATER:

Mile 5.6, Ward Creek. Mile 11.6, Whipple Creek. Mile 15.1, First Waterfall Creek. Mile 15.7, Second Waterfall Creek, water inaccessible.

CAMPING/TRAILS:

Mile 5.5. Ward Lake, see Sideroads. Mile 17.2, Settler's Cove State Recreation Site. This campground has 12 campsites, campground hosts and trails.

FOOD/LODGING:

Mile 11, The Mecca. Bar, restaurant, and laundry facilities.

ROADSIDE SIGHTS:

Mile 3.2, The Elmer Wolff Memorial Viewpoint. This viewpoint is dedicated in memory of Elmer Wolff. Through his personal campaign what once was a garbage dump is now a community asset. Mile 7.6, Louisiana Pacific Pulp Mill Entrance. Mile 10, Totem Bight State Park. Here are 14 totems and a community house. The Tlingit and Haida poles are arranged in a path overlooking the Tongass Narrows. The community house, a replica of an early 19th century clan house, was constructed by the CCC. The Alaska Division of Parks has an office and a brochure which describes each totem. Totem Bight is a historical park; no camping or fires are allowed. Mile 12, Guard Island Viewpoint. There is a lighthouse on this island.

SOUTH TONGASS HIGHWAY

ROAD CONDITIONS/TERRAIN:

The road, 13 miles in length, has a narrow shoulder and is paved to Mile 8.6. Mostly flat with some rolling hills.

WATER:

Mile 8.9, Whitman Creek.

ROADSIDE SIGHTS:

Mile 2.3, Saxman Totem Park. Mile 3.4, Rotary Beach Picnic Area. Mile 5.4, Mountain Point. Good fishing according to USFS Interpreter Jim Case. Mile 10.4, waterfall.

SIDEROADS:

Ward Lake Road to Harriet Hunt Lake. The road has a gravel surface and is rolling. Mile 0.8, USFS Signal Creek Campground on shore of Ward Lake. Wood available at campground entrance. Mile 1, USFS 3 C's Campground. Very small campground. Mile 2.9, USFS Last Chance Campground, 23 sites. Mile 3.1, Connell Lake Road. Road leads 0.6 miles to man-made lake and dam. Mile 3.6. Wooden pipe constructed in 1950's brought water from Connell Creek to the pulp mill. At Mile 7.2 the road forks, keep left to get to Harriet Lake. Mile 10.1, Harriet Hunt Lake. Medium sized lake, good blueberry picking spot. The recreation area is jointly managed by the Cape Fox Native Corporation and the Government.

CHAPTER 3: PRINCE OF WALES ISLAND

BACKGROUND

Prince of Wales Island, the third largest island in the U.S., has over 1,000 miles of logging roads, making it an excellent place to bicycle. Prince of Wales Island has a cold, moist maritime climate. The temperature varies from 46°F-70°F in the summer months. The island is dominated by the northward moving Pacific Ocean high pressure system. Precipitation varies, with June and July being the driest months. Winds blow mainly from the northeast or southeast in the summer, although directions vary depending on the topography. Fall and summer gale winds can last several days.

Each spring thousands of migratory waterfowl and shorebirds pass through Prince of Wales Island on their way to their northern breeding grounds. The estuaries and wetlands provide critical resting and feeding habitats.

The big game species found on Prince of Wales Island include mountain goats and Sitka black tail deer, which in the summer prefer the island's mountainous terrain. Bears feed along fish streams in the summer. There are wolves on POW Island. Smaller mammals include mink, land otter, racoon, short tailed weasels, red and flying squirrels, voles, shrews and bats.

Prince of Wales Island's warm waters support a variety of marine invertebrates including non-reef building coral, sea fans, sponges, and sea anemones as well as jelly fish, starfish, and sea cucumbers. Stellar sea lions, harbor seals, sea otters, Dall and harbor porpoises, and killer and humpback whales frequent the island's near shores. (All marine mammals are protected from harvest by the Marine Mammal Protection Act of 1972, except for traditional use by Natives.)

Although the island has been heavily logged, it still has a large and diverse tree and plant ecosystem. The forests include western hemlock, Sitka spruce, and yellow cedar. Stands of red cedar, lodgepole pine, mountain hemlock, and alder are interspersed among them. Salmonberries, huckleberries, blueberries, currants, and cranberries and plentiful.

Developed camping areas are scarce. According to the Thorne Bay Forest Service Ranger Station staff, there are four FS campgrounds and four picnic areas available for public use. As for undeveloped sites, it's illegal to camp on Native lands without permission. These areas are marked by signs. FS cabins are also available.

There are nine communities on Prince of Wales Island. Information on the southern road system communities of Hollis, Hydaburg, Klawock, Craig and Thorne Bay is provided.

HOLLIS

BACKGROUND

Because Hollis is the island's Ferry Terminal site, most people visiting the island arrive here. The town is located about a mile from the Ferry Terminal. There are no visitor facilities in Hollis.

HYDABURG

BACKGROUND

The first known inhabitants of Hydaburg (pop. 475) were the Haida Indians who migrated up to Tlingit occupied Prince of Wales Island from the northwest area of Graham Island in Western Canada in the 17th century. By 1910, the villages of Howkan, Klinkwan and Sukkwan were the major Haida population centers. In 1911, the site of present day Hydaburg was chosen and the three villages merged into one. Hydaburg's economy is based upon commercial fishing and timber harvesting. There are no visitor facilities or bicycle stores in Hydaburg.

MEDICAL SERVICES:

For medical assistance telephone 285-3462 or 285-3111.

GROCERIES:

Do Drop In Grocery, located on the town's main street, carries groceries, but no fresh produce.

LODGING/CAMPING:

There are no hotels or hostels in Hydaburg, but some folks rent rooms. Locals advise asking around.

EATING/DRINKING ESTABLISHMENTS:

Sandwiches Etc. is owned by Sandra and Warren Peele. The small cafe has a grill and is located opposite the grocery store.

POST OFFICE:

The Post Office is located at the top of the hill. Go right at the bridge when entering town. Zip Code: 99922.

KLAWOCK

BACKGROUND

Klawock (pop. 760) is located where the Klawock River empties into the Klawock Inlet, and where Road 924 (Hollis-Craig Road) intersects Road 929 (Big Salt Road). In 1779, Klawock was called "La Galleria," or the gallery by the Don Ignacio Arteaga Expedition because it was surrounded by water during high tides.

In 1869 a trading post and salmon saltery were established and in 1878 the first cannery in Alaska was built. Soon after, several canneries were operating in the Klawock area during peak salmon runs.

In a park overlooking the town are a collection of memorial and mortuary totem poles. These replicas and restored originals were found at abandoned sites further north on the island and transported to Klawock.

MEDICAL SERVICES:

For medical assistance telephone 755-2900 or 755-2918.

GROCERIES:

At the junction is a small but complete grocery store (no fresh produce). The store is owned by Pete and Pauline Ruzgis. Hours: 8 a.m. to 9 p.m. daily.

BICYCLE/OUTDOOR STORES:

Klawock has no bicycle shop. However, the Log Cabin Resort at Mile 0.2 on Highway 929 carries limited parts, including tubes and pedals.

LODGING/CAMPING:

Nearly all of the land around Klawock is privately owned. Camping is available at the Log Cabin Resort. The $15.00 nightly fee includes a shower, kitchen and TV.

POST OFFICE:

Zip Code: 99925.

LAUNDRY/SHOWERS:

Klawock's laundromat is located next to the store. Showers are coin operated.

CRAIG

BACKGROUND

Craig (pop. 1,167) is the largest town on Prince of Wales Island. Fishing has played a prominent role in Craig's history. Even before the establishment of a permanent community, the Tlingit-Haida Indians occupied village sites and fish camps on the land. A light salting operation on Fish Island, started by Craig Millar in 1907, was the start of the permanent city. Fishing continued to provide an economic base for the community and by the 1930's Craig's houses and businesses were connected by a network of wooden sidewalks.

Craig's growth is due in part to its increased use as an economic and transportation center. It now has a small boat harbor, built by several Native organizations.

MEDICAL SERVICES:

For medical assistance telephone 826-3257.

VISITOR'S CENTER:

Located at Third and Main Street, the Craig City Hall has information on Craig and the surrounding area. There is also a bank on the corner. Write: Box 23, Craig, AK 99921. Phone: 826-3275.

FOREST SERVICE INFORMATION:

The Craig District Ranger office of the USFS is at 900 Ninth Street. Camping, fishing, public use cabins, the timber industry and land ownership information is available. The office also has a free island road map. There are six recreation cabins in the Craig District. For information write: USFS, Pouch 500, Craig, AK 99921. Phone: 826-3271.

GROCERIES:

Thompsen House Supermarket is located outside of town on the Craig-Hollis Road. The supermarket has a full selection of groceries and fresh produce at reasonable prices.

LODGING/CAMPING:

The land around Craig is privately owned, thus not available for camping. Outside of town, about half way around the Hamilton Loop Road, there is a picnic area with a wooden shelter. There are also two small hotels in town.

POST OFFICE:

The Craig Post Office is located on the corner of First and Main Streets. Hours: 8 a.m. to 5 p.m. Monday through Friday and 10 a.m. to 2 p.m. Saturdays. Zip Code: 99921.

THORNE BAY

BACKGROUND

The body of water known as Thorne Bay was named after Frank Manley Thorn, Superintendent of the U.S. Coast and Geodetic Survey from 1885 to 1889. In 1953, Ketchikan Pulp Company established a logging camp at Hollis. In 1960, road construction began and a small floating logging camp was built on Thorne Bay to replace the Hollis facility. Engineers planned the new campsite in 1961. By 1962 the move from Hollis to Thorne Bay was complete. Roads connecting Thorne Bay to Hollis, Craig, and Klawock were constructed in 1973. Most employment in Thorne Bay (pop. 475) is still related to the logging industry.

MEDICAL SERVICES:

Thorne Bay has a health clinic. Phone: 828-3906.

VISITOR'S CENTER:

The Thorne Bay City Hall has information about the town and surrounding area. The staff are very helpful. Write: Box 19110, Thorne Bay, AK 99919.

FOREST SERVICE INFORMATION:

The Thorne Bay District Ranger office has information on area rental cabins. The Control Lake, Sweetwater Lake and Stanley Creek cabins are road accessible. There are 11 other cabins in the district. Staff also has videos on the Tongass National Forest ecosystems and information on archeological sites, (recently ancient petroglyphs have been found in some caves on the northern part of the island) land ownership, fishing and the timber industry.

GROCERIES:

Clear Cut Market has a good selection of groceries and some fresh produce.

LODGING/CAMPING:

About six miles past Thorne Bay is the Sandy Beach Picnic Area. There are four USFS picnic sites in the Thorne Bay Ranger District. All the picnic sites have shelters.

EATING/DRINKING ESTABLISHMENTS:

Gallagher's Galley is owned by Jerri Gallagher. The cafe was originally started by a group of women who ran a weight watchers program. The present menu includes hamburgers and pizza.

POST OFFICE:

The Thorne Bay Post Office is located at Mile 0 of the Thorne Bay Road (Road 30). Zip Code: 99919.

PRINCE OF WALES ISLAND ROAD INFORMATION

ROAD INFORMATION: HOLLIS-KLAWOCK-CRAIG ROAD (ROAD 924)

SECTION 1: MILE 31.5 (HOLLIS)-MILE 0 (CRAIG)

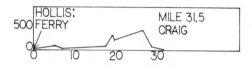

ROAD CONDITIONS/TERRAIN:

Mileposts are from Craig to Hollis, but because most people visiting the island start in Hollis, road information is provided from Hollis to Craig.

Hollis is at Mile 31.5. There is a gravel road from Hollis to Mile 19.5, the Harris River. The road from Harris River to Craig is paved. Locals indicate that the road from Harris River to Hollis will be paved in the near future. The road is rolling, climbing to 480 feet before dropping down to sea level.

JUNCTIONS:

Mile 20.5, Hydaburg Road (Road FH13.) Mile 7.5, Big Salt Road (Road 929).

WATER:

The road to Hollis begins 0.3 miles from the Hollis Ferry Terminal. About 0.2 miles from the junction, there's a water spigot on the left. Mile 28.5, Maybeso Creek. Mile 19.5, Harris River. Mile 17.4, Klawock Lake, private property. Mile 6.9, Klawock River. Numerous unnamed creeks in the area.

CAMPING/TRAILS:

Old Hollis Ferry Terminal. Acceptable spot for camping if the ferry arrives late. Go to the junction of Hollis Road, Mile 31.2. Follow the road to where it forks, take the right fork, which leads to a flat open area. There might be construction equipment, and the ground's uneven. Mile 28.5, Maybeso Creek. Rocky but scenic. Bicycles must be lifted over guardrail. From Mile 24.6 to Mile 18.2 is the Tongass National Forest. Private Native land from Mile 18.2 to Craig.

FOOD/LODGING:

No food or lodging on this road, except at Klawock and Craig.

ROADSIDE SIGHTS:

Mile 9.1, Klawock Lake State Fish and Game Hatchery.

ROAD INFORMATION: HYDABURG ROAD (ROAD FH 13)

SECTION 1: MILE 0 (MILE 20.5, ROAD 924)-MILE 21.6 (HYDABURG)

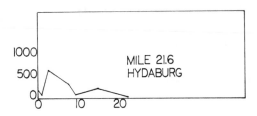

ROAD CONDITIONS/TERRAIN:

21.6 mile gravel surfaced, winding and narrow road leads from Road 924 to Hydaburg. The road is rolling, with its highest point being 675 feet at Mile 2.7. Hydaburg is at sea level.

JUNCTIONS:

Mile 9.8. Road 21 leads to 12 Mile Arm.

WATER:

Mile 0.3, Harris River. Mile 0.9, Fubar Creek. Mile 4.1, West Fork Trocadero Creek. Mile 6.4, Gulch Creek. Mile 6.7, Cable Creek. Mile 7.5, Trocadero Creek. Mile 9.7, Beaver Creek. Mile 15.1, unnamed creek.

CAMPING/TRAILS:

Mile 2.5, Duck Trail. Alpine shelter 1.5 miles up trail. Forest Service land for the first 15 miles, private Native land follows. No official campgrounds.

FOOD/LODGING:

No food or lodging on this road.

ROADSIDE SIGHTS:

Mile 6.7. Cable Creek, where salmon fry are released by the Klawock Hatchery.

ROAD INFORMATION: BIG SALT ROAD (ROAD 929)

SECTION 1: MILE 0 (KLAWOCK)-MILE 17 (JCT. ROADS 20 AND 30)

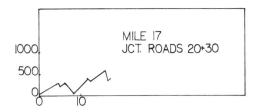

ROAD CONDITIONS/TERRAIN:

Gravel road parallels Big Salt Lake for approximately 7 miles. The road is rolling with some moderate hills. The highest point is 575 feet at Mile 16.

JUNCTIONS:

Mile 17, end of road. Junctions with Roads 20 and 30.

WATER:

Mile 1.6, Bennett Creek. Mile 3.7, Little Salt Creek. Mile 5.5, Duke Creek. Mile 9.5, Black Bear Creek. Mile 12.3, Steelhead Creek.

CAMPING/TRAILS:

Mile 16.5, trail leads to Control Lake. Forest Service boundary begins at Mile 13.5. Private Native land before that. No official campgrounds.

FOOD/LODGING:

No food or lodging on this road.

ROAD INFORMATION: THORNE BAY ROAD (ROAD 30)

SECTION 1: MILE 18 (JCT. ROADS 929 AND 20)-MILE 0 (THORNE BAY)

ROAD CONDITIONS/TERRAIN:

Gravel surface, parts of the road are narrow and rocky. The 18 mile road connects the junction of Road 929 to Thorne Bay. Mileposts read from Thorne Bay to the junction. Since most bicyclists will start at the junction, road information is from the junction to Thorne Bay. The road leads mostly downhill to Thorne Bay, dropping 400 feet.

JUNCTIONS:

Mile 6.8. Road leads to North Pole and Lake Number Three USFS Campground. The campground is 4.3 miles on this road. There are two campsites in the middle of a clearcut. The unsheltered, open campsites have picnic tables, fire pits, and an outhouse.

WATER:

Mile 17.7, Control Creek. Mile 16.6, Balls Lake. Mile 13, Rio Roberts Creek. Mile 12.7, New Loonberry Creek. Mile 10.8, Rio Beaver Creek. Mile 6.8, Goose Creek. Mile 5, Thorne River. Mile 4.3, Gravelly Creek.

CAMPING:

Mile 4.3, Gravelly Creek Picnic Area. Nice picnic area with large trees and picnic shelters. The second growth trees follow logging operations that were completed sixty years ago. The entire road is within the boundaries of the Tongass National Forest and therefore open to camping.

FOOD/LODGING:

No food or lodging on this road.

Dozer camping, Old Hollis Ferry Terminal

CHAPTER 4: WRANGELL

BACKGROUND

Wrangell (pop. 3,112) is located 85 miles northwest of Ketchikan and 150 miles southeast of Juneau. To the east is Canada which can only be reached by boat via the Stikine River.

The original inhabitants of Wrangell may have been the Tlingit Indians, who came to the area by way of the river. However the discovery of stone petrogylphs in the area has led some to believe that another group of people may have preceded the Tlingits by as much as 8,000 years.

The U.S. Government purchased Alaska from the the Russians in 1867 and the community was named Fort Wrangell, after Baron Ferdinand Von Wrangell. Wrangell is the only town in Alaska to have been ruled under three flags: the Russian, British and American.

The Klondike Gold Rush brought people to Wrangell, but ultimately it was the fishing, canning, and lumber industries which provided the town with a stable economic base. In the late 1800's the Wilson and Sylvester Sawmill, believed to be the first in Alaska, was built in Wrangell. The mill produced building lumber and packing boxes for the canneries. Later it produced high-grade timber for airplane construction. Today the timber industry is Wrangell's major employer. Wrangell Forest Products is located about five miles outside of town.

Commercial fishing is a secondary industry. Salmon, herring, shrimp, crab, and halibut are all fished from the Wrangell waters. Many locals are involved in the tourism and construction trades, while others are government employees.

Wrangell is one of the friendliest towns in Alaska. Even Police Chief Brent Moody is eager to chat. In an article in the June 16, 1988 issue of the *Wrangell Sentinel*, Moody said "I'm always ready to talk. The coffee pot is on."

The average July temperature in Wrangell is 57° F. The July average rainfall is 5 inches.

VISITORS INFORMATION

VISITOR'S CENTER:

The Wrangell Visitor Information Center is located downtown, near the waterfront, in an A-Frame structure by Wrangell City Hall. It is open when cruise ships and ferries are in port and at other times throughout the summer. At the Center are copies of the *Wrangell Guide,* which has a listing of the area businesses, a walking tour map, and information on Stikine River charter boat trips. The Wrangell Museum on Church Street has brochures and maps of Wrangell and other Southeast towns. For additional information write: Box 1078, Wrangell, AK 99929. Phone: 874-3901.

FERRY TERMINAL:

The Wrangell Ferry Terminal at Stikine Avenue and Second Street, one block north of the Stikine Inn, has a staffed information desk and printed visitor information. The office opens two hours before ferry arrivals and is open from 10 a.m. to 4 p.m. most weekdays. For 24 hour recorded message phone: 874-3711. For reservations phone: 874-2021.

FOREST SERVICE INFORMATION:

The Wrangell Area Ranger Station is located at 525 Bennett Street. The office has information and maps. 23 FS cabins are available for rental. For reservations write: Wrangell Ranger District, Box 51, Wrangell, AK 99929. Phone: 874-2323.

TRAVELLER'S NEEDS

MEDICAL SERVICES:

The Alaska Public Health Nurse's office is in the Kadin Building, at 215 Front Street. Phone: 874-3615.

GROCERIES:

The City Market on Front Street sells groceries and has 24 hour film processing. Hours: 8 a.m. to 6 p.m. Benjamin's Market at 223 Brueger Street also sells groceries.

BICYCLE/OUTDOOR STORES:

Wrangell doesn't have a bicycle store.

LODGING/CAMPING:

Wrangell doesn't have a Youth Hostel. There are at least two lodges which offer meals and charter trips. Check the Visitor's Center or the *Wrangell Visitor's Guide* for more information.

The City Park is south on Zamovia Highway, about one mile outside of town. The waterfront park is immediately south of the cemetery and city baseball field. Turn into the ballfield parking lot to enter. The park has picnic tables, picnic shelters, a covered bar-be-que pit and restrooms. 24 hour camping only. The tenting area is close to the road; there are no marked sites.

Shoemaker Bay Boat Harbor and Recreation Area is located about five miles south of Wrangell on the Zamovia Highway. Tent camping is allowed here; sites are close together. There are picnic tables, but no shelters. This a popular RV area.

Pat's Lake is not maintained by the city or state and is often filled with RV's. The camping area is located about 11 miles south of downtown Wrangell, near the point where the Zamovia Highway ends and becomes a narrower Forest Service road. When you come to two roads going to the left, take the second of the two. To obtain water, follow the short trail from the campground area to Pat's Creek. Campfires permitted.

POST OFFICE:

The Wrangell Post Office is located on Second Street, opposite the library. Mail pick-up and delivery is at the post office only; there are no drop boxes around town. Zip Code: 99929.

LAUNDRY/SHOWERS:

Showers are available at the Thunderbird Hotel on Front Street. $3.00 includes a towel and soap.

The Thunderbird Laundromat next to the hotel has Zanussi Double loaders. There is no sign indicating that bicycles cannot be brought into the laundromat. However, this is not allowed, or so says the man sitting in the back room observing the laundromat via the two closed circuit cameras mounted above the front door.

ENTERTAINMENT AND RECREATION

TRAILS:

There is a network of unimproved, single-lane roads throughout the island. Many of these roads are suitable for mountain biking. For more information contact Dennis Reed at the USFS.

MUSEUMS/HISTORICAL SITES:

The city-run Wrangell Museum, at Second and Bevier Streets, is operated by the Wrangell Historical Society. The building has been a doctor's office, a morgue, a library, and a city hall. The structure was turned into a museum in 1967. Phone: 874-3770.

In the Communications Room is the old Campbell's press and linotype that was once used to print the *Wrangell Sentinel*, the state's longest continuously published newspaper. The last page printed is still in the press. Also in this room are a propeller and tail skid from a damaged World War I biplane, one of four that landed in Wrangell in 1920. The Wrangell Museum is open from 1 to 4 p.m. Monday through Saturday and at least an hour when ships and ferries are in port. Suggested admission for adults is $1.00.

The Our Collections Museum, owned by L.C. (Bolly) and Elva Bigelow is a private museum, housed in the Bigelow's garage. The museum contains Bigelow family artifacts, as well as a plaster of paris replica of the City of Wrangell, made for the 1967 Centennial. "Our Collections Museum" is located on Stikine Avenue, which turns into Evergreen Avenue . Phone 874-3646 during the day for an appointment.

There are several old churches in Wrangell. St. Philip's Episcopal Church at the intersection of Episcopal and Church Streets, was built by local Natives in 1903. The church also operated the first hospital in Wrangell which is listed on the *National Register of Historic Places*. The First Presbyterian Church was founded in 1879 by Rev. S. Young Hall. Next to it is the St. Rose of Lima Catholic Church, established at about the same time.

There are several places in town where totem poles have been preserved or recreated including Shakes Island, near the Wrangell Boat Harbor. The poles and the adjacent Chief Shakes House, were constructed by the Civilian Conservation Corps as a part of the 1930's totem restoration project.

Recently the Wrangell Cultural Heritage Committee, funded with $250,000 in state and federal grants, hired individuals to carve new and restore old totems. A pamphlet entitled *The Authentic History of Shakes Island and Clan* by E.L. Keithahn provides background information on many of the Shakes Island totem poles. A copy can be obtained from the Wrangell Museum. The Chief Shakes House is open from 3:30 to 6:30 p.m. Tuesday, 10 a.m. to 1 p.m. Wednesday, and 1 to 2:30 p.m.

Saturday. To view the house at other times, phone 874-3747. A $1.00 donation is requested.

Totem Poles are also on display in the Totem Park on Front Street. The park was purchased and donated to the community by Sealaska Corporation, one of Alaska's Native corporations. On July 4, 1987, the local Tlingit people invited local residents and Natives from Southeast Alaska to attend the raising of the Kiksadi Pole, the one nearest Front Street. Other totem poles are located in the front of the museum, by the Post Office, and near the Wrangell City Hall.

Approximately 40 stone carvings or petrogylphs have been etched on the rocks at Wrangell Beach. Some of these carvings, which may have been boundary markers, are at least several thousand years old. Some look like animals or faces while others appear to be scribbles. Its not known who created them, but one widely held theory is that the petrogyphs were carved by the early Stikine Tlingits. Removing the rocks is forbidden, but rubbings can be made. The best materials to use are black wax and rice paper, which are available in local stores.

To reach the petroglyph beach, go past the Ferry Terminal and turn left on Evergreen Avenue. Go north on Evergreen Avenue about three quarters of a mile to a boardwalk leading to the beach. Head down the boardwalk, and turn right at the beach. Walk up the beach toward the big rock outcropping on the north, high-tide limit of the beach. Most of the petrogyphs tend to face the sea although three also face the nearby wooded area. They are most easily found when the tide is below 12-feet. Other petrogyphs are on display at the library and the museum.

SIDE TRIPS:

The Stikine River begins its 330 mile-long journey inside British Columbia at the headwaters of the Spatsizi Wilderness and runs 30 miles into Alaska. Its endpoint is the Pacific Ocean, five miles north of Wrangell.

One of the river's most spectacular features is the 55-mile long Grand Canyon of the Stikine, about 200 miles upstream from Wrangell. Some sections of this canyon are considered unnavigable by kayak or raft. Mount Edziza Provincial Park and Recreation Area is south of the canyon. The park contains lava flows, basalt plateaus, cinder and sand fields, and symmetrical cinder cones.

The only town along the Stikine is Telegraph Creek , B.C. (pop. 300) which is at the west end of the Grand Canyon. Several buildings from the goldrush era, including the former Hudson's Bay Company store, are here. (Telegraph Creek is accessible via a 75 mile road off the Cassiar Highway.)

At Chief Shakes Hot Springs, about 22 miles from Wrangell, there are two hot tubs available for public use.

The Le Conte Glacier is the southernmost tidewater glacier on the North American continent and is a part of the 1,300 mile Stikine Icefield. It continuously calves large chunks of blue ice into Le Conte Bay, a favorite site for seals and other wildlife. The glacier is located about 25 miles north of Wrangell, on the mainland.

The garnet ledge is located on the mainland about five miles northeast of Wrangell by boat, near the mouth of the Stikine River. The ledge is a landmark which belongs to the Boy Scouts. Only Wrangell children may collect and sell the garnets. Adults may collect them if they obtain special permits at the museum. The garnets can be purchased from children, who relentlessly hawk them at the ferry dock.

PUBLIC RECREATION:

The Wrangell Pool is located on Church Street on the Wrangell High School campus. The pool is open for general swims. The pool building also includes a racquetball court and weight room. There is a public gymnasium at the Wrangell Community Center, next to the pool building. For hours and fees, phone: 874-2444.

ROAD INFORMATION: ZAMOVIA HIGHWAY

SECTION 1: MILE 0 (WRANGELL)-MILE 11 (END OF PAVEMENT)

ROAD CONDITIONS/TERRAIN:

The Zamovia Highway leads south from the Wrangell Ferry Terminal, first via Second Street, then via Church Street. Pavement for the first 11 miles. After Mile 11 the highway is a gravel Forest Service logging road. The road has a narrow shoulder and gently rolling hills.

WATER:

Mile 8.8, spring.

CAMPING:

Mile 1.9, City Park. Mile 4.5, Shoemaker Park. Mile 10.9, Pat's Lake.

ROADSIDE SIGHTS:

Mile 4.8, Wrangell Institute. Former school for Natives now owned by the the Cook Inlet Native Corporation. Mile 6.3, Wrangell Forest Products. For tour information phone 847-3371.

SIDEROADS:

The Zamovia Loop Road ride is only 2.9 miles in length. The road is paved, and is narrow, but has a marked white line shoulder. At the Wrangell Ferry Terminal, turn left onto Zamovia Loop Road. Mile 0.3, the Our Collections Museum. Mile 0.6. The boardwalk leads to the Wrangell petroglyphs. (For directions see section on petrogylphs.) Mile 0.8, the Wrangell Landfill entrance. The Wrangell Convention and Visitor's Bureau handout *Things To Do in Wrangell*, lists the dump as a bear watching site. Mile 1.1, airport. Mile 1.7, USFS. Mile 2.3, public radio station. Mile 2.8, loop ends at the Wrangell Ferry Terminal.

Chapter 5: Petersburg

BACKGROUND

Petersburg (pop. 3,282) is situated on the northern tip of Mitkof Island on the Wrangell Narrows. For the past ninety years, fishing has been the little town's main industry. In 1897, Peter Buschmann, a Native born Norwegian from Tacoma, Washington moved to the area. Soon under his direction, bunkhouses, shipways, a sawmill, a dock, a wharf and living quarters had been built. By 1900 the Icy Straits Cannery, which Buschmann managed, had put out 32,750 cases of salmon. By 1923, 150,000 cases of canned salmon were packed in Petersburg.

In the summer months, the smell of salt water and fresh fish is strong in the Petersburg air. The town processes crab, herring, and ships over 150,000 pounds of shrimp to market each year. Petersburg has the largest home based halibut fleet in Southeast Alaska, and has four canneries. In 1987 the Petersburg fishermen harvested $36.9 million worth of fish. The total value of fish landed ranked Petersburg tenth among U.S. ports. The town's secondary industry has always been logging.

The residents of Petersburg are fastidious about their surroundings. The houses are freshly painted and their lawns well tended. The only drawback for the traveller is that the town has not made provisions for the campers that arrive in town on the late night ferries. The USFS campground is 22 miles away. However, going to Petersburg is worth the intial hassle of finding a place to stay. The Mitkof Highway ride is one of the best Southeast Alaska has to offer.

Petersburg's average July temperature is 56° F. The average July rainfall is 5.3 inches.

VISITORS INFORMATION

The Petersburg Visitor's Center is located on the North Harbor dock next to the Harbormaster's office on Harbor Way, across the street from Sears. The Center, operated by the Chamber of Commerce has fishing, lodging, dining and local history information. The *Viking Visitor's Guide* as well as a free cookbook are available. Write: Box 649, Petersburg, AK 99833. Phone: 772-3646.

FERRY TERMINAL:

The Petersburg Ferry Terminal, located about 1/2 a mile south of downtown Petersburg on Nordic Drive, contains printed material and the *Viking Visitor's Guide*. There are no lockers at the terminal but travellers may leave bags under the seats in the waiting room. The terminal is only open during business hours.

FOREST SERVICE INFORMATION:

The Petersburg District Ranger's Office is located in the Federal Building, behind the post office on the corner of Nordic Drive and Haugen Drive. Enter through the rear of the building. Trail information is available. For FS cabin information write: Box 1328, Petersburg, AK 99833. Phone 772-3871.

TRAVELLER'S NEEDS

MEDICAL SERVICES:

The Petersburg General Hospital is located on Second Avenue and Excel Street at 201 Fram Street. Phone: 772-4291.

GROCERIES:

Trading Union Inc. is situated on the north end of town at Nordic Drive and Dolfin Street. Hammer and Wikan Grocery is in the middle of town on Nordic Drive. These supermarkets carry similar items in the same price range.

Helse Restaurant and Health Food Store, located in Sing Lee Alley, has vegetarian soup, and bulk food items such as nuts and granola. Phone: 772-3444.

The Icicle Seafood local sales office is just north of town on Nordic Drive. They have good deals on fresh and frozen fish and crab, as well as canned salmon; a perfect food for ferry travel.

BICYCLE/OUTDOOR STORES:

Petersburg has no bicycle shop. Tubes and cables are available at the Trading Union Sports and Hardware Store (phone: 772-3881) and at Hammer and Wikan, a grocery, hardware and sporting goods store (phone: 772-4811).

LODGING/CAMPING:

Petersburg has no hostels. Hotel and Bed and Breakfast information is available at both the Ferry Terminal and at the Visitor's Center. There is no official in-town camping.

Tent City, which has 38 platform sites, is located next to the airport. From the Ferry Terminal, travel north, about half a mile to Haugen Drive. (This road isn't marked but ends at where the City Hall and police station are located.) Go up Haugen Drive. The road turns left at the airport terminal, then winds around the airport. Keep going— Tent City is on the right. See narrative for additional information. The USFS Ohmer Creek Campground is located at Mile 21.8, Mitkof Highway. See Road Information: Mitkof Highway.

POST OFFICE:

The Petersburg Post Office is in the Federal Building at Nordic and Haugen Drives, across from City Hall. Zip code: 99833.

LAUNDRY/SHOWERS:

Glacier Laundry at Nordic Drive and Dolfin has 8-minute showers which cost $1.50. The Petersburg Harbormaster's Office also has coin operated showers. Scandia House at 110 Nordic Drive, has showers, hot tubs and saunas.

ENTERTAINMENT AND RECREATION

TRAILS:

There are numerous logging roads in Petersburg. Information is available at the Forest Service office.

MUSEUMS/HISTORICAL SITES:

The Clausen Memorial Museum contains pioneer and fishing industry artifacts. The museum also has two stuffed trophy fish on display: a 126.5 pound Chinook, and a 36 pound chum salmon. The museum is located at 203 Fram Street. Phone 772-3598.

The Little Norway Festival is held annually on the weekend closest to Norwegian Independence Day, May 17th. The popular three-day event features dancing and a Norwegian fish feed. Many locals wear authentic Norwegian costumes.

BOOKSTORES:

Bibliomania is located at 206 Sing Lee Alley.

MOVIES/PLAYS:

The Viking Theatre is located at 306 Nordic Street: Phone: 772-4204.

PUBLIC RECREATION:

The Roundtree Memorial Swimming Pool has a public swim schedule. Phone: 772-3304.

ROAD INFORMATION: MITKOF ISLAND HIGHWAY

SECTION 1: MILE 0 (PETERSBURG) - MILE 21.8 (OHMER CREEK CAMPGROUND)

ROAD CONDITIONS/TERRAIN:

For a ways the two-lane road parallels both the Wrangell Narrows and Petersburg's residential district. Further out is the Tongass National Forest, where evidence of old clearcuts and mature second growth forests can be seen. There are numerous roadside picnic areas and recreation sites. The *Mitkof Island Road Guide* has detailed information.

Leaving town, the road is paved. The shoulder becomes narrower at Mile 3.8. There are flat sections and gradually rolling hills most of the way, except for a steep drop from Mile 13.4 to Mile 13.6. Gravel road surface begins at Mile 17.4.

JUNCTIONS:

Mile 0.7, Petersburg Ferry Terminal. Mile 2.9, Scow Bay Loop Road. Mile 7.5, Twin Creek Road. Mile 10.7, Three Lakes Loop Road. Mile 21.8, Woodpecker Cove Road. The roads leading past the Ohmer Creek Campground to Woodpecker Cove have a gravel surface. They provide excellent views of the Sumner Straits and Zarembo Islands.

WATER:

Mile 10.7, Falls Creek, fishing prohibited.

CAMPING/PICNIC AREAS/TRAILS:

Mile 7.5, Twin Creek RV Park, owned by Phil and Darlene Clausen. Tent sites $9.00. Showers $2.00. Water, laundry facilities available. Limited groceries include canned goods, some fresh produce and Haagen Daz Ice Cream. These are nice people. Darlene in particular sympathizes about the lack of town tenting facilities. Mile 12.3, Blind River Rapids Trail. Mile 12.8, Blind River Island picnic area. Boardwalk trail goes through meadow to picnic area with seven sites. Mile 19.5, Manmade Hole picnic area. Tables, firepits, short trail and swimming here. Mile 21.8. USFS Ohmer Creek Campground has 15 well secluded sites, running water, and picnic tables.

ROADSIDE SIGHTS:

Mile 0.1, Hammer Slough Bridge. Mile 3, Scow Bay. Mile 3.4. Old Mill, now owned by Mitkof Lumber Company. Mile 7.2, B. Frank Heintzleman Forest Tree Nursery. For tours, phone 772-3841. Mile 10.8, Falls Creek and fish ladder. Papke's Landing, public boat dock and USFS terminal transportation facility. Mile 14, beginning of Tongass National Forest. Mile 15, Blind River Rapids fishing area. Mile 16.3, Trumpeter Swan observatory. Mile 17.5, Blind Slough Recreation Area, Crystal Lake Hatchery. (Impromptu tours depend on how busy employees are.)

Author at Control Lake USFS Cabin, Prince of Wales Island

Tent City

A low lying mist nearly covers the mountains in the distance, and gnarled pine trees off the road to the right seem to be holding up the dark grey sky. Tent City is where the summer cannery workers live, and where hikers and bicyclists who disembark the late ferry are directed to go. As Pete and I have just discovered, camping at the boat harbor parking lot near town is for RVs only.

Riding into Tent City at 3 a.m., I see all shapes and sizes of tents pitched above the muskeg on wooden platforms. Some of the tents are covered with visqueen while others are surrounded by wood planks. Roofing material is tacked onto boardwalks which lead to each site. A few people in a shelter sit by a fire. One fellow strums on a guitar and sings off-key. This is what I think the world will be like after a nuclear holocaust. Too tired to talk, Pete and I pick a platform, pitch our tent, and crawl into it.

The sound of a jet screaming overhead wakes me in the morning. Remembering that Tent City is located at the end of an airport runway, I unzip the tent door and look outside. The tents that earlier appeared to be a uniform grey are enshrouded in flapping, brightly colored plastic and nylon. Pete makes breakfast on the embers of the wood fire the cannery workers partied next to hours before. I eat my oatmeal. A fellow with short hair and puffy cheeks, wearing a dark hooded sweatshirt, sits next to his boom box, which is blasting Ozzie Osborn. Nearby, a slightly built woman with short, curly, black hair reads a book called *Communion*, and puffs on a cigarette. I notice her left wrist is bandaged. When I ask her what happened to it, she looks up, says she developed a tendon problem while sliming fish. She sighs, flips a page, and begins reading again.

After eating breakfast Pete and I go to town. When we return to the shelter a few hours later, the guy is still listening to music and the woman is still reading. Bored, we wander around. We converse for a while with a soft spoken fellow whose tent is pitched near ours. He gives us the particulars on Tent City.

He tells us that the occupants, mainly cannery workers, are charged $100.00 a month for their platforms and the use of the shelter. The campsite is monitored by Police Chief Bob Oszman, who makes 50 percent on each unit he rents. There is a bunkhouse in town which rents for $350.00 a month.

Those who are staying there, we are told, will soon be displaced by former workers, who will arrive in town shortly. The evicted will then share platform space with the people already living in Tent City. We are warned that the sheriff will ask for a $25.00 deposit from us if we stay another night.

We decide to stay at Tent City because Ohmer Campground is 22 miles away. Also, a sign tacked to the men's room door indicates that the Bahai's are going to provide a free spaghetti feed. As promised, at 7 p.m., a number of heavy-set women arrive by car. Some have kids, all laugh loudly. They dish out spaghetti with meat sauce, serve corn bread and rolls. Frankfurters and marshmallows also appear from the inner recesses of their cars. Conversations about genetics, fishing, the bears at the garbage dump, and hiking trails follow. Some of the workers sit quietly and read Bahai pamphlets. A few have pinned buttons that say "One Planet, One World," to their shirts.

The sheriff does not put in an appearance. I'm both relieved and disappointed. I want to meet this guy. He might be interesting to write about. On the other hand, I'd rather not. I think the $4.00 a person fee and the $25.00 deposit are a little steep.

The next day while I'm riding the Mitkof Highway, Pete meets Chief Oszman. When he stops his vehicle in front of the Ferry Terminal, Pete asks him if it's true that he makes half of the Tent City camping fee. Oszman replies that yes, that is correct. According to Pete he justified his high salary by saying that there are a lot of drug dealers and losers up at Tent City. "It's a tough job. I have to weed out the crap," Oszman tells Pete.

CHAPTER 6: SITKA

BACKGROUND:

Sitka, (pop 8,160) on the west side of Baranof Island, facing Sitka Sound, is located about 90 miles south and west of Juneau. Sitka was founded in 1799 by Alexander Baranof, head of the Russian American Company under a charter from the Czar. Baranof built his settlement, Michael St. Redoubt, at old Sitka near the present Ferry Terminal, but this was destroyed in 1802 by the Tlingit Indians. The Russians retaliated and two years later defeated the Tlingits. Baranof then rebuilt the town on its present site.

In 1806 Sitka replaced Kodiak as the capital of Russian Alaska, and was soon the center of trade, industry, and Russian culture in the New World. Ships from Spain, France, Russia, England and the United States regularly visited Sitka. Until 1867, Sitka, called New Archangel by the Russians, was an important center for the fur trade. But, mainly because of a diminishing fur market, Russia decided to sell Alaska to the U.S. The price was $7,200,000 or less than 2 cents an acre. Thus Sitka was the first town in Alaska to display an American flag. Secretary of State William H. Seward, who arranged the purchase, was heavily criticized. For a long time after, Alaska was called "Seward's Icebox," "Walrussia" and "Seward's Folly."

Sitka was the seat of military government until 1884, and the District of Alaska civilian government until 1900. Government functions were moved to the new capital of Juneau in 1906.

During World War II, Sitka was a major link in Alaska's defense system. At that time a U.S. Naval Air Station was built on Japonski Island, across Sitka harbor. After the war the Naval Air Station became the Bureau of Indian Affairs Mt. Edgecumbe Boarding School.

Sitka is the largest city-borough in the U.S. with 4,710 miles lying within its municipal boundaries. In the center of the town is St. Michael's Cathedral, a replica of a Russian Orthodox Church. The original, built in 1844-48 by Bishop Innocent Veniaminov, was destroyed by fire in 1966. Priceless icons were saved by the townspeople and are now on display in the rebuilt cathedral.

The average July temperature in Sitka is 55° F. The July average rainfall is 4.7 inches.

VISITOR'S INFORMATION

VISITOR'S CENTER:

The Sitka Visitor's Center, run by the Sitka Chamber of Commerce, is in the same building as the Sitka Historical Society Museum and Sitka City Council Chambers. All three are in the Centennial Building on Harbor Drive, next to the downtown Crescent Boat Harbor. Write: Box 1226, Sitka, AK 99835.

FERRY TERMINAL:

The Sitka Ferry Terminal at Mile 7.1 Halibut Point Road has printed visitor's information. The terminal has no storage lockers, but according to the 1988 American Youth Hostel houseparents Barbara and Jack Taylor, items may be left at Sitka Police or Fire Station offices. Phone: 747-8787.

FOREST SERVICE INFORMATION:

The Sitka District Ranger Station has local trail and FS cabin information. There are 17 recreation cabins in this district. For information write: Sitka District Ranger, 204 Siginaka Way, Box 504, Sitka, AK 99835. The Forest Service office is located at Siginaka Way and Katlian Streets. Phone: 747-6671.

TRAVELLER'S NEEDS

MEDICAL SERVICES:

The Sitka Community Hospital is located on the corner of Brody Street and Halibut Point Road. Phone 747-3241.

GROCERIES:

The supermarket closest to the Ferry Terminal and the nearby campground is Seamart, at Mile 2.2 Halibut Point Road. Seamart has a bakery and health foods section. Hours: 9 a.m. to 9 p.m. Monday through Saturday and and 11 a.m. to 6 p.m. Sunday. The Granite Creek Store is at Mile 4.6 Halibut Point Road . Market Center at 210 Baranof is open from 7 a.m. to 11 p.m. Monday through Saturday and 10 a.m. to 7 p.m. Sunday.

BICYCLING/OUTDOOR STORES:

Southeast Diving and Sports has been owned by Bob and Corky Boes for five years. The Boes' carry Shimano and Suntour parts and can do most repairs. Bicycles, quality outdoor and diving gear is sold. Diving gear rental and classes are offered. Hours: 10 a.m. to 5 p.m., Tuesday through Saturday. If the store doesn't open at 10 a.m, be patient. The Boes' often dive in the morning. Southeast Diving and Sports is located on Lincoln Street. Phone: 747-8279.

LODGING/CAMPING:

The Sitka Youth Hostel is about five miles from the Ferry Terminal at 303 Kimsham Street, on the corner of Kimsham and Edgecumbe Streets. The hostel is in the basement of the United Methodist Church. From the Ferry Terminal, follow Halibut Point Road into town. Turn left at Peterson Street (at Prewitt's Funeral Home) and follow Peterson a half block to Kimsham. (Left at fork in road.) The hostel is at the top of the hill on corner of Kimsham and Edgecumbe Streets. The hostel requires a sleeping bag, but has no cooking facilities. Hours: 6 p.m. to 8:30 a.m. Lights out and no admission after 11 p.m. The hostel can accommodate up to 20 on a first come, first serve basis. AYH members are charged $5.00. For more information write: Box 2645, Sitka, AK, 99835. Phone: 747-8356. Check at the Visitor's Center for information on Sitka bed and breakfasts. For camping information, see Sitka Road Information.

POST OFFICE:

The Sitka Post Office is located in the south end of town at Mile 1 Sawmill Creek Road. Zip code: 99835.

LAUNDRY/SHOWERS:

Suds 'n Duds is located at about Mile 1 Halibut Point Road across the street from McDonalds. Showers are $1.25. Homestead Laundry is next to the Thomsen Boat Harbor on Katlian Street. Showers are $2.00.

ALTERNATIVE TRANSPORTATION:

Prewitt Enterprises has sightseeing tours and meets the incoming planes and ferries. The charge for a ride into town or to the hostel is $2.50. Phone: 747-8443.

ENTERTAINMENT AND RECREATION

TRAILS:

Sitka has a small number of logging roads. Check with the Forest Service for more information.

MUSEUMS/HISTORICAL SITES:

The Isabel Miller Museum, operated by the Sitka Historical Society, is located in the Centennial Building on Harbor Drive. The museum features exhibits from Sitka's Russian, Native and pioneer American past.

The Sheldon Jackson Museum is located on the campus of Sheldon Jackson College. The museum has exhibits on the culture and art of Alaska Natives as well as a quality collection of artifacts. The octagonal museum building was built in 1895, and a large number of the items on display were collected by Dr. Sheldon Jackson. Hours: 9 a.m. to 5 p.m. daily. Admission is $1.00.

Both Sitka's Tlingit and Russian cultures are well represented at the Sitka National Historic Park. The park consists of two sites. The Russian Bishop's House, restored by the National Park Service to its 1853 appearance, is located on Lincoln Street near the Crescent Boat Harbor. Built in 1842 by the Russian-American Company for use by the Orthodox Church, it was recently renovated and opened for public viewing. It is the last major Russian log structure in Sitka and one of the few remaining ones in Alaska. Exhibits focus on the house's history, the Russian fur trade, and the church. The fort site is located 0.5 miles from town on Metlakatla Street. Here once stood the Tlingit fort that was burned by the Russians after the 1804 Battle of Sitka. There is a Visitor's Center with audio visual programs and exhibits of Indian and Russian artifacts. A trail leads to the fort site and battleground. A totem pole collection which stands along the trail contains original pieces collected in 1901-03 and some replicas.

Baranof Castle Hill Historic Site or Castle Hill is the site of Baranof's Castle. This is the site of the October 18, 1867 transfer of Alaska from Russia to the U.S. In the Old Russian Cemetery behind the Pioneer's Home, lies the grave of Princess Maksoutoff, the wife of Alaska's last Russian governor. Totem Square, across Katlian Street from the Pioneer's Home, contains a totem, petroglyphs, a cannon and three large anchors found in Sitka harbor.

PIONEER'S HOME:

The Sitka Pioneer's Home, the first built in the state in 1934, is conveniently located near the waterfront at Katlian and Lincoln Streets. Visitors are welcome and crafts made by the residents are sold in the basement.

BOOKSTORES:

The Observatory, owned by Dee Longenbaugh, specializes in rare and out of print books, maps, prints and Alaskana. Dee also sells contemporary books. Dee is a great person to talk to about Alaskana. The Observatory is located at 202 Katlian Street. Write: Box 1770, Sitka, AK 99835. Phone: 747-3033 or 747-3457.

Old Harbor Books, on Lincoln Street, has paperback and hard back titles as well as topographical maps. Phone: 747-8808.

MOVIES/PLAYS/MUSIC

The annual Sitka Summer Music Festival is held the first three weeks in June at Centennial Hall. Twice weekly concerts and workshops are presented by performing artists from all over the world. One of Alaska's premier musical events. Make reservations early, as seats sell out quickly. Write: Box 907, Sitka, AK 99835.

SIDE TRIPS:

In 1980, about 90 percent of Admirality Island was set aside as a national monument, with 937,000 square acres designated as wilderness. Much of the island is a spruce-hemlock rain forest with muskeg patches.

Angoon, the only town on Admiralty Island, is located on the southwest coast in Mitchell Bay facing Chatham Strait. Angoon (pop. 639) is a Native community, predominately Tlingit.

The Seymour Canal Inlet contains the world's largest population of bald eagles. There are also numerous coastal brown bears, which is why the Tlingits refer to the area as "Fortress of Bears."

Ferries serve Angoon year round; there is boat and plane service from Sitka and Juneau.

There are twelve public recreation cabins available. Write: Admiralty Island National Monument, Box 2097, Juneau, AK 99802 or City Office Building, Flagstaff Road, Angoon, AK 99820.

ROAD INFORMATION: HALIBUT POINT ROAD

SECTION 1: MILE 7.7 (ROAD'S END)-MILE 0 (SITKA)

ROAD CONDITIONS/TERRAIN:

The 7.7. mile Halibut Point Road begins at the center of Sitka, and ends just beyond the Sitka Ferry Terminal. State mileposts run from town to the end of the road. Because the Sitka Ferry Terminal is at Mile 7.1 and most cyclists start from here, route information begins at the road's end. The entire road is paved, with a wide shoulder and bike lane from Mile 7.1, the Ferry Terminal, to Mile 1.7. From Mile 1.7, the road narrows.

WATER:

Mile 7.3, Starrigavan Creek. Good fishing at high tide. Mile 4.6, Granite Creek. Mile 2.3, Cascade Creek. Mile 2.2, Pioneer Park.

CAMPING/PICNIC AREAS/TRAILS:

Mile 7.6, USFS Starrigavan Campground. Camping on both sides of the road. The campground on the east (right) side of the road has water. The campground on the west (left) side of the road has tent sites. The campground host is in the east campground, check here for clamming information. Mile 4.2, Harbor Mountain Road. Winding gravel road 4.9 miles. Elevation 2,100 feet. A short steep trail leads to an old lookout. Another short trail leads to an overlook at Harbor Mountain Peak. Bicycles are allowed, motorized vehicles are not. Mile 2.2, Pioneer Park. Covered tables, enforced no camping. Trails lead to beach where there is often a view of Mt. Edgecumbe.

FOOD/LODGING:

Mile 4.6, Granite Creek General Store sells liquor and some groceries. Hours: daily from 7 a.m. to midnight.

ROADSIDE SIGHTS:

Mile 7.5, Old Sitka. A *National Register of Historic Places* landmark and site of the Russian American Company. Interpretative signs.

ROAD INFORMATION: SAWMILL CREEK ROAD

SECTION 1: MILE 0 (SITKA)-MILE 7.5 (ROAD'S END)

ROAD CONDITIONS/TERRAIN:

The 7.5 mile road is paved to Mile 5.5, then has a gravel surface. The road has a bike path for the first mile, then narrows. There is a gate at Mile 7.5. It is approximately 10-12 miles to Green Lake Dam. This is presumed to be a nice ride.

JUNCTIONS:

At Mile 5.5, on the left, just before the pulp plant, a steep uphill road leads to Sawmill Campground. The campground is not well tended, and reeks of pulp plant smoke.

CAMPING/TRAILS:

Mile 0.7, Indian River USFS trail. Walk up the dirt road adjacent to State Trooper's Academy; the trail begins at the pump house. The trail extends 2 miles to the fork of the river and 5 miles to a trail leading through Indian River Valley to the falls at the base of the Sisters. Mile 3.7, Thimbleberry Lake and Heart Lake Trails. Trail leads 2.8 miles to the lakes. Trail connects at Heart Lake to another short trail leading to Blue Lake Road. Mile 5.5, Sawmill Creek Road, see camping. USFS Beaver Lake trail begins at Sawmill Creek Campground at Blue Lake Road. Trail starts at bridge across campground and leads 0.5 miles to Blue Lake.

FOOD/LODGING:

No food or lodging on this road.

ROADSIDE SIGHTS:

Mile 0.5. Sitka National Cemetery is open from 8 a.m. to 5 p.m. daily. In 1924 President Calvin Coolidge designated the site. Until World War II, it was the only national cemetery west of the Rockies. Civil War veterans, veterans of the World War II Aleutian Campaign as well as many other notable Alaskans are buried here. Mile 0.9, University of Alaska Southeast Islands Community College. Mile 5, Alaska Pulp Company. Mile 6.2, asbestos disposal site, don't linger!

SIDEROADS:

The Japonski Island Loop

After crossing the O'Connell Bridge, turn right at hospital road. The 1,225 foot long bridge was the first cable-stayed, girder-span bridge in the U.S. The mountains of Baranof Island and the volcanic cone of Mt. Edgecumbe on Kruzof Island are visible. Mile 0.9, Mt. Edgecumbe School. At Mile 1.1, you'll come to stairs and guard rail. Hike over gravel for 50 yards then turn left at the fork. A right turn leads to John Brown's grave, and John Brown's Beach. At the rock strewn beach is another excellent view of Mt. Edgecumbe. Mile 1.7, Airport. Mile 2.9, peak of bridge. Mile 3.1, loop's end.

The Sitka Raptor Rehabilitation Center

In a small shed behind the Sheldon Jackson Museum, Jerry Deppa, wearing a brown welder's apron and a glove, both talked and kept his eyes on one of the two eagles he was feeding. Quasimodo, either bored or not hungry, looked skyward. Jerry stroked the bird's beak with a piece of fish. Quasimodo, two months before, had been caught in a steel trap. Subsequently, frostbite and gangrene had indirectly caused the loss of some of his primary flight feathers.

The eagle flapped his wings and shifted his weight from one foot to the other. "I wish he'd get down here and preen," Jerry said, pointing to the bird's side. The raptor moved away from his hand.

"Oh, I know, I know, don't touch the new feathers!" he said. Not bothered by the bird's disinterest, Jerry put the fish head on a tray the volunteer was holding and moved over to the second bird.

"Eagles have a reputation as carrion feeders but they're gourmet feeders. They know the difference between fresh fish and pretty fresh fish. "Halibut? They love it!"

A second bird, Crackers, crouched in a corner and eyed Jerry. Standing above her, he slowly lifted his arms above his head, made a wooshing sound and brought them down to his sides.

"I'm imitating the mama bird," he said. As Jerry, the current Sitka Raptor Rehabilitation Center president later explained, neither bird was able to feed itself. Crackers was being fed like a baby bird because she was physically, and mentally incapable of eating normally. Quasi, a little healthier, could take offered food. Crackers flopped around a bit, backed further into the corner, and opened her cracked beak. Jerry dropped the food in her mouth and she swallowed it. Noticing the disgruntled look in the eagle's yellow eyes, he said to her, "that was a mean trick, wasn't it!"

When Crackers had been brought to the Raptor Center two months before, volunteers and the Alaska Department of Fish and Game thought she might be suffering from DDT poisoning. Since she had shown no signs of improvement, it was suspected she might have a brain tumor or some other neurological disorder.

For the past eight years over 150 volunteers have worked with injured raptors. They've spent countless hours administering medication, giving flying lessons and coercing finicky birds to eat. Roughly 40 percent of their patients have been returned to the wild. Others have been placed in breeding programs, educational facilities, and animal parks and zoos. Those that haven't responded to treatment have been humanely destroyed.

The Center's main goal is to rehabilitate injured birds. But as Lynn Owens, the former Raptor Center president explained, the volunteers are also in business to educate people.

80 percent of the birds that are brought into the Sitka Raptor Center have injuries that are caused by humans either directly or indirectly. Fishing line and hooks, guns, poisons, automobiles, power poles and steel traps all injure raptors. Five to ten percent of the injuries are of an undetermined cause, including obscure toxins in the environment. "It would be great if we could put ourselves out of the rehabilitation business," Owens said.

"We try not to get involved with diseased birds. We're not trying to impact the regular eagle population. That would be presumptuous of us," said Jerry.

Athena, a Western Screech Owl, is mainly kept at the Center for educational purposes. As Jerry explained, she was found in a tree downed by loggers. With the help of Raptor Center volunteers, she was able to recover partial use of her right foot. Because of her injury, volunteers realized she'd have a difficult time surviving in the wild. She has also imprinted on people.

"She's terrifically innocent. She'll let a cat stalk her. Anyone can pick her up," said Jerry.

The owl, because of her small size and easy going disposition, is often taken on walks, for car rides and to area schools. It's hoped that when they meet Athena, "little boys thinking of shooting off a bee-bee gun might think differently. That's a big part of why we should exist," Jerry said.

The Sitka Raptor Rehabilitation Center was started in 1980 by Jim Tigan and Dan Mueller, two Sitka residents who had an interest in raptors, and saw the need for a facility. After obtaining the proper state and federal permits, two small enclosures were built and the Raptor Center began treating bald eagles and other birds of prey. In 1983 the Center moved to its present location on the Sheldon Jackson College campus. A larger facility with a 450 square foot flight cage, an isolation enclosure for newly received, possibly infectious birds and a small office for health checks and treatments was constructed by volunteers. Currently the Center has tax-exempt status from the IRS which is important because it is financed entirely through membership fees and contributions.

Owens and the other volunteers would like to see the Raptor Center's facilities grow so they can accept more birds. They want to build an interpretive center and have a staff member run the Center. But added Owens, further growth would take a huge volunteer effort.

"The birds take an incredible amount of care. The responsibility falls on the self-employed and the unemployed. The Raptor Center can take over your life," she said.

Jerry, who has been involved with the Center for three years, works very closely with Crackers and Quasimodo. When Quasimodo was first brought in, he was dehydrated and had to be given fluid with a stomach pump. Gradually he was put back on a fish diet. The drawback that Jerry and the other nine volunteers had in dealing with Quasimodo was that any handling would break the bird's new incoming flight feathers.

"A great deal of time has been put into training him to accept us," said Jerry. Because Quasi lost two toes while in the steel trap, the eagle has needed daily foot massages. This has helped to increase circulation and reduce swelling.

"He'll let me have his feet as long as I'm careful with them. I've filed down his talons. He'll let me do that," he said.

Quasimido will soon be trained to stand confidently on a person's hand. Then after his flight feathers grow in, he'll be given flight lessons on a long line.

"I'll be tickled if he flies 100 feet!" said Jerry.

When asked what would happen to Crackers if she didn't recover, Jerry said that a committee would decide what should be done.

If Jerry and the committee decide that Crackers can't be rehabilitated, she'll be euthanized and an autopsy will be performed by the Department of Fish and Game. Although the death of the bird will be a loss, the Center will have a more complete file to refer to if another bird with similar symptoms is brought in.

"You shouldn't consider euthanasia in this operation as a failure, but as a reasonable alternative. We have a problem in our species making those decisions. We don't have the right to project our interspecies problems on them. They would have settled problems out there by dying," said Jerry. "Even our best efforts will only bring her up to a certain level. Crackers is a good bird, but they're all good birds."

JUNEAU

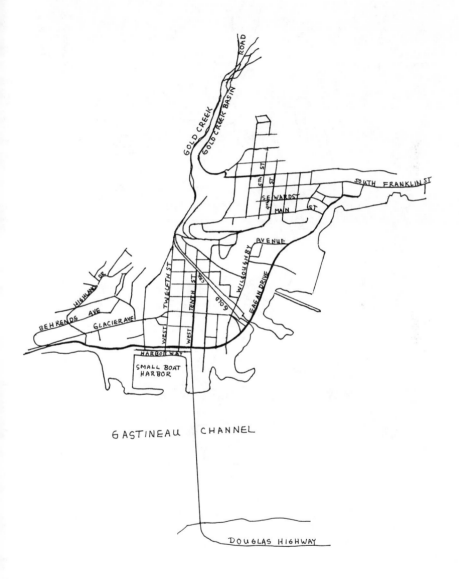

GREATER JUNEAU

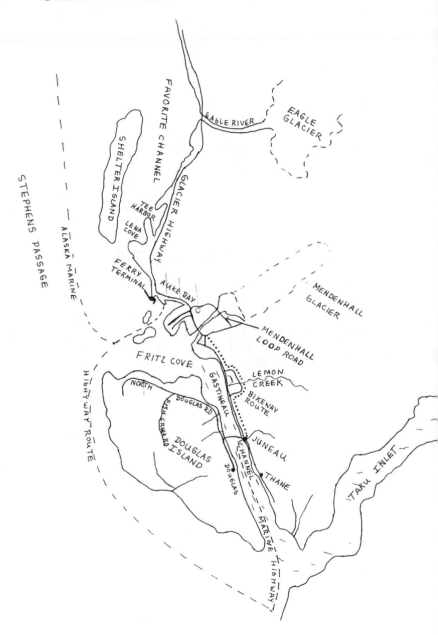

Chapter 7: Juneau

BACKGROUND

Juneau, (pop. 27,270) Alaska's third largest city, has been the state capital since 1906. It is the only U.S. capital (with the exception of Honolulu) that is not connected to the North American road system. Built along the shores of Gastineau Channel in the shadows of Mt. Juneau and Mt. Roberts, Juneau is a busy port with the arrival of hundreds of cruise ships each summer. A significant number of Juneau's residents are government employees. Others are involved in the fishing, transportation and tourism industries.

The first published account of exploration in Gastineau Channel was written in 1793-1794 by Captain George Vancouver. Another account was penned by naturalist John Muir. Upon his return to Sitka after visiting the Gastineau Channel and meeting with the Chilkat Tlingits, Muir noted the mineralized character of the mainland shore in the area that was later known as the Juneau Gold Belt.

Mining engineer George Pilz, receiving word of Muir's sightings, secured more detailed knowledge about them after Chief Kowee, a Tlingit Indian, brought him ore samples. Pilz then grubstaked Joe Juneau and Richard Harris. They returned to Pilz six weeks later, empty-handed. A second search effort was funded after Chief Kowee again visited Pilz, bearing more ore samples. The second time around, Harris and Juneau found gold at what Harris named Silver Bow Basin.

The Treadwell Mine on Douglas Island was discovered by "French Pete" Erussand and developed under the leadership of California gold miner John Treadwell. By 1915, the 960 stamp mill was crushing a record 5,000 tons of ore a day. In 1917, all but the Ready Bullion mine flooded with seawater. When this mine closed in 1922, hard rock mining on Douglas Island ended. Although many of the buildings have deteriorated and are now buried under heavy vegetative undergrowth, it is still possible, on a walking or mountain bike tour, to get an idea of what the operating Treadwell Mine was like.

The area's second mine, the Alaska Juneau Mine or A-J mine, was incorporated in 1897, and closed fifty years later. Juneau's mining era ended with the closing of the A-J. A third area of consolidated mining activities took place in Silver Bow Basin. The Perseverance Mine, established in 1885, grew until the quality of retrievable ore dropped to an unprofitable level in 1921. Recent events indicate that mining will again play an important part in Juneau's future.

The Gastineau Channel separates Juneau from Douglas. In 1910, mainly because of mining activity, Douglas's population had grown to 1,722. However, between 1911 and 1937 the town was struck by a series of fires which by 1939 reduced the population to 522. Today Douglas is a residential area.

Juneau's average July temperature is 57° F. and average rainfall is 6.2 inches.

VISITORS INFORMATION

VISITOR'S CENTER:

The Davis Log Cabin Information Center is located at the corner of Third and Seward Streets. The Visitor's Center is a recreation of an 1881 structure which was the town's first church. The original building, which served as a school, carpentry shop and brewery office, is located a block away from its replica.

The Center has information on lodging, horse and buggy tours, guided day hikes, walking tours, fly-in fishing, flightseeing, restaurants, hotels, bed and breakfasts, local buses, salmon bakes, museums and art galleries. Hours: 8:30 a.m. to 5 p.m. Monday through Friday, 10 a.m. to 2 p.m., Saturdays, and 2 to 5 p.m. Sundays. Phone : 586-2201 or 586-2284. For additional information write: Convention and Visitor's Bureau, 76 Egan Drive, Juneau, AK 99801. The Southeast Alaska Bed and Breakfast Association phone number is 586-2959

FERRY TERMINAL:

The Auke Bay Ferry Terminal at Mile 14 Glacier Highway has printed visitor information. Also, when not pressed for time, the staff can provide information. Baggage lockers available. Phone: 465-3941.

FOREST SERVICE INFORMATION:

The USFS Information Center in Centennial Hall at Egan Drive and Willoughby Avenue has information on USFS cabins and hiking trails. The Forest Service maintains about 24 recreation cabins in the Juneau vicinity of the Tongass National Forest. The cabins are accessible by foot, float plane or boat in salt water areas. The Center has video tapes and films and cultural, historical, and natural history exhibits. Alaska Natural History Association publications and maps are available. Hours: 9 a.m. to 6 p.m. daily. Phone : 586-8751. For cabin reservations write: Juneau District Ranger, Box 2097, Juneau, AK 99802.

COOPERATIVE EXTENSION OFFICE:

The Cooperative Extension Service has brochures on wild and edible berries and plants, preparing fish and game, gardening and sourdough cooking. The office is located on the first floor of the Federal Building, Room 137. Hours: f8 a.m. to 5 p.m. Monday through Friday. Phone: 586-7102.

TRAVELLER'S NEEDS

MEDICAL SERVICES:

Bartlett Memorial Hospital is located at 3260 Hospital Drive. Phone: 586-2611.

GROCERIES:

Foodland Supermarket, which also has an adjacent pharmacy, is located in downtown Juneau at 631 Willoughby Avenue. Fred Meyers, at 8181 Old Glacier Highway, outside of town, is open 24 hours a day. There are several other food stores in Juneau.

BICYCLING/OUTDOOR STORES:

Adventure Sports, 9105 Mendenhall Mall Road, carries some Shimano and Suntour parts and has a large inventory of children's bicycles and mountain bikes. Repair work is done here. The shop is owned by mechanic Tom Mayer, Lynn Mayer and Bill

Gissel. They can provide information on the half dozen or so local biking events that take place each summer. Phone: 789-5696 for store hours.

The Foggy Mountain Shop at 134 Franklin Street has expensive quality outdoor equipment. They carry Northface tents, sleeping bags and clothing, as well as Coleman, Svea, and MSR stoves. Hours: 10 a.m. to 7 p.m. Monday through Friday, Saturdays, 10 a.m. to 6 p.m. and Sunday, 12 a.m to 5 p.m. Owners are Scott and Betsy Fischer. Phone: 586-6780.

LODGING/CAMPING:

The Juneau International Youth Hostel is located in a three story downtown historic home built in the 1920's. Overnight fees are $7.50 per night for AYH members and $9.50 for non-members. The hostel has 40 beds. Reservations are accepted if accompanied by a non-refundable deposit of the first night's fee. Houseparents Bill and Shirley Keller enforce the standard AYH rules.

Registration is from 5 p.m. to 10:30 p.m. and check-out time is 9 p.m. The hostel is closed from 9 a.m. to 5 p.m. Pets, smoking, drugs and alcohol are prohibited. The maximum stay is three days, and each guest is assigned a daily chore. According to Shirley, the hostel is not set up for bicycle storage. However, a limited number can be stored on the porch. Reservations are required for large groups. Phone: 586-9559. The hostel is located at 614 Harris Street on the corner of Sixth and Harris Streets.

There are no camping facilities in the city proper. However, there are Forest Service campgrounds on the Mendenhall Loop Road and near Auke Bay. See Road Information.

POST OFFICE:

The Juneau Post Office (main branch) is located on the ground floor of the Federal Building at 709 West 9th Street. Hours: 9:30 a.m. to 5 p.m. Monday through Friday. Zip Code 99801.

LAUNDRY/SHOWERS:

Showers are available at the Alaskan Hotel, 167 S. Franklin Street (phone: 586-2055) and the Zach Gordon Youth Center, 306 Whittier Avenue (phone: 586-2635). Shower and laundry facilities are available at the Harbor Washboard, Alaska Laundry, 1100 Glacier Avenue. Phone: 586-2055. Hours: Monday through Friday, 8 a.m. to 9 p.m., Saturday from 9 a.m. to 9 p.m. and Sunday from 9 a.m. to 6 p.m. Laundry facilities are available at The Dungeon, Mendenhall Apartments (basement), 326 Fourth Street. Phone: 586-2805.

ALTERNATIVE TRANSPORTATION:

A privately owned company, Mendenhall Glacier Transport (MGT) has a 1-1 1/2 hour tour which goes to both the Mendenhall Glacier and the Chapel by the Lake at Auke Bay. For ticketing and departure times phone 789-5460. MGT meets all ferries with their shuttle bus. For $3.00 they'll take passengers from the Ferry Terminal to the airport, and for $5.00, from the Ferry Terminal to downtown Juneau. They do not transport bicycles. Check at the Log Cabin for information on other motorized and horse-drawn transportation.

ENTERTAINMENT AND RECREATION

TRAILS:

The trails on the Forest Service lands are presently open to bicyclists. However, it is illegal to ride on the Perseverance, Mt. Roberts, Mt. Juneau, Granite Creek or Sheep Creek Trails which comprise the Juneau State Trail System. Locals say many of the trails, because of roots, muskeg and mud, are unsuitable for riding. Exceptions are the Herbert Glacier and Amalga trails, both former mining roads. Trails throughout the Mendenhall Glacier Recreation Area lead to points of interest. They include the Moraine Ecology Loop and Nugget Creek Trails which are both 1.5 miles long, and the East Glacier loop and West Glacier Trails, two 3.5 mile hikes.

The Forest Service publication, *Juneau Trails Recreation Opportunity Guide* provides maps, profiles, and trail descriptions. The book is available from the FS Information Center, local book stores and the Mendenhall Glacier Visitor Center. Another description and historic overview of the local trails is included in *In the Miner's Footsteps* by Willette Janes (available at the J-D City Museum).

GLACIER VIEWING:

The Mendenhall Glacier was formed during the ice age about 3,000 years ago. Before 1750, the Mendenhall Glacier was advancing; its face was 2.5 miles down valley from its present position. Due to slightly warmer temperatures, land under ice is being exposed. The average rate of forward flow is about two feet per day, but the Mendenhall Glacier is receding at a slightly faster rate.

Opened in 1962, the Mendenhall Glacier Visitor's Center was the first one built in Alaska by the USFS. Guided trail walks are given daily starting at 9:30 a.m. When the salmon spawn in mid-July, walks are given daily at 3 p.m. Brochures, maps, books pamphlets, and visual aids are available at the staffed information desk. Hours: 9 a.m. to 6:30 p.m. daily. For directions, see Road Information, Mendenhall Loop Road.

MUSEUMS/HISTORICAL SITES:

The Juneau Douglas City Museum has detailed information on local mining history. A model of the A-J Mine shows the extensive system of tunnels that run through Gold Mountain. The museum has historic photos, slides and videos and a library. Temporary exhibits and an ongoing lecture series focus on additional areas of Juneau's history, wealth, natural world, and culture. The museum is located in the old Juneau Memorial Library building on Main Street

The Juneau Douglas City Museum also has several walking tour maps. The Historic Juneau Downtown Walking Tour gives an overview of the town. The Totem Pole Walking Tour identifies the figures on the City's twenty totem poles, their dates of carving and their carvers. The *National Register of Historic Places* Walking Tour has the location and a brief description of eleven local buildings on the National Historic Register.

Many of these buildings, including the House of Wickersham, are open to the public. The Wickersham House, a turn of the century residence, was the retirement home of Alaska pioneer Judge James Wickersham. Artifacts from the Judge's ethnographic collection are on display and guided tours are available. Hours: 10 a.m. to 5 p.m. Sunday through Friday. The building can be rented for special occasions. Phone: 586-9001.

The Last Chance Basin Walking Tour leads to the remains of the Alaska-Juneau Gold Mining Company's portal camp. A few buildings, trains, and the No. 1 mining tunnel are left. Completed in 1913, the compressor building, made of heavy timber and corrugated iron, is 18 feet tall from concrete floor to wood truss. It holds an Ingersoll Rand Compressor and other mining equipment. The compressor building, a part of the Last Chance Basin Museum, may be open in mid-1989. Check at the City Museum.

Admission to the Juneau Douglas City Museum is free, but donations are welcome. Hours: 9 a.m. to 5 p.m. Monday through Friday and 11 a.m. to 5 p.m. Saturdays and Sundays. Phone: 586-3572.

Created by the Congress in 1900, the Alaska State Museum began exhibiting in 1920. In 1967, the City and Borough of Juneau funded the construction of the museum's current site and presented the building to the state in honor of the Alaska Purchase Centennial celebration. The Alaska Native Gallery has extensive exhibits on the four major Alaska Native cultural groups: the Northwest Coast Indians, the Athabaskans, the Aleuts, and the Eskimos. The Governor's North Galleries contain temporary exhibitions.

The 13,000 square foot white house on Calhoun Street with the six columns in front and the totem pole at the side is the current home of Governor Steve Cowper, first lady Michael Cowper, and their son Wade. Recently the Governor's Mansion underwent a $2 million renovation. The house, originally built in 1912, was restored to an early 1900's decor. In addition, structural and security improvements were made. The Governor's Mansion is only open to the public one day during the Christmas season.

The State Capital is on Fourth Street between Main and Seward Streets. The marble interior panelling and columns on the outside came from the Tokeen quarry on Marble Island near Prince of Wales Island. Built in 1932, the capital served as a territorial building and housed the post office, courtrooms, library and museum. Today it is the home of the Alaska State Legislature, which meets from January to May. Free guided tours of the Capital are available every half hour. Hours: 8:30 a.m. to 5 p.m. daily.

The State Office Building has two main entrances. One is diagonal from the Capital Building on Fourth Street and the other is on Willoughby, across from Bullwinkle's Pizza Parlor. The Alaska State Library, on the eighth floor, includes the state historical library. The Old Witch Totem Pole and a 1928 Kimball Pipe Organ are on this floor. The totem pole, carved in the 1880's, came from a Haida village on Prince of Wales Island. Free organ recitals are held on Fridays at noon.

The Juneau Public Library is located atop the Municipal Garage on Marine Way. The new 18,000 square foot facility opened in January, 1989.

Alaska Pioneer's Home:

Visitors are always welcome at the recently opened Alaska Pioneer's Home, located at 4675 Glacier Highway. Phone: 780-6422.

Eating/Drinking Establishments:

At The Channel Bowl, 608 Willoughby Avenue, trucker sized meals are served adjacent to a bowling alley. One of Channel Bowl's best known breakfast specials is Mount Jumbo. This concoction of eggs, scallions, zucchini, celery, potatoes, cheese, and spices comes with salsa and a side order of toast. Burgers, fries, cajun pork roast, clam strips and meat loaf are also served in the cramped little diner.

The Channel Bowl, located across from a local supermarket parking lot, has been owned for the past five of its twenty years by Lauri Borg. According to one of the Bowl's waitresses, Borg has encouraged her customers to contribute to the unusual decor. On the walls above the tables are old black and white photos of local bowlers. One bowler, hunched over with his ball at eye level, wears paper rabbit ears. Another, a Santa Claus hat. The Channel Bowl opens at 6:30 a.m. and serves breakfast until 11:30. Closing time, in the summer, when the legislature isn't in session, is "around 5."

The soups, salads, burgers, and croissants at the Fiddlehead Restaurant and Bakery are excellent although it would be costly for a hungry bicyclist. The background noise is Windham Hill music, not bowling pins, and there's a no smoking area. There's also a beer and wine list. The Fiddlehead, which has a full lunch and dinner menu, is at 429 Willoughby Avenue, around the corner from the Alaska State Museum. The Fiddlehead is open from 7 a.m. to 9 p.m. Monday through Saturday and from 9 a.m. to 9 p.m. Sundays.

The Federal Building Cafeteria has the basic cafeteria fare--tuna and egg salad sandwiches, Jello, salads, and muffins from a mix. But for those on a limited budget, the food will fill the hole. Around noon the window seats are often occupied by federal employees, but before 10 a.m. or after 2 p.m. the dining area is a good place to watch the ships, gulls, and float planes cruise along the Gastineau Channel.

Another eatery is the Tex-Mex Cafe on South Franklin across from the downtown former Ferry Terminal. Everything from chili to cajun food is served here.

Chinook Alaskan Brewing is open on Tuesday and Thursday, from 11 a.m. to 4 p.m. or by appointment. Phone: 780-5866. See Juneau Road Information, Glacier Highway for directions. For more information see the narrative in this chapter

There are scores of restaurants, fast food places as well as two salmon bakes. Check the *Juneau Empire* or ask at the Log Cabin.

BOOKSTORES:

The Alaskan Heritage Bookshop at 174 South Franklin (in the Emporium Mall) is a small antiquarian bookshop which claims to have the world's largest stock of books on the Yukon poet Robert Service. The store has a large selection of fine old bird prints, rare maps, photos, postcards, 18th and 19th century prints, and Alaskana. Phone: 586-6748.

Big City Books, at 100 North Franklin Street, is a good general interest bookstore with numerous contemporary Alaska books and USGS maps. Phone: 586-1772.

On the same block, at 254 Front Street, is Hearthside Books, a smaller general bookshop. They have a larger branch at the Nuggett Mall, out the road. Phone: 586-1726. Staff at Big City and Hearthside are helpful and knowledgeable.

MOVIES/PLAYS:

There are two multiplex movie theatres, one in town and one in the valley.

The Perseverance Theatre, a nationally recognized theatre company, has an ongoing summer play, "The Lady Lou Revue." The show is presented at the downtown Elks Club, 109 N. Franklin Street. Show time is 8 p.m. daily. Occasional shows are at 2 p.m., depending on cruise ship schedules. Phone: 586-3686. The main stage is located at the home of Perseverance Theatre, at 914 Third Street, Douglas. Phone: 364-2421.

Public Recreation:

The Juneau Parks and Recreation Department summer schedule (available at the Log Cabin) includes information on athletic events, outdoor classes and library and pool hours.

The Augustus Brown Swimming Pool, located at 1619 Glacier Avenue, between Juneau Douglas High School and the Marie Drake Middle School, has open and lap swimming hours. The pool building has a sauna, showers and weight equipment. Unfortunately, it is anticipated the pool will be closed for repairs during summer, 1989. Phone: 586-2055.

Environmental Concerns:

The Southeast Alaska Conservation Council (SEACC,) located at 419 Sixth Street, has information on current environmental issues. Phone: 586-6942.

JUNEAU ROAD INFORMATION

GLACIER HIGHWAY

Background

The Glacier Highway extends north from Juneau along the shores of Gastineau Channel, Auke Bay and Favorite Channel to Eagle River, with branches leading to the Mendenhall Glacier, Mendenhall Penninsula and Lena Point. Spur roads lead to Tee Harbor and Dotson's Landing.

The highway starts in Juneau at Main Street, Mile 0 and is 40.3 miles long. Road conditions are variable. Egan Drive becomes Glacier Highway, which later has a gravel surface. Bicycles are not permitted on Egan Drive and cyclists must use the bicycle path which at times is difficult to follow.

The Juneau Bikeway begins at the outskirts of Juneau and continues to where the Glacier Highway crosses the Mendenhall River. Since most cyclists initially disembark at the Ferry Terminal, the directions given lead from the Auke Bay Ferry Terminal to the city of Juneau. Next, road information is given from the Mendenhall River, Mile 10, to the end of the road.

ROAD INFORMATION: BIKE ROUTE TO TOWN

Section 1: Mile 14.2 (Ferry Terminal) - Mile 0 (Juneau)

The terminal is located 14.2 miles north of Juneau. Mileposts run from Juneau north. Cyclists follow the highway for about four miles or until the Mendenhall River Bridge. From here, the divided highway is known as Egan Drive, and bicycles are restricted. To continue to town, turn right (west) on Sunset Drive (just past the Mendenhall River Bridge). To go to Adventure Sports, instead of turning right on Sunset Drive, turn left (east) and enter the Mendenhall Mall. The bike shop is located within the mall complex.

Going to town--follow Sunset Drive about 0.1 miles then turn left (south) on Del Rae Road. Follow Del Rae Road until it intersects Mendenhall Loop Road (about 0.5 miles; it's a busy street). Turn left (east) and follow Mendenhall Loop Road about 0.3 miles to the bike path just on the other side of Egan Drive. See Sideroads for information on the Mendenhall Loop Road.

To get to Juneau International Airport: instead of turning left (east) on Mendenhall Loop Road, turn right (west). Go straight to the Old Glacier Highway. Turn left, follow signs to airport terminal.

Going to town--we will designate the start of this bike path Mile 0. Turn right (south) on the bike path and parallel Egan Drive for about 0.8 miles where at Fred Myers (24 hour grocery and general merchandise) the path ends and a road begins. Follow this road. Mile 3. The road turns left (east) and becomes Lemon Creek Loop Road. Mile 3.7, road crosses Lemon Creek. Mile 3.9, Aika Road, turn left to get to the Chinook Brewery. Go to Shaume Road, and turn right. Brewery is on the left. At Mile 4.5 the Lemon Creek Loop Road returns to Egan Drive. Turn left (south) on the road here and again parallel Egan Drive. Mile 4.7, Juneau Pioneer's Home is on the right. Mile 5.1. The bike path resumes and enters Twin Lakes Park. Mile 6.1, bike path ends at the road. This end of Twin Lakes Park has restrooms and a picnic shelter. Turn right (west) on to the road, then immediately left (south) and back on the bike path. Continue on the bike path to Mile 6.6 where the bike path ends and Glacier Avenue begins. Glacier Avenue leads into town, where it becomes Willoughby Avenue.

ROAD INFORMATION: GLACIER HIGHWAY

SECTION 1: MILE 10 (MENDENHALL RIVER) - MILE 42 (END OF THE ROAD)

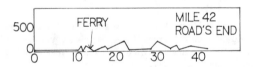

ROAD CONDITIONS/TERRAIN:

Paved road with shoulder to Mile 32.8. Gravel road for the remainder. Rolling hills most of the way, with the highest point being about 240 feet at Mile 29.9.

JUNCTIONS:

Mile 12.3. North terminus of Mendenhall Loop Road. Mile 14, Auke Bay Ferry Terminal.

WATER:

Mile 10, Mendenhall River, Brotherhood Bridge. The river is named after the Mendenhall Glacier. Water not recommended for drinking. Mile 27.6, Herbert River. Mile 27.9, Eagle River. Mile 33.8, Bessie Creek. Mile 40.1, Kowee Creek. Private land, no camping.

CAMPING/TRAILS:

Mile 15.5. USFS Auke Bay Campground. Running water, flush toilets. Mile 27.6, Herbert Glacier Trail. (4.6 miles). Mile 27.9, Amalga (Eagle Glacier) Trail.

Approximately 7 miles, some planking evident. Both trails are old mining roads, and suitable for bicycling.

Food/Lodging:

Mile 11.3, De Hart's Liquor and Grocery. Limited groceries, Blazo fuel, some fishing gear.

Roadside Sights:

Mile 11.7, University of Alaska, Southeast. Mile 15.2, Yax-te totem pole and interpretive sign. Mile 15.3, interpretive sign describing AHNCH-GA-TSOO village area and Auke-kwan village site. Mile 19.6, Inspiration Point in Tee Harbor. View across Favorite Channel and Lynn Canal to the Chilkat Range. Good sport fishing here. Mile 22.7, Shrine of Saint Terese. The shrine chapel, constructed of cobblestones and native timber, is on an island which is joined to the mainland by a 400 foot causeway. On the mainland is a caretaker's residence and a log retreat lodge. The two story lodge has sleeping accommodations for five, kitchen facilities and may be reserved for $20.00 a night. For more information write: Shrine of St. Terese, 5933 Lund Street, Juneau, AK 99801. Phone: 780-6112. Mile 28.5, Eagle Beach Picnic Area.

SIDEROADS

Mendenhall Loop Road:

The road begins at Mile 9 Glacier Highway or where the bikepath intersects Mendenhall Road when travelling north. At Mile 2.2 is a junction for the Mendenhall Glacier Spur Road. (To reach the Mendenhall Glacier, follow this road 1.4 miles.) Steep Creek near the Mendenhall Glacier parking lot is a good place to observe spawning salmon. From July to December, sockeye, coho and chum salmon enter the creek from nearby salt waters.

Mile 3.3, the Mendenhall River. Mile 2.7, junction with Montana Creek Road. 0.8 miles up Montana Creek Road is the USFS Mendenhall Lake Campground. Non-vehicular camping is allowed. Mile 4.6, Montana Creek. Mile 5.7, Lake Creek. Mile 6.5, junction with Mile 12, Glacier Highway.

Douglas:

The 0.3 mile bridge crosses the Gastineau Channel at 10th Street and Egan Drive. Turn left to go to the city of Douglas. There are two Douglas Highways, one goes north and the other south. The North Douglas Highway begins at the bridge on Douglas Island. It parallels the Gastineau Channel to Mile 11.3, False Outer Point Beach, then turns inland for an additional two miles. In June, Lupines line portions of the road. Gently rolling hills to Mile 7, Eaglecrest Ski Resort. Steep five mile gravel road leads to the ski slopes. Mile 8.2. Fish Creek, Mendenhall Wetland State Game Refuge is to the right. Fishing not allowed. Mile 11.3, False Outer Point Beach. Mile 13.3, blueberry picking in season.

The South Douglas Highway starts at Egan Drive on the mainland and ends in the town of Douglas. After crossing the bridge, a bicycle path leads 1.9 miles to a primary school. Mile 2.3 Douglas Post Office. To reach the Treadwell Mine area and historic trail, continue through town and turn left where St. Anne's intersects with Harbor Road. Continue through Savikko Park, and look for walking tour signs.

Mountain biking trails in this area. Residential properties line both the North and South Douglas Highways.

THANE ROAD:

Thane Road begins at the junction of Egan Drive and South Franklin Street. The roadside is lined with salmonberries. Rolling hills for 5.5 miles. Avalanche area. Portions of road closed in January, 1989 due to avalanche. The last two miles go through the Thane residential area. At Mile 4.2 is Sheep Creek and Sheep Creek Fish Hatchery. Note the fish weir beside the bridge. Point Bishop/DuPont Trail begin at the road's end.

View from Last Chance Basin Mining Museum

The Chinook Brewery

In June 1987 and 1988 at the Great American Beer Festival, the largest one of its kind in North America, 160 American-brewed beers were judged by a panel of experts. In 1988 the top overall vote getter during the two-day event was Alaska brewed Chinook Beer. In both 1987 and 1988 Chinook also received the gold medal in the alt competition, one of 18 categories recognized by the judges.

The award was the culmination of seven years of hard work on the part of Jeff and Marcelle Larson, the owners of the only operating Alaska brewery. Marcelle, wearing jeans and a Chinook tee-shirt, took a break from doing the books, and talked about their now successful business venture.

Jeff graduated from the University of Maryland with a degree in Chemical Engineering. His first job upon graduating involved designing and installing alcohol manufacturing plants. Marcelle had a degree in accounting from Furman University in South Carolina. . Because of their related skills, the pair often joked about starting a brewery. However, it was when job pickings began to look slim for Jeff that the pair seriously thought about starting their own company. Said Marcelle, "There weren't a lot of chemical engineering jobs out there. Brewing looked a heck of a lot better."

Their musings became a reality when the Larsons found a 1940's bottling unit in Iowa. Even though it was slow, the old Coca Cola bottler suited their needs. "These bottlers are like an old car— they don't die, they're just too slow for larger operations," said Marcelle, glancing through the plate glass window at the row of dark brown bottles slowly moving like soldiers in formation under the taps of the old machine.

Soon after acquiring this bottler, the Larsons were putting out 500 cases of beer a week. Recently they upped this to 1,000 cases a week. In their short career as brewery operators, the Douglas couple has found that putting out a quality product is more expensive in Alaska than in the Lower 48. A single brew of Chinook beer requires roughly 1,000 pounds of malt. Because in-state grain has too much protein, the Larson's use malt from the Saskatchewan grain belt. Thus the shipping costs are higher than they would be if locally grown grain was used.

Special labels that stick to wet bottles and cardboard boxes also cost more in Alaska than elsewhere.

The bottling is done locally by six full time and six part time employees. The company also has over 100 investors, who often help bottle in exchange for some of the rejects.

The Chinook Beer recipe is based on one used by the Douglas Brewing Company, which produced beer in Alaska from 1899 to about 1907. The water is advertised as coming from local mountains and glaciers.

The label on the bottle, which shows a fishing seiner making its way out of Elfin Cove, was designed by Lauren Giusti, a former Juneau artist. Marcelle explained how the name Chinook was selected. "We wanted a name for the beer, one word that meant a lot to the area, but we didn't want to localize it. It's not just a Juneau beer, but an Alaska beer. A Chinook is a mountain wind, an ocean fish, and a trading language. There is even a Chinook dictionary."

In December 1988, the Larsons produced a special seasonal beer, a smoked porter. The 200 test cases sold out in five hours. The brewers are now planning to produce more seasonal beers.

Visitors are welcome on Tuesdays, brewing days, and Thursdays bottling days, between 11 a.m and 4 p.m. or by appointment (phone: 780-5866). Free samples are available.

Chapter 8: Haines

BACKGROUND

Haines (pop. 1,151) is located on a narrow peninsula between the Chilkoot and Chilkat Inlets, 75 miles northwest of Juneau and 14 boat miles south of Skagway. The first inhabitants of the area were Chilkat Tlingit Indians. Their principal village, still in existence, is Klukwan on the Chilkat River.

The town of Haines was settled around 1880 by S. Hall Young, a Presbyterian missionary. The Tlingit Chiefs offered Hall a site on Portage Cove between the Chilkat River and Chilkoot Inlet. The Tlingit name for the site was Dei-Shu or "End of the Trail." When the mission school opened the following year, it was named Haines after Mrs. F.E.H. Haines, secretary of the Presbyterian Home Mission Board.

During the Klondike Gold Rush, adventurer Jack Dalton developed a toll road from Haines to the Yukon along an old Indian trade route. The Dalton Trail, which leads from Pyramid Harbor on the Chilkat Inlet to the vicinity of Whitehorse in the Yukon, was used as a pack route into the Klondike. This was a longer but easier alternative to the Chilkoot and White Pass trails until the White Pass and Yukon Railroad out of Skagway was completed in 1900.

In the early 1900's the army constructed Fort William H. Seward in Haines. The completed buildings housed two companies of soldiers. Not to be confused with the town of Seward, and to "commemorate the pass over which the pioneers of Alaska made their way in the days of the Gold Rush," Fort Seward was named Chilkoot Barracks in 1922. Between 1922 and 1939, the Chilkoot Barracks was the only army post in Alaska. It served as an induction and rest camp during World War II. In 1947, the property was purchased by a group of veterans who established the community of Port Chilkoot. The post was designated a national historic site in 1972, and renamed Fort Seward. Most of the buildings have been restored and are now private residences.

For a while the Chilkat-Chilkoot Inlet area supported a cannery industry. Chinese laborers, white cannery workers and fishermen imported from San Francisco made up the bulk of the seasonal employees. Haines Packing Company at Letnikoff Cove was the only successful company. The cannery was in operation until 1970, and for a few years served as a grocery store.

The fishing and timber industries have been the community's principal means of employment. Many Haines residents fish commercially for sockeye and chum salmon, and halibut. For the past several years the timber industry has been unstable and Haines mill owners have come and gone.

Most of the Haines residents have accepted the fact that catering to the innumerable RVers and cruise passengers for four months a year allows them to live year-round in one of the most beautiful areas of the world. Haines is a short ride from Mile 18 Haines Highway, where over 3,000 eagles come in the fall and winter to feed on the late salmon run. The area contains the 48,000 acre Chilkat Bald Eagle Preserve which was made a sanctuary in 1982.

The average July temperature in Haines is 57° F. The average July rainfall is 1.7 inches.

VISITORS INFORMATION

VISITOR'S CENTERS:

The Haines Visitor's Center, located on Second Avenue near Willard Street, has a complete listing of town activities, including walking tours, and numerous town restaurant menus. Hours: 8 a.m. to 8 p.m., Tuesday through Saturday, 8 a.m. to 6 p.m. Sunday and 8 a.m. to 10 p.m. Monday. Write: Box 518, Haines, AK 99827. Phone: 766-2202.

FERRY TERMINAL:

The Haines Ferry Terminal is located at Mile 4.5 Lutak Road, about five miles from town. The terminal is open two hours before the ferry arrives and one hour following its departure. The Terminal has baggage lockers. Phone: 766-1222.

FOREST SERVICE INFORMATION:

The Haines Area Ranger Station is located at 245 Main Street on the second floor above Helen's Gift Shop.

EAGLE CENTER:

The Dave Olerud Eagle Preserve Visitor Center is currently under construction. The completed center will provide interested visitors with visual and written information on the Chilkat Bald Eagle Preserve. Dave Olerud, whom the center will be named after, has been instrumental in getting funding and community support for the facility. The center will be located near the Haines City Hall.

TRAVELLER'S NEEDS

MEDICAL SERVICES:

The Haines Public Health Nurse's office is located above Helen's Gift Shop at 245 Main Street. Phone: 766-2125.

GROCERIES:

Howsers Supermarket, on Main Street, is a full service supermarket. Hours: 9 a.m. to 8 p.m. Monday through Saturday and from 10 a.m. to 7 p.m. Sunday. The Food Center Supermarket at Third Avenue and Dalton Street has comparable goods and prices.

Panhandle Produce, open from 9 a.m. to 5:30 p.m. has fresh produce and bulk food items. The store is located at Mile 1 Haines Highway. Hours: 9 a.m. to 5:30 p.m. Monday through Saturday.

Bible Believers Food carries natural foods and grains and is located at Sixth and Main Street. Haines Quick Shop, open later then the supermarkets, is located at Mile 0 of the Haines Highway, next to the Post Office.

BICYCLING/OUTDOOR STORES:

Sockeye Cyclery is in the Gateway Building behind Howsers Supermarket. Owner Tom Ely sells bicycles and does repair work. The store was formerly owned by Harold Hopper. In addition to stocking Shimano and Suntour components, Ely has a "ten year supply of Schwinn parts." Ely may be able to provide road service for cyclists stuck up the road. He offers tours, and is a good local road and trail resource. Phone: 766-2441. Tee shirts of a sockeye salmon riding a bicycle are sold here. The shirt design is the work of local artists Greg and Teri Bastable-Podsiki.

The Alaska Sport Shop on Main Street has camping gear and film, and carries Coleman stoves, but is geared more for hunters and fishing enthusiasts than bicyclists.

LODGING/CAMPING:

The Bear Creek Camp & Hostel is an AYH Hostel. The hostel has two dormitories, a common room, a kitchen, and can accommodate 22 travellers. Showers cost $2.00. The nightly fee is $8.00 for members. Tent camping is $3.25. To find the hostel, follow Third Avenue south. Keep on this road and it is a straight shot from town to the hostel. When the paved road turns to dirt the hostel is less than a mile ahead. The road bends to the left uphill. The hostel is at the top of the hill, on the left. Late arrivals permitted if they phone ahead. Paid reservations aren't accepted. Write: Alan and Lucy Miller, Box 1158, Haines, AK 99827. Phone: 766-2259.

Lenores' Cot and Coffee has a dormitory with showers and cooking facilities and is located at 391 Allen Road near Union Street. Phone: 766-2866 The Summer Inn Bed and Breakfast, owned by Bob and Ellen Summer, is located at 247 Second Avenue. If it's raining, this is a nice alternative to camping. Phone: 766-2970.

The Portage Cove State Recreation Site is located in town, at Mile 1 Beach Road. (The Haines Highway becomes Beach Road.) The open area campground offers a great view of the Lynn Canal. The campsite is for backpackers and cyclists only.

Located at Mile 7 Mud Bay Road, The Chilkat State Park Campground has 32 campsites and a picnic shelter. The shelter is about a quarter mile from the campsites near the boat launch. The campground is a ways from town and there are some steep hills leading to it. Also, it tends to be crowded in late May and early June during the two weekends when the Haines Salmon Fishing Derby is underway.

The Chilkoot Lake State Recreation Site is located five miles past the Ferry Terminal at Mile 10 Lutak Road. The scenic campground has 32 campsites and a picnic shelter. Information on the four private campgrounds and other accommodations is available at the Visitor's Center.

POST OFFICE:

The Haines Post Office is located on the Haines Highway near the City Hall. Hours: 9 a.m. to 5:30 p.m. Monday through Friday, and 1 to 3 p.m. Saturdays. There is a 24-hour stamp machine and drop box. Zip code: 99827.

LAUNDRY/SHOWERS:

Laundry and shower facilities are available at Suzy Q's, on Main Street across from the Sheldon Museum or at the Port Chilkoot Camper Park behind the Hotel Halsingland.

ALTERNATIVE TRANSPORTATION:

Alaska Sightseeing Company has tour service to Anchorage. Phone: 766-2819. Alaskon Express Motor Coaches provide service to Skagway, Whitehorse and Fairbanks. Phone: 766-2030.

ENTERTAINMENT AND RECREATION

TRAILS:

One of the most popular hiking trails is the Mt. Ripinski Trail. Its 3.6 miles to the summit, and the last 1,000 feet are steep. Locals advise Ripinski hikers to carry food, water, and raingear.

The summit of the Mt. Riley Trail, a 2.1 mile hike, is 1,760 feet. This hike isn't as strenuous as the Mt. Ripinski climb, and takes about half as much time. The fairly easy 5.4 mile Seduction Trail through Chilkat Park is also quite scenic. People at the Forest Service or the Visitor's Center have information about these and other trails.

Tom Ely of Sockeye Cyclery knows of several riding trails. If interested in glacier trekking or a guided hike, contact Ice-Field Ascents. Phone: 766-2409 or 766-2441.

FISHING:

At Mile 9 Lutak Road, half way between the Ferry Terminal and the Chilkoot Lake Recreation Site, there is a Department of Fish & Game fish weir. From the first week of June through October, Fish & Game employees count the salmon, take scale samples and measure the fish. This helps the Department forecast the strength of future runs.

For information pertaining to fishing in the Haines-Skagway area, contact the Alaska Department of Fish and Game. Phone: 766-2625.

MUSEUMS/HISTORICAL SITES:

An excellent overview of the history of Haines can be obtained at the Sheldon Museum and Cultural Center, located on Main and Front Streets, just above the Small Boat Harbor. Handcrafted cases by local artist Jon Carlson hold spruce root baskets, beadwork, carving and trade items. There is a replica of an early Tlingit tribal house, and other exhibits center around Haines' pioneering era and the histories of the Alaska Marine Highway and Alaska Highway.

Paintings by local artists are featured on the upper level. The museum's curator, Elisabeth Hakkinen, whose pioneer family ran a trading post in Haines' early days, knows a lot about the history and the people of Haines. If Hakkinen is unavailable, there is an audio cassette which includes some of her anecdotes and related background information on the museum's artifacts. Books and quality arts and crafts are sold. Slides and movies, including "The Last Stronghold of the Eagles," a locally produced Audobon Society movie on the Chilkat bald eagles, are shown. Admission: $2.00.

EATING/DRINKING ESTABLISHMENTS:

Hazel's Chuckwagon, a trailer next to the Ferry Terminal, has fast food. The Cutter, located on Main Street up a few blocks from the Small Boat Harbor, has pizza, sandwiches, and seafood. Porcupine Pete's at Second Avenue and Main serves pizza. The Catalyst International Cafe on Main Street has an excellent salad bar. The Chilkat Bakery on Fifth Street, up a block from Main, serves breakfast, lunch and dinner and sells fresh baked goods.

BOOKSTORES:

The Gutenberg Dump, owned by Susie and Ron Scollon, has a wide variety of titles, and an excellent literature section. Classical music tapes are also available. The store is located on Second Avenue next to the Summer Inn Bed and Breakfast. General Interest books may be purchased at Bell's Store at Second Avenue and Main Streets.

FAIRS:

The Southeast Alaska State Fair is held in Haines during the third week in August. The fair, one of the biggest events in Southeast Alaska, features livestock, art exhibits and live entertainment. Haines is very crowded during Fair week.

MOVIES/PLAYS:

"Lust for Dust," is a light hearted melodrama based on local history. Produced by the Lynn Canal Players, performances are on Friday and Sunday evenings at the Chilkat Center. Admission: $5.00.

PUBLIC RECREATION:

The Haines High School swimming pool, at Mile 0.5 Haines Highway, is open to the public Monday though Saturday. Phone: 766-2666.

Rand McDonald and his penny farthing

Randy McDonald's Penny Farthing

It was easy to get Randy McDonald, known around Haines, as "the guy who owns that funny large wheeled bicycle" to talk bicycles. The Haines mason was once a self-proclaimed bicycle junkie who owned more than 200 bicycles. Now down to four bicycles and a number of books on the subject, he's more of a bicycle historian. Wearing wire rim glasses and sporting a bushy brown mustache that droops over the corners of his mouth, Randy even looked the part.

One by one he proudly wheeled his collection of two-wheeled vehicles out of his study. The first two bicycles were heavy duty cruisers, which had vintage frames and seats. Randy built them both from parts that he found in junk yards and stores. He took components from old Flying Arrows, Schwinns, Hiawathas, and Clevelands and made completely new bicycles. "A piece here, a piece there, people thought I was crazy," Randy said.

Randy next wheeled out a spotless mirror bright chrome plated Schwinn Le Tour. On this machine, "randified" for long distance races, he once bicycled from Bend to Burns, Oregon in 6 hours. On the same machine in the same state, he also rode from Burns to Crater Lake, a distance of 326 miles, in 24 hours.

Lastly, out of the study rolled the Boneshaker, a replica of a 1903 penny farthing. Randy first saw the bicycle in a shop window in Corvallis, Oregon. It was one of 50 made by the Boneshaker Company in Cleveland for the 1976 Bicentennial.

The price of the penny farthing was $1,000, too much for Randy, and the store owner wouldn't lower the price. So he swapped the store owner five Schwinn bicycles, which he had rebuilt, for the Boneshaker.

Randy then rebuilt the Boneshaker which had been made to ride in parades and hang in store windows. "I machined it out, pulled the bushings and put in bearings," he said, pointing to the front hub.

An accident made Randy realize that the penny farthing is a dangerous machine. One day, while out on a spin, the slightly out of true front wheel collapsed and he went flying. "It folded under just like a pretzel," he said. Randy was not hurt badly, but it took five years to get the penny farthing back in working order. The wheel had to be rebuilt from ordered parts. The spokes came from Mexico, the rim strap from Pittsburg Steel and the tire rubber from a wheel chair company in San Diego.

Randy won't let anyone else ride the Boneshaker because it's dangerous and would be costly to repair. However, he does give demonstrations.

"I'm being stingy because I just put $300 into it," he said, hopping up onto the seat.

"A penny farthing," Randy explained, as he started down his dirt driveway, "has no brakes. And this," he added, leaning back, and pushing down on the pedals with his heavy leather soled boots, "is how you stop."

Until recently, Randy thought that riding in Fourth of July parades was the most dangerous thing he'd ever done. As the father of three children explained, its hard to stop quickly when kids dart out in front of him.

"July Fourth is my birthday. I guess I'd rather be a spectator," he said.

Randy has recently learned that quiet back roads can be as dangerous as crowded main streets. This June he had an encounter with a bear when he was out for a ride on Mud Bay Road.

"He came around the corner—I stopped and stared at him— he looked at me and I looked at him. It seemed like an eternity. I thought I'd be charged." Then, as Randy told it, a glacier rumbled and the bear startled, ran off.

"Why do you continue to ride such a dangerous machine?" I asked. "Oh, people love it and it makes great pictures," he said, pushing the penny farthing back into the study.

Deb and Dylan Smith camping in Skagway

CHAPTER 9: SKAGWAY

BACKGROUND

Skagway (pop. 712) was founded in 1887 by William Moore, a steamboat operator and prospector who landed at the mouth of the Skagway River and staked a 160-acre claim.

Moore, thinking that there was a need for a port city which would connect the Yukon with the outside world, constructed a cabin and wharf in Skagway. Ten years later gold was discovered in Rabbit Creek, a tributary of the Klondike River in the Yukon. Shortly after, the S.S. *Queen* docked at Mooreville's wharf. Eager to establish claims, her passengers pushed aside Skagway's first settler. A group of surveyors, led by Frank Reid, laid out a new townsite on Moore's land and named it Skaguay, after the Tlingit word Skagua meaning "windy place."

Skagway came into its own in the fall of 1897 and the winter of 1898 when the gold stampeders landed from the steamships. Their goal was to get to the Dawson Goldfields. However, over 10,000 would-be miners who arrived late, couldn't get over the pass and ended up wintering in Skagway. A tent city sprang up in the town. Soon Skagway had streets, framed houses, dance halls, and wharves.

The town acquired a reputation as a rowdy, lawless place. For a while Skagway was run by Soapy Smith, a gambler, con-artist, and thief. In 1898, after a prospector was robbed by Smith's gang, some locals decided to clean up the town. Frank Reid shot and killed Soapy, though Reid would die of gunshot wounds a few days later. The two are buried in Skagway's Gold Rush Cemetery, about a mile north of the main part of town. (A gold rush cemetery guide is available at the Visitor's Center.)

After the goldrush, Skagway's population dwindled, but it fared better than neighboring Dyea, which became a ghost town. Skagway survived because it was selected as the southern terminal for the White Pass and Yukon Railroad, a narrow gauge line that carried freight into the Yukon. Construction of the 110 mile railroad was completed on July 29, 1900. The WP&YR carried passengers and freight between the coast and navigable waters of the Yukon, creating a stable economy in Skagway. The WP&YR ceased operations in 1982 when ore shipments from the Yukon Territory stopped. The line resumed limited service in the spring of 1988.

As part of the Klondike Gold Rush National Historical Park, many of the buildings along Broadway, Skagway's main street, have been restored to their turn of the century appearance. While Skagway is no longer an entrance and departure place for miners, it remains a hub for travellers.

The majority of Skagway's residents are now financially dependent on tourism. This is unlikely to change, so the locals are making big plans for the future. They're currently putting in their bid to be the home of the 1998 Winter Olympics. The theme of the Skagway Olympics will be "Going for the Gold."

Skagway's average July temperature is 57° F. Average July rainfall is 1.5 inches.

VISITORS INFORMATION

VISITOR'S CENTER:

The Skagway Visitor Center is located on Broadway Street between Second Avenue and Third Avenue in the Arctic Brotherhood Hall. On the building's front is a mosaic made from over 20,000 pieces of driftwood. Write: Box 415, Skagway, AK 99840.

FERRY TERMINAL:

The Skagway Ferry Terminal is conveniently located at the edge of town on Broadway Street. Phone: 983-2941.

NATIONAL PARK SERVICE:

The Klondike Gold Rush National Historical Park Visitor Center is in the big refurbished red building on the corner of Second Avenue and Broadway Street. Many of Skagway's downtown buildings are owned and being restored by the National Park Service, as part of the Klondike National Historical Park. In addition to photographs and interpretive information, the Visitor's Center offers a guided walking tour of town, slide shows, and films. Write: Box 517, Skagway, AK 99840.

TRAVELLER'S NEEDS

MEDICAL SERVICES:

Skagway has a Health Center. Phone: 983-2255.

GROCERIES:

Fairway Market, on the corner of Fourth Avenue and State Street, has a full selection of groceries.

BICYCLING/OUTDOOR STORES:

A trip to Skagway wouldn't be complete without a visit to J.D.'s Bicycle Shop. J.D. True, a semi-retired railroad engineer, fixes bicycles as a hobby. The author of *Along the White Pass High Iron* (Lynn Canal Press, 1988) has all kinds of parts including patch kits, master links, brake and derailleur cables, tubes, seat posts, Suntour derailleurs, and "tires galore." J.D. can lace up rims and do major repairs. His hours are varied. "Anytime anyone needs help I'm around," he said. Phone: 983-2687.

LODGING/CAMPING:

There are no hostels in Skagway. There are many hotels; check with the Skagway Visitor Center for locations and prices. Hanousek Park at Fourteenth Avenue and Broadway is a city owned campground. The park attendent collects the $6.00 fee at odd hours. The campground is not well maintained. The Dyea Campground, run by the National Park Service, is located nine miles out of town in Dyea. (See Road Information on the Dyea Road.)

POST OFFICE:

The Skagway Post Office is located in the same building as the National Bank of Alaska, on the corner of Broadway Street and Sixth Avenue. Zip Code: 99840.

LAUNDRY/SHOWERS:

Goldrush Laundry, owned by Duff and Karla Ray, is located at Fifth Avenue and Broadway. Hours: 11 a.m. to 8 p.m. Monday through Saturday and from noon to 7 p.m. Sunday. Coin operated showers are available at Hoover Chevron Service Station across from the State Street Market.

ALTERNATIVE TRANSPORTATION:

Horse and carriage tours of Skagway are offered by Skagway Hack, owned and operated by Michelle Kennedy and family. A point to point taxi ride costs $5.00; a tour of the town $14.00. Phone: 983-2472. There are numerous motor vehicle tours of Skagway and vicinity. An up-to-date listing may be obtained at the Visitor's Center.

Alaskon Express motor coaches provide service to Haines, Whitehorse and Fairbanks. Phone: 456-7741.

ENTERTAINMENT AND RECREATION

TRAILS:

The most popular trail in the area is the 33 mile Chilkoot Trail. The route was the shortest, quickest, and most dangerous way to the Klondike Gold Fields. The trail runs from Dyea to where the trail intersects with the White Pass and Yukon Railroad tracks 69 miles from Whitehorse. The Chilkoot starts near sea level and climbs to 3,700 feet in 16.5 miles. The Chilkoot Trail is within the Klondike National Historical Park. As in all National Parks, the Chilkoot is closed to vehicles (including bicycles). A brochure on the Chilkoot Trail, available at the NPS Visitor's Center, gives detailed historical and route information. The NPS Visitor Center has a map of Skagway area hikes.

Frontier Excursions provides daily transportation to the Chilkoot trailhead in Dyea, and also has information on return trips from Lake Bennett. Their office is located off Broadway, between Second and Third Avenues. Their 24-hour hotline phone number is 983-2512.

MUSEUMS/HISTORICAL SITES:

The Trail of 98 Museum and the Skagway City Hall are located in an attractive stone building, two blocks east of Broadway Street on Seventh Avenue. In addition to items taken over the Chilkoot and White Pass trails, the museum has a blanket made from the skins of ducks necks. Hours: 8 a.m. to 8 p.m. daily. Admission: $2.00.

Corrington's Alaska History Museum, located on Broadway Street between Fifth and Sixth Streets is adjacent to Corrington's Alaska Ivory Store. The museum's historical Alaska exhibits begin with the Bering Land Bridge and end with the Alaska Pipeline. There are also a number of related Alaska and Yukon books for sale. The store and museum are owned by Dennis and Nancy Corrington. Admission: $2.00.

Located in an alley off Broadway Street between Second and Third Avenues, Miss Kitty's has hats and other Gold Rush style costumes, as well as massage oil. Miss Kitty's is owned by archivist Glenda Choate. Choate is eager to talk about Juneau, Haines, and Skagway's historic structures and cemeteries.

MOVIES/PLAYS:

The historic gay 90's melodrama "Skaguay in the Days of 98," is held most evenings at 9 p.m. at the Eagles Dance Hall at Sixth and Broadway. The live show features 1890's song and dance numbers and live comedy. Phone: 983-2234.

SIDE TRIPS:

The White Pass and Yukon Railroad, back in operation after six years, takes passengers from Skagway to the summit of White Pass. Trip time is three hours. The trains leave Skagway between two and four times a day, at least once early in the morning and once in the early afternoon. Tickets for the train are available at the White Pass Depot just off Broadway in downtown Skagway. For reservations telephone (800) 343-7373 or write: WP&YR, Box 435, Skagway, AK 99840.

SIDEROADS

DYEA

BACKGROUND

The town of Dyea, located 9 miles west of Skagway at the head of the Taiya Inlet, like Skagway was a staging place for miners who needed to get their year's supplies over the mountains before completing the remainder of their journey on water. It is roughly 33 miles from Dyea to Lake Bennett over the Chilkoot Pass, or to Lake Linderman from Skagway over the White Pass. Still, it took an average of three months for the stampeders to pack their "outfits," shuttling many trips over the mountains.

Before the completion of the White Pass & Yukon Railroad, Dyea rivaled Skagway as Alaska's largest town. The towns competed for stampeders dollars, offering them gambling halls, women, room and board and an array of expensive supplies. Because of a tramway which ferried supplies up the steep Chilkoot pass, Dyea began to surpass Skagway economically. With the coming of the railroad, Dyea was quickly abandoned. Its buildings were dismantled and moved to Skagway.

What's left of Dyea are a few scattered foundations and some posts which originally made up the town's extensive wharf. Some of the wharf posts can still be seen in Taiya Inlet.

There are a couple of short but interesting roads which wind around the old town site. The wooded area that was stripped for stove fuel is now overgrown with willows and aspens. Signs along one of these short wooded roads lead to the Slide Cemetery. Sixty people, killed by the April 3, 1898 Palm Sunday avalanche, are buried here.

To reach Dyea, travel north up the Klondike Highway 2.1 miles to the Dyea Road. The 6.5 mile narrow, hilly, windy gravel road has several sharp turns. At Mile 6.5 there is a NPS information sign. The Dyea Ranger Station and the Dyea campground are at Mile 6.6. The well-tended campground has 22 sites.

II: Interior Alaska, Yukon Territory and British Columbia

KLONDIKE HIGHWAY AND

OTHER YUKON ACCESS ROUTES

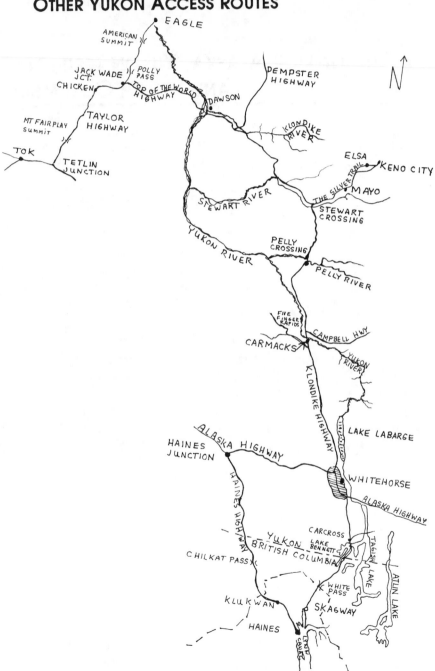

Chapter 10: The Klondike Highway

BACKGROUND

The 448.2 mile/720 kilometer Klondike Highway (Alaska/Yukon Route 2) begins at Skagway, Alaska and ends in Dawson City, Yukon Territory. For the most part, the route follows old trails used by miners traveling to and from the Klondike goldfields. The first 14 miles of the highway are within the U.S., and the remainder are within Canada's British Columbia and Yukon Territory. Because kilometer posts instead of mileposts are used in Canada, Yukon information is given in kilometers.

In addition to cars, trucks, and RV's, there are ore trucks on the road, hauling lead-zinc concentrates on the Klondike Highway from Carmacks to Skagway. In Carmacks one of the truck drivers said that the trucks, "run approximately every 50 minutes." The vehicles, which look like they're carrying large yellow-green margarine tubs, are eight and a half feet wide, 85 feet long, and have eight axles. Be careful: these trucks throw rocks and create a lot of wind, making cycling difficult.

The Klondike Highway is divided into two parts by the Alaska Highway near Whitehorse. The South Klondike Highway, 162 kilometers long, leads from Skagway, Alaska to the Alaska Highway in the Yukon Territory. The North Klondike Highway, 558 kilometers long, leads from the Alaska Highway, south of Whitehorse, north to Dawson City.

ROAD INFORMATION: KLONDIKE HIGHWAY

Section 1: Mile 0 (Skagway)-Km 108.3/Mile 67 (Carcross)

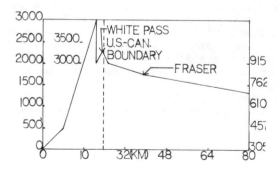

Road Conditions/Terrain:

The Southern portion of the Klondike Highway is divided into two sections. The first section is from Skagway to Carcross (108 km). The second section is from Carcross to the Klondike Highway's junction with the Alaska Highway near Whitehorse (54 km). The road is paved with a wide shoulder to Mile 14.6/Km 23.5 (U.S.-Canada Border). Hard pack gravel and chipseal from the border to Km 44.3. Rough pavement, narrow shoulder, occasional potholes, and frostheaves to Km 88. Chipseal to Km 105.1. Pavement with narrow shoulder to Km 108.3. From Skagway the highway climbs 3,992 feet/1,195 meters to Whitepass, then descends, with some rollers to Carcross, 656 meters.

JUNCTIONS:

Mile 2.1, Dyea Jct. Mile 5.8, U.S. Customs. Mile 22.4/Km 36, Fraser, Canadian Customs. Km 108.3, Carcross Jct.

WATER:

Mile 1.3, Taiya River. Mile 11.2, Moore Creek. Km 64.9, Tutshi Lake. Km 77.1, Dall Creek. Km 84.6, Pooly Creek. Km 88.9, Conrad Creek. Km 107.8, Nares River.

CAMPING:

Km 64.9, Tutshi Lake Recreation Area. B.C. Forest Service has a small campground with minimal facilities. Carcross campground. See Road Information, Section Two.

FOOD/LODGING:

Km 108.3, Carcross.

ROADSIDE SIGHTS:

Mile 5.4, historical exhibit on the White Pass & Yukon Railroad. "Give me enough snooze and dynamite and I'll build you a road to hell." Michael J. Heney, railroad construction contactor. Mile 9.1, Dead Horse Gulch Memorial. Because White Pass was not as steep as the Chilkoot Pass, it was favored by wealthy stampeders who could afford pack animals. Unfortunately, many of the gold crazed prospectors drove their animals to death. This memorial is in memory of the thousands of horses that died along this trail. Mile 11.2, Captain William Moore Bridge. Mile 11.9, view of Pitchfork Falls. Mile 14.2, White Pass Summit, elevation 3,922 feet/1,195 meters. Mile 14.6/Km 23.5, U.S.-Canada Border. Km 24.3, Watershed Divide. Water south of the divide flows into the Pacific Ocean. Water north of the divide travels 2,300 miles/3,700 kilometers down the Yukon River to the Bering Sea. Km 43.8, Log Cabin. The old railroad tracks of the WP&YR cross the road. Km 71.2, road parallels Tutshi Lake. Km 81.3, British Columbia-Yukon Territory border. Km 83.2, Venus Mine interpretive sign and viewpoint. Mill and tramway are still visible. Km 100, the road closely parallels the Windy Arm of Tagish Lake. To the west is Montana Mountain. Km 107.8. The Carcross Bridge spans the Nares River, known to the Tagish Indians as the Na Ta Sa Heenie or River of Clear Water. When the temperature drops to -40° F, the river remains ice-free, even though the nearby lakes freeze solid.

CARCROSS

BACKGROUND

Carcross (pop. 300) is located on the shores of Lake Bennett, next to the narrows which separate Lake Bennett and Nares Lake. Before the Klondike Gold Rush, the area was a seasonal fishing and hunting camp for the Tagish Indians, an Athabaskan tribe. Since a large caribou herd used the narrow passage during their twice annual migration, Carcross was originally called Caribou Crossing.

Rt. Rev. William Carpenter Bompus, an Anglican Bishop, is responsible for Carcross's present name. In 1901, he arrived in Carcross from Selkirk and established an Anglican Mission. Under Bompus's direction, St. Saviour's Church was built in 1904 on the south shores of the narrows. It was moved to its present location, next to the stern-wheel boat *Tutshi*, in 1914. The S.S. *Tutshi*, built in 1917 by the WP&YR, was originally used to transport people and supplies from Carcross to the Atlin goldfields. Because of the spectacular scenery and easy railroad access from Skagway, the stern-wheeler trip was popular with tourists. The excursions continued until the *Tutshi's* retirement in 1955. The vessel is now owned by the Yukon Department of Tourism, Heritage, and Cultural Resources. Carcross is now primarily a tourist town.

The average July temperature in Carcross is 55.4° F. The yearly average rainfall is 4.5 inches.

MEDICAL SERVICES:

The Carcross Health Station and Royal Canadian Mounted Police telephone number is 821-4441.

VISITOR'S CENTER:

Adjacent to the boat, which is being refurbished, is the Carcross Visitor's Center which has historical exhibits as well as a free map of the Yukon.

GROCERIES:

Matthew Watson General Store sells limited groceries and souvenirs.

LODGING/CAMPING:

The Caribou Hotel, the oldest operating hotel in the Yukon, has a cafe, bar, and rooms with showers down the hall. Cafe hours: 6 a.m. to 10 p.m. daily. See Section 2 for Carcross Campground.

ROAD INFORMATION: KLONDIKE HIGHWAY

SECTION 2: KM 108.3 (CARCROSS)-KM 161.9. (JCT. OF THE ALASKA HIGHWAY)

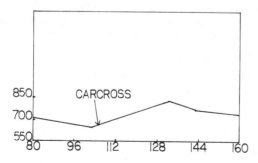

ROAD CONDITIONS/TERRAIN:

161.9 kilometers from Skagway the Klondike Highway intersects with Km 1455.5 of the Alaska Highway. Travellers continuing on the Klondike Highway to Dawson City must travel 32.7 kilometers northwest on the Alaska Highway to Km 1488.2 before again going north on the Klondike Highway. For information on this portion of the Alaska Highway, see the Alaska Highway section.

This section of the Klondike Highway is paved, has occasional gravel and chipseal sections, and a narrow shoulder. The highway is rolling with a slight overall gain in elevation.

JUNCTIONS:

Km 108.9, Tagish Road Jct. (leads to the Atlin Road and the secondary route to the Alaska Highway).

WATER:

Km 115.5, Dry Creek. Km 131.6, Lewis Lake Road. Km 156.3, Kookatsoon Lake.

CAMPING/PICNIC AREAS:

Km 108.9, Carcross campground. Just past town next to the airport with 14 campsites. Some sites are surrounded by shrubbery, providing a needed windbreak. No shelter. Km 156.3, Kookatsoon Lake Picnic Area has firepits, wood, tables, and outhouses.

FOOD/LODGING:

Km 115.3, Spirit Lake Lodge. Rooms, tent camping ($3.00), showers ($2.00), and homemade pie. Km 161.9. Carcross Corner Services, owned by M. De Villiers, is located at the junction of Klondike and Alaska Highways. The cafe is open from 8 a.m. to 8 p.m.

ROADSIDE SIGHTS:

Km 111.1, the Carcross Desert. "The world's smallest desert" was once a large lake bottom. After the lake dried, sandy soil and shifting sand dunes remained. Lodge pole pine uncommon to the surrounding areas, grows here. Km 89.1. In 1899, the WP&YR built a staging area and named it Robinson. A few years later, gold was discovered in the nearby hills. Robinson, a small town with a post office, was abandoned when little gold was discovered here.

The second half of the Klondike Highway begins at Km 1488.7 Alaska Highway and continues north to Dawson City. On this portion of the Klondike Highway, the kilometer posts continue to show the distance from Skagway.

ROAD INFORMATION: KLONDIKE HIGHWAY

SECTION 3: KM 192.4 (JCT. WITH ALASKA HIGHWAY)-KM 271.3

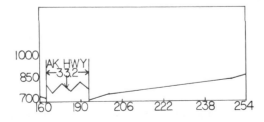

Road Conditions/Terrain:

The Klondike Highway from the junction of the Alaska Highway to Dawson City has mostly a chipseal and asphalt surface. Portions of the road are gravel. This section is rolling, with most hills being less than one kilometer. The overall elevation gain is approximately 200 meters. There is no shoulder.

Water:

Km 195.6, Takhini River. Km 228, Fox Creek. Km 248, Fox Lake Campground. Km 237.3-Km 264.5, road parallels Fox Lake.

Camping:

Km 197.8, Takhini Hot Springs. Turn at the sign on Klondike Loop Road at about Km 5 and follow Takhini Hot Springs Road to Km 10. Admission is $2.00. The pool temperature is maintained at 96° F. The nightly campsite fee is $5.00. Cafe, and guided trail rides for $7.00 an hour. Km 224.5. The Lake Laberge Yukon Government Campground has 22 campsites. Follow the gravel road 1.9 miles downhill to reach the lake and campground. Km 248. Fox Lake Yukon Government Campground contains 19 campsites. The campground is close to the road and noisy.

Food/Lodging:

Mom's Bakery, owned and run by Tracie E. Harris, is about a mile down the Lake Labarge campground road on the right. Harris, a former wolf biologist and naturalist, is familiar with the area wildlife. Her guard dog Rebel starred in the movie *Never Cry Wolf*. Harris sells homemade breads, rolls, and other baked goods in her kitchen, as well as fresh eggs and her own art work. Since Harris's business is home-based, it is best to call during the day.

Roadside Sights:

Km 197.8, Takhini Hot Springs (see Camping this section). Km 208.4, Northern Splendor Reindeer herd. Turn east (right, northbound) on Shallow Bay Road. Follow signs to the road's end. Hours: 8:30 a.m. to 9 p.m. daily.

Road Information: Klondike Highway

Section 4: Km 271.3- Km 351.2

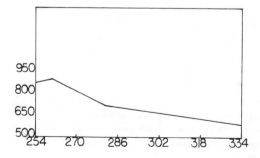

Road Conditions/Terrain:

The road has a chipseal surface, and is rough. There are some long, level areas broken up by rolling hills. There is an overall loss in elevation of 177 meters.

WATER:

Km 280.4, Braeburn Lodge. Km 308.2, Twin Lakes Campground.

CAMPING:

Km 308.2. Twin Lakes Yukon Government Campground has eight campsites, no shelter.

FOOD/LODGING:

Km 280.4, Braeburn Lodge. The cafe has huge cinnamon buns, sandwiches, and homemade pie. German spoken here.

ROADSIDE SIGHTS:

Km 297.1. Conglomerate Mountain, elevation 3,361 feet/1,024 meters. Interpretive sign reads: "The Laberge Series was formed at the leading edge of volcanic mud flows some 185 million years ago (Early Jurassic). The flow solidified into sheets several kilometers long, about 1 km wide and 100m thick. This particular series of sheets stretches from Atlin British Columbia to north of Carmacks, a distance of about 350 km. Other conglomerates of this series form Five Fingers Rapids." Km 322.9, Montague Road House. The dilapidated structure was one of several roadhouses which at one time were located every 30 kilometers along the 500 kilometer long winter trail from Whitehorse to Dawson City.

ROAD INFORMATION: KLONDIKE HIGHWAY

SECTION 5: KM 351.2-KM 431.5 (MINTO LANDING ROAD)

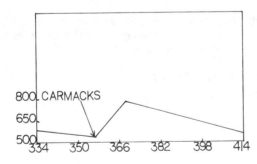

ROAD CONDITIONS/TERRAIN:

The ride is fairly easy to Carmacks. After crossing the Yukon River at the far end of Carmacks, the road climbs steeply 250 meters for about 8 kilometers. 32 kilometers of moderate rollers follow. The road then heads gradually downward, dropping 320 meters. The road has a narrow shoulder and a chipseal surface, except when it passes through Carmacks.

JUNCTIONS:

Km 360.4, Campbell Highway Jct. Ore trucks use this road. Km 361.3, Tantalus Butte Road.

Water:

Km 357, Carmacks. Km 383.4, Tatchun Creek. Km 402.1, McGregor Creek. Km 431.5, Minto Landing Campground.

Camping:

Km 357, Carmacks Campground (see Camping Information, Carmacks). Km 383.4, Tatchun Creek Yukon Government Campground. Located about 25 kilometers north of Carmacks, the small campground has 13 campsites. Water is available from the creek. Km 402.1, McGregor Creek. Not an official campground, but camping possible. Km 431.5, Minto Landing Yukon Government Campground. The large grassy area on the banks of the Yukon River was originally a camp for the Tutchone Indians. Later it became an RCMP post and a wood stop for riverboats. The campground is located about a mile off the road. There are interpretive signs, as well as an old wagon road which follows the river to where the Pelly River enters the Yukon, close to Fort Selkirk.

Food/Lodging:

Km 357, Carmacks. Km 424, Midway Lodge. In the 1970's the original roadhouse burned down. The roadhouse, like the present lodge, was halfway between Whitehorse and Dawson. The Kruse family has owned it since 1980. Homemade pie is served. The house specialty is the Midway burger. Fresh salmon is on the menu when in season, and smoked salmon is for sale. The Midway Lodge is open from 8 a.m. to midnight. A radio phone is available for emergencies. The Midway Lodge has no shower or camping facilities.

Roadside Sights:

Km 354.7. Carmacks interpretive sign and rest stop. Km 361.3, Tantalus Butte. This hill was named in 1883 by Lt. F. Schwatka, U.S. Army. In 1897 Charles E. Miller built the Yukon Sawmill in Dawson and ran the riverboats *Clara* and *Reindeer*. After the *Reindeer* burned in 1900 he mined coal. Km 380.8, Five Finger Rapids and interpretive sign.

CARMACKS

Background

Before the Klondike Gold Rush, Carmacks (pop. 250) was an Indian camp situated on one of several trading routes used to connect the coastal Chilkats with the Interior Athabaskans. In its early years, Carmacks provided roadhouse facilities for the Dalton Trail and the Whitehorse-Dawson winter road, and serviced the river boat steamers. The settlement was originally the Tantalus Police Station.

In 1893, George Washington Carmacks found a seam of coal near Five Fingers Rapids and another near Tantalus Butte. Carmack, Skookham Jim, and Tagish Charlie discovered gold at Bonanza Creek in 1896. This was the beginning of the Klondike Gold Rush.

Carmacks survived while other river ports didn't because of its strategic location on the Klondike Highway. Completion of the highway from Whitehorse to Mayo in 1950 transformed Carmacks into a roadside service center. Large numbers of Native people moved into town from river settlements. The Campbell Highway (unpaved from Carmacks to Watson Lake, BC) was completed in 1969.

Carmacks is surrounded by a boreal forest of spruce, aspen, cottonwood, birch, and willow. Carmacks is now primarily a service center for travellers and area miners. The July average temperature in Carmacks is 58° F. The average yearly rainfall is 6.8 inches.

MEDICAL SERVICES:

The Carmacks Health Center phone number is 863-5501.

GROCERIES:

Datchum Center Grocery and General Store. Esso Gas Station and General Store. Because of political differences, half the town goes to one store, and half to the other store. Both stores have similar items.

LODGING/CAMPING:

Carmacks has three hotels. The Carmacks Yukon Government Campground is located on the river next to the bridge, on the far end of town. There are 20 campsites. Four river bank sites are for tents only. The campground is close to town and drunks often frequent the area. Don't leave your belongings here unattended.

LAUNDRY/SHOWERS:

A laundromat and showers are available at the Esso Gas Station and General Store.

ROAD INFORMATION: KLONDIKE HIGHWAY

SECTION 6: KM 431.5 (MINTO LANDING ROAD)-KM 512.4

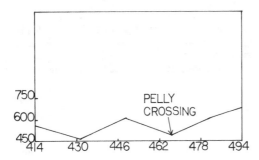

ROAD CONDITIONS/TERRAIN:

The road has a chipseal surface and a narrow shoulder. It is rolling, and initially gains 137 meters before dropping 100 meters to the Pelly River. From the Pelly River the road climbs 292 meters to Km 512.4.

WATER:

Km 465, Pelly River. Km 467.4, Willow Creek. Km 589.9, Jack Fish Lake Road.

CAMPING:

Km 465. The Pelly River Campground is a small wayside located across the road from town, next to the Pelly River. No shelter.

Food/Lodging:

Km 464.9, Pelly Crossing.

Roadside Sights:

Km 466.3, interpretive sign and Pelly River overlook. Km 482.5, marsh area with many birds.

Pelly Crossing

Background

Pelly Crossing (pop. 150) is located where the Pelly River met the overland trail. The trail, built in 1892, ran from Whitehorse to Dawson. The community is located in a broad river valley between the Dawson Range and the Tintina Trench, within sight of ancient volcanoes. The surrounding forest is mainly boreal evergreen and birch.

Pelly had two roadhouses and a trading post run by Ian Van Bibber and his partner Woolen. The trading posts were abandoned around 1952 when the riverboats were beached and the road to Dawson was finished. Indian families from Minto and Fort Selkirk were encouraged to move to Pelly Crossing where the government had built houses and a school. In 1958, the Pelly River ferry was replaced by a bridge. Pelly Crossing's primary economic activities are hunting, fishing, outfitting and guiding. Pelly Crossing's average July temperature is 58° F. The average annual rainfall is 6.8 inches.

Medical Services:

The Pelly Crossing Health Center. Phone: 537-3241.

Groceries:

The Fort Selkirk store, owned by the Selkirk Indian Band, sells groceries and ice cream. Hours: 10 a.m. to 9 p.m.,

Laundry/Showers:

The Pelly Crossing Laundromat is located in "downtown" Pelly Crossing in building #28. This facility, mostly used by locals, has showers for $1.00.

Road Information Klondike Highway
Section 7: Km 512.4- Km 592

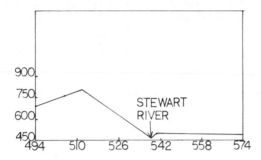

ROAD CONDITIONS/TERRAIN:

The highway is rolling, but drops about 220 meters to the Stewart River. After crossing the Stewart River, the road is still rolling, but with little gain or loss in elevation. The road has a narrow shoulder and a chipseal surface.

JUNCTIONS:

Km 537.9, the Silver Trail. This road, also known as the Mayo or Keno Road, leads east up the north side of the Stewart River to Mayo, then via a loop road to the towns of Elsa and Keno City. Keno City is roughly 130 kilometers from the Klondike Highway.

The towns of this region are often bypassed by tourists. Hence, area residents have formed the Silver Trail Tourism Association. The Silver Trail Visitor's Center is located across the road from the Stewart Crossing Lodge. Inside this small, attractive A-frame building is a staffed desk which has information on area services and history. The center also has an excellent and free road guide, Chris Burn's *Guide Book to the Surface Geology and Environmental History of the Silver Trail.* (Ottawa, Carleton University Press, 1985.)

WATER:

Km 537.6, Stewart River. In June 1851, Explorer Robert Campbell, under order from Governor Simpson, was floating down the Yukon River when he and his men passed a large tributary. Campbell named it after John Green Stewart, whom Campbell had left in charge of the fort. Km 548.6, Dry Creek. Km 561.8, Moose Creek. Km 582.9. McQuesten River, a tributary of the Stewart River. McQuesten and Alfred Mayo operated a string of trading posts along the Yukon River. McQuesten was elected the first mining recorder of the Stewart River area in 1883.

CAMPING:

Km 526.8, Ethel Lake Yukon Government Campground. Located 24 kilometers from the highway with 15 sites and no shelter. Km 538.3. Five-Mile Lake Yukon Government Campground, located on the Silver Trail, (59 km from the Klondike Highway) has 20 campsites and swimming. Km 562, Moose Creek Yukon Government Campground, has two sections. The first, a newer area, is for RV's. The second area, an older tenting section, is perched on a bluff. To reach the tent section, keep left when entering the campground. A walking trail parallels a nearby Creek.

FOOD/LODGING:

Km 537.5, Stewart Crossing. The Stewart Crossing Lodge and RV Park are owned by the same people. There are lodging, laundry facilities, showers ($3.00), a cafe, and a small grocery store, all of which are open from 7 a.m. to 10 p.m. Km 561.8, Moose Creek Lodge. Sourdough pancakes, bakery fresh bread, sandwiches, and homemade soup are available. Fresh produce (bread and eggs) are for sale, just ask. There are walking trails on the grounds. The lodge has cabins for rent. Hours: 7 a.m. to 10 p.m. daily. Moose Creek Lodge owners Chris and Nancy Sorg also run Nancy's Bakery in Dawson.

MEDICAL SERVICES:

A hospital and a health center are located at Mayo, Km 57 on the Silver Trail. Phone: 996-2345.

ROAD INFORMATION: KLONDIKE HIGHWAY

SECTION 8: KM 592-KM 671.2 (SIGN ON THE KLONDIKE RIVER)

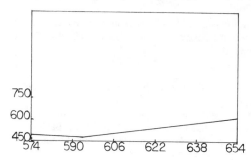

ROAD CONDITIONS/TERRAIN:

The road has a narrow shoulder, a chipseal surface, and is rolling with little elevation change.

WATER:

Km 598.4, Clear Creek (muddy). Km 617.9, Beaver Dam Creek. Km 621.6, Willow Creek. Km 626.6, Gravel Lake. Km 631.2, Meadow Creek. Km 642.9, Stone Boat Swamp. Km 667.4, Flat Creek.

CAMPING:

Km 622.7, camping possible on road above Willow Creek. Km 667.4, Flat Creek.

FOOD/LODGING:

None.

ROADSIDE SIGHTS:

Km 658.2, Tintina Trench interpretive sign. This important geological feature extends thousands of kilometers across the Yukon and Alaska. Here geologists have proof of the concept of Plate Tectonics.

ROAD INFORMATION: KLONDIKE HIGHWAY
SECTION 9: KM 671.2-KM 720 (YUKON RIVER FERRY, DAWSON CITY)

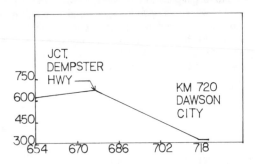

ROAD CONDITIONS/TERRAIN:

The road has a narrow shoulder and a chipseal surface, and is rough in places to just before Dawson where the pavement begins. There is about a 250 meter loss in elevation in this section.

JUNCTIONS:

Km 677.4. The Dempster Highway leads 725 kilometers to Inuvik, NWT. (For more information, see Chapter 33). Km 702.9, Hunker Creek Road. Km 703.7, Bear Creek Road. Km 715, Bonanza Creek Road. The 100 kilometer road runs through the heart of the Klondike gold country. (See Chapter 11, Side Trips.) Beside the road is a Visitor's Center and a dredge. Km 717, Dome Road. From the top, a good view of Dawson City. See Dawson Trails for more information.

WATER:

Km 686.7, Goring Creek (overgrown, no water). Km 713, Klondike River Bridge.

CAMPING:

Km 698. Klondike River Yukon Government Campground has 28 campsites and a hiking trail.

FOOD/LODGING:

Km 677.4. The Klondike River Lodge is located at the junction of the Klondike and Dempster Highways. The lodge, for sale in 1988, has a licensed cafe. Km 719, Dawson City.

ROADSIDE SIGHTS:

Km 704.2, Bear Creek Gold Dredge Support Camp. This 62-acre community owned by the Yukon Consolidated Gold Corporation has recently reopened. Until 1966, gold was cleaned, melted down, and poured at a rate of 800 ounces every two weeks. Guided tours given from 12 to 5 p.m. daily. Admission: $3.00. Interpretive signs are located at Km 704.4, Hunker Creek Road and Km 705.5, Yukon Ditch.

CHAPTER 11: DAWSON CITY

BACKGROUND

Dawson City (pop. 1,200) was named after George Mercer Dawson, a director of the Geological Survey of Canada who explored the region in 1887. The original townsite was staked out by Joe Ladue in 1896. In the spring and summer of 1897, the Canadian Government surveyors, foreseeing a population increase, laid out a grid pattern on a local moose pasture. As they mapped out the townsite they didn't realize that Dawson would become the largest Canadian city west of Winnipeg. Gold discoveries in 1896 turned the Indian summer fish camp at the junction of the Klondike and Yukon Rivers into "The Paris of the North." Soon the town of 40,000 had telephone service, running water, and steam heat.

Few of the town's early buildings remain today, for most of them were poorly designed. The exceptions were the large commercial buildings like the Bonanza, the Palace Grand, and the hotels, theatres, saloons and stores that lined Front Street. To encourage miners to spend money, business owners put fine furnishings inside and ornate decorative work on the building fronts. Behind the facades were log structures, for Dawson, a gold rush town, was considered to be a transient community.

At the turn of the century, attitudes about building changed. In 1899 the stampede for gold came to an end, and 8,000 people left Dawson for the Nome goldfields. But many who'd arrived during the gold rush remained. In 1901 Dawson became an incorporated city. The rich built elaborate houses. Today, decorative spindle and ball fretwork and fancy eave barge boarding can be seen on Fifth, Sixth, Seventh, and Eighth Avenue houses.

The average July temperature in Dawson is 60° F. The average yearly rainfall is 7.2 inches.

VISITORS INFORMATION

VISITOR'S CENTER:

The Dawson City Visitor's Center, open from 9 a.m. to 9 p.m. daily, is located at the corner of King and Front Streets. The large center has displays on historic sites, videos, and information on eating establishments, riverboat trips, and bus tours. Walking tours are given at 10:30 a.m., 1 p.m. and 4:30 p.m. daily. Phone: 993-5566.

FOREST SERVICE INFORMATION:

The Yukon Forestry staff, familiar with the area's mining roads, will provide trail information. The office is located on the Second Floor of the Federal Building, adjacent to the Mining Recorder office.

MAP INFORMATION:

The Mining Recorder office on the second floor of the Federal Building has topographic maps.

TRAVELLER'S NEEDS

MEDICAL SERVICES:

The Dawson City Nursing Station is located at Seventh Avenue and Front Street. Phone: 993-5333 or 993-5444.

GROCERIES:

Groceries and fresh produce are available at the Dawson General Store at Front and Queen Streets. Hours: 8:30 a.m. to 9 p.m. daily and Sundays, 10 to 6 p.m. The Dawson Farmer's Market has fresh local produce. They're located on Second Avenue near Front Street and open from 8 a.m. to 8 p.m. Monday through Friday, and Saturday and Sunday from 12 noon to 6 p.m. Tommy and Ann Taylor sell inexpensive fresh salmon. Look for a sign that says "Fresh Salmon," or ask locals for their address.

BICYCLING/OUTDOOR STORES:

There are no bicycle or outdoor stores in Dawson City.

LODGING/CAMPING:

There are no hostels in Dawson. There are a number of hotels, which tend to be expensive in the summer months. Check at the Visitor's Center for more information.

Across the river at Km 0.3 Top of The World Highway is the Yukon River Yukon Government Campground, the territories' largest campground with 20 tent sites, 97 campsites total. Check the board at the campground entrance for tent site locations. The Top of the World Highway begins on the campground side of the Yukon River. The free ferry, which leaves from Front Street, runs 24 hours a day and takes bicycles.

POST OFFICE:

The central post office is located in the Federal Building on Fifth Avenue between Princess and Queen Streets. The historic 1901 post office can be found at the corner of King and Third Avenue. Postal Code: YOB 1GO.

LAUNDRY/SHOWERS:

At the Dawson Laundromat it costs $1.50 to run a load of wash and 75 cents to dry the same for 10 minutes. The laundromat, at Front and York Streets, has coin operated showers. Hours: 9 a.m. to 8:30 p.m. Monday through Friday, and Saturday and Sunday from 9 a.m. to 5 p.m. The hours of the adjacent soda fountain are the same. The Fifth Avenue Laundromat and Video Arcade at Princess and Fifth Avenue charge $1.50 for a wash and 75 cents for 21 minutes to dry. Hours: 11 a.m. to 10 p.m. Monday through Thursday, 11 a.m. to 11 p.m. Friday and Saturday and 2 to 10 p.m. on Sunday.

ALTERNATIVE TRANSPORTATION:

Dawson City International Airport is located at Km 701, on the Klondike Highway just before town.

ENTERTAINMENT AND RECREATION

TRAILS:

Since Dawson, at latitude 64 degrees north, is 150 kilometers south of the Arctic Circle, there is almost continuous daylight during June and July. There is a panoramic view of Dawson City, the Yukon and Klondike River Valleys, the mining creeks, Ogilvie Mountains, and the Sixty-Mile area at the Dome's summit. Turn off at road junction at Km 717 of the Klondike Highway and continue to the top. The summer solstice is often celebrated here.

See the Forestry Office for information on rideable mining roads.

MUSEUMS/HISTORICAL SITES:

The Dawson City Museum, located in the former territorial administration building on Fifth Avenue, has photos and Gold Rush artifacts, as well as exhibits on mining, Athabaskan life-styles, and early Dawson city life. Of interest to cyclists is a wooden bicycle wheel with metal spokes. The interpretive information beneath it says: "By the 1890's the bicycle craze had gripped the nation. With the rush of gold seekers to the north came "the wheel," as the bicycle was known. A few hardy wheelman actually travelled by bicycle from Skagway to Dawson during the winter months over the frozen lakes and rivers. With the rush to Nome in 1899 the wheel was again the means of transportation chosen by an adventurous few." A silent film is presented daily. The museum has a gift shop, a Klondike Reference Center and special exhibits in the historic court room. Hours: 10 a.m. to 6 p.m. daily. Admission is $3.00.

The Riverboat *Keno* once travelled up and down the Stewart River, bringing lead, silver, and ore concentrates from the mines around Mayo to the confluence of the Yukon, where larger riverboats, such as the *Klondike* II, picked them up for transport to Whitehorse and the railhead. In 1960, the *Keno* was moved to her present berth on Dawson's waterfront beside the Canadian Bank of Commerce. The boat is open to the public.

The cabin where Yukon Poet Robert Service lived from 1909-1912 is located on the hillside on Eighth Avenue. Service is best known for his poems, "The Cremation of Sam McGee," and "The Shooting of Dan McGrew." Service's poetry is recited by an actor twice daily. Hours: 9 a.m. to 6 p.m. daily.

Readings and tales of adventurer and author Jack London's life are told at his restored cabin every day throughout the summer. London's cabin is also located on Eighth Avenue.

On Front Street, next to the S.S. *Keno*, on the second floor of the Canadian Imperial Bank of Commerce is the Gold Room, where gold transactions were once made. Foreign currency may be exchanged for Canadian bills at the wicket once staffed by Robert W. Service. The bank is open Monday through Thursday from 10 a.m. to 3 p.m. and Fridays from 10 a.m. to 6 p.m.

The Yukon Gold Panning Championships are held on July 1, Canada Day, and the annual Dome Marathon Foot Race is run on the third Sunday in July. Discovery Day festivities begin on the third Monday of August. The Great International Outhouse Race takes place on Labor Day weekend.

BOOKSTORES:

Maximillan's Goldrush Emporium, located on Front Street, on the Ladue Block, includes many Alaska and Yukon related books. Souvenirs are sold here.

MOVIES/PLAYS:

Diamond Tooth Gertie's Gambling Hall has legal gambling and twice-nightly cancan shows. Gertie's opens nightly (except on Sundays) at 8 p.m. Admission is $3.00.

The Gaslight Follies perform nightly (except Tuesdays) at 8 p.m. in the Palace Grand Theatre on King Street.

The Dawson City Music Festival is held the last weekend in July.

SIDE TRIPS:

The 100 kilometer Bonanza Creek Loop Road leads to historic dredge #4, Discovery Claim and a visitor's gold panning operation on Claim #6. Bonanza Creek Road has a hard packed gravel surface and is hilly. The first section is heavily travelled. There is much devastation as this road follows Eldorado Creek, past the White Channel, an ancient gold bearing creek bed.

Fowlerville, (pop. 14) was established in 1980. A sign here reads "No vacancy, ever." A sign at Km 10, Boulder Hill indicates the location of the first dredge in the Yukon. There is a small store at Guggie Ville. Souvenirs, goldpanning, soda and snacks are sold inside; outside are interesting mining artifacts. Km 12, Fox Gulch Interpretive Sign. Dredge #4 is 13 miles from the Klondike Highway on the 100 kilometer loop. The Parks Canada Interpretive Centre provides hourly guided dredge tours.

PUBLIC RECREATION:

The Dawson Public Pool has an outdoor pool and showers. The facility fee is $2.00 for adults and $1.50 for students. Hours: 1 p.m. to 10 p.m. daily, closed from 5 to 6 p.m.

I had been prepared to see a large stream, but had formed no conception of the reality. Neither pen nor pencil can give any idea of the dreary grandeur, the vast monotony, or the unlimited expanse we saw before us.

Travel and Adventure in the Territory of Alaska
—Frederick Whymper (1868)

The Yukon River

About a dozen people are clustered in small groups on the Dawson City side of the bank of the Yukon River. To my left, three people are talking rapidly in Dutch. On this particular day a fellow named Roel, from Holland, is going to swim across the Yukon. He is, we are told by one of his companions, about a mile upriver from us.

Someone shouts, and we see at the distance, a motor boat, and next to it, two shiny black arms, alternately slicing through the murky grey water. Roel swims with the current and slowly makes his way diagonally across the river. As he passes, the crowd on the riverbank trots along beside.

It takes Roel approximately half an hour to cross the Yukon. At the Dawson City shore, he rises up like a sea monster out of the murky water, sputters something in Dutch and gingerly peels off the duct tape holding his orange gloves in place. Little droplets of water cling to his vasoline smeared face. When the crowd thins, I talk to Roel. He tells me he's in the process of swimming all the major rivers in the world. He's swam 35 already, including the Hudson and the Missouri. A week before he'd "done" the Mackenzie.

When I ask him why he is doing this he smiles and says, "I like to collect rivers. "

As he heads back to his hotel room, I realize that I have no desire to do what he is doing. I wouldn't want to be swept downstream by a river's strong current. There would be nothing to see but water and nothing to think about but death. Swimming a river might be a good way to get to know it, but it wouldn't give a person a good mental picture.

When it comes to rivers, I'd rather observe than collect them. It always seems easier, even on a bicycle, on shore, to move along with a river than to go upstream, against its current. The wind usually pushes me forward, and as I ride, I watch as the rivers show me small fragments of their multi-faceted personalities.

Specific waterways come to mind. There is the Kenai, turquoise blue, in places bulging with red sockeye salmon, slowly making their way upstream to spawn. There is the Teklanika, in Denali National Park, grey, murky, braided, gurgling and gushing over rocks and gravel. There is the Mackenzie, blue grey, banking around a turn on the way to Inuvik. There is the Tanana, expansive, slow moving, its shallow shores pocked with downed trees. As I left these rivers behind, they rose and fall, and changed color and shape.

After my bicycle tour was over, my attention was drawn to a Alaska-Yukon map on my kitchen wall. I looked at the Yukon River, a squiggly blue line that in places widened, and then narrowed. Its points of origin and termination were vague. Lakes outside of Whitehorse drained into it, and it branched into several smaller thin lines that ran into the Bering Sea. As I studied the map, scattered bits and pieces of visual and historical information come back to mind.

In early May I arrived at the Yukon's shore in Circle. Large chunks of bluish white ice, streaked with brown silt, moved ponderously downstream. Occasionally a sweeper, pulled by the river's strong current, passed by. I'd been told by a local that I'd just missed break up. The loud din of ice ramming ice had been replaced by the muffled sound of rapidly running water. "This is the mighty Yukon," I said to myself, thinking that it would not be right if the Yukon was called the Smith, Jones, or Parker River.

The name Yukon was given to the river by the Hudson Bay Company trader John Bell. He called it the "Youcon," his version of the Loucheaux Indian word "Yuchoo," meaning "The Greatest River," or "Big River." The estuary of the Yukon had been explored in the 1830's by the Russian Explorer Glasunov, who named it "Kwikhpak," an Aleut Eskimo word meaning "Great River." The Tanana Indians call it "Niga-To," which means the same thing.

But as I stood beside the river in Circle, I was unaware of all this. I did, however notice the first warm winds of spring coming off the water and inhaled deeply. I felt more energetic and thought that others who'd been near the Yukon at this time year must have felt similarly.

In late May, while riding the Dalton Highway, I camped on the shores of the Yukon. In the early evening it was pinkish orange and illuminated by the setting sun. Patches of snow lined the banks, and occasionally a large chunk of ice aimlessly bobbed by. A fishwheel, in need of repair, sat on the bank. The river's mumbling lulled me to sleep. The next morning when I awoke, it was raining, and a thick blanket of fog cloud covered the silent river. Disoriented, I felt as though I had awoken in a completely different place. A gull flying overhead confused me even more. I realized later that the Yukon, like other rivers, was always changing. Even if I stayed in one place for a great length of time, I'd never know it completely.

One evening in July, after leaving Carmacks, I bicycled uphill. I was rewarded at the end of a steep climb with a view of Five Fingers Rapids. The water, which snaked its way in five parts through four columns of basalt rock outcroppings, was fast moving. This, said the interpretive sign, was a treacherous stretch for riverboats before the most dangerous rocks were blasted loose in 1902-03.

As I'd learned at the Carcross Visitor's Information Center, more than 250 steamers navigated the 2,000 mile Yukon River during the 90 years they served as the area's principle form of transportation. These boats hauled passengers, ore and other supplies between Dawson City and Whitehorse. Squinting, I imagined these riverboats being tossed about in the current like little toy boats.

I came upon the Yukon again in August. From the river bank in Eagle, I saw the river was wide, languid, slow moving, and coffee colored. I stuck my hand in the current. The water was cold, but not numbing. Sensing something was near, I looked up. A red canoe, heavy with gear, floated slowly downstream. Two passengers, holding paddles, waved. I waved back. At the Yukon-Charlie National Park and Preserve office, downriver from the town of Eagle, park rangers told me that Peregrine falcons had raised their young on the Yukon's nearby bluffs. Park Ranger Pat Heath said that the previous summer they watched a hawk learn to fly. We looked at a map together, and she told me a little about the river villages. Other cyclists I learned, had lashed their bicycles to rafts and floated down to Circle. This, I think, would be an excellent way to travel this water highway.

But now, looking at my map, I'm glad I have seen the Yukon from the vantage point of a bicycle. I have ridden beside it during three different seasons and caught this particular river, almost by surprise, in several moods. Next summer if I raft, canoe or kayak the Yukon I'll get to know it even better. But I won't swim it. Getting to know a river that way is best left for collectors like Roel.

Winner, Whitehorse to Dawson Winter Bicycle Race, 1903.
Credit: University of Alaska, Fairbanks, Archives

Top of the World and Taylor Highways

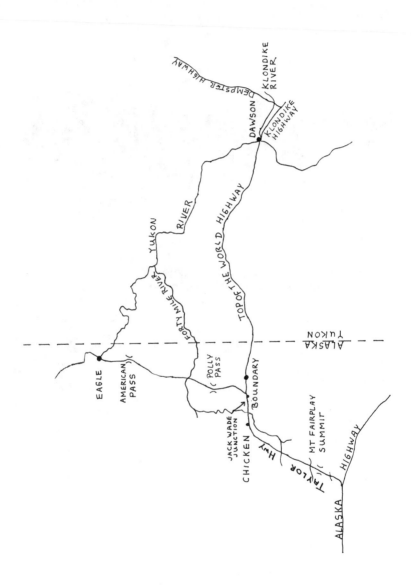

Chapter 12: The Top of the World Highway

BACKGROUND

The 128.7 kilometer/80.4 Mile Top of the World Highway (Yukon Route 9) was constructed to provide overland access to the rich Cassiar Asbestos Mine, which was in operation from 1967-79. Today the highway links Dawson City with the Taylor Highway and provides a short access route between Canada and Alaska. The surrounding land is semi-arid. Since the highway is almost entirely along ridgetops, it is often above treeline and provides views of a dry, parched landscape. Since the area is so dry, the road surface is often dusty. Cyclists riding the Top of the World Highway should carry extra water.

ROAD INFORMATION: TOP OF THE WORLD HIGHWAY

Section 1: Km 0 (Dawson)-Km 128.7/Mile 80.4. (Jack Wade Jct.)

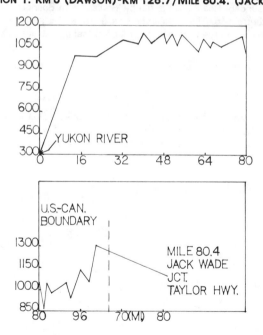

ROAD CONDITIONS/TERRAIN:

From the highway's beginning at the Yukon River, the road climbs 672 meters during the first 18 kilometers. After the initial climb, the highway is rolling with elevation gains and losses of 100 and 200 meters. Towards the border the road climbs steeply to its highest point at 1,320 meters, then descends to the border and Boundary Lodge in Alaska.

In Canada, the gravel road is hard packed and smooth. In Alaska the road has not been well maintained and is more difficult to ride.

JUNCTIONS:

Mile 65.4, U.S.-Canada Border. Neither customs station is open 24 hours. This is the northernmost land boundary between the U.S. and Canada. Mile 80.4, Jack Wade Junction. End of the Top of the World Highway with its junction with the Taylor Highway (Alaska Route 5)

WATER:

Km 97.2. If it's been raining, there may be water in this area.

CAMPING:

There are no official campgrounds on this road. Camping is permitted at Boundary Lodge, Mile 69.2.

FOOD/LODGING:

Mile 69.2, Corbett's Boundary Roadhouse is run by 'Boulder from Boundary,' Jack "Action Jackson" Corbett's son. The roadhouse has a bar and a jukebox, and serves sandwiches. There's a green cabin on the property that cyclists may stay in for free.

In Boundary, Alaska, the average July temperature is 55° F. The average July rainfall is 2.6 inches.

ROADSIDE SIGHTS:

Km 66.1. Road leads about 25 miles to the deserted Cassiar Asbestos Mine and town of Clinton Creek. The confluence of the Yukon and Forty Mile Rivers is about 5 kilometers from Clinton Creek. Km 85.4, old sod roof cabin could provide shelter in inclement weather.

CHAPTER 13: THE TAYLOR HIGHWAY

BACKGROUND

The 163 mile Taylor Highway (Alaska Route 5) begins at Tetlin Junction, south of Tok, where it leaves the Alaska Highway (Alaska Route 2), north through the gold-bearing Forty Mile country, and ends at the town of Eagle on the Yukon River. At Mile 96 of the Taylor Highway is Jack Wade Junction, which marks the end of the 80 mile/129 kilometer Top of the World Highway.

The Taylor Highway partially follows the route of the old Valdez-Eagle Trail, first blazed in 1885 by Lt. Henry Allen. Gold was discovered along the Forty Mile River in 1886. A telegraph line which linked Fort Liscum in Valdez with Fort Egbert in Eagle was constructed in 1901.

The Taylor Highway, completed in the 1950's, has a gravel surface, can be dusty, and is narrow, winding and hilly. Recently the Alaska Department of Transportation widened portions of the road, removed some sharp turns, and leveled a few of the hills. More upgrading will be done in the near future. A warning about the drinking water: this stretch of the Forty Mile country may contain the cysts of the parasite *Giardia lamblia*.

ROAD INFORMATION: TAYLOR HIGHWAY

SECTION 1: MILE 0 (TETLIN JUNCTION)-MILE 49.3 (49 MILE CAMPGROUND)

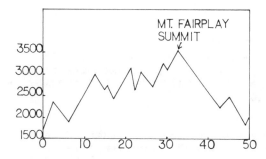

ROAD CONDITIONS/TERRAIN:

In the first portion of this section, the highway crosses old sand dunes created by winds blowing off the Tanana River. The road is rolling for the first 33 miles, but up 1,830 feet to Mount Fairplay Summit, elevation 3,560 feet/1,085 meters. From the summit, the road descends to Mile 49.3.

WATER:

Mile 6.2, spring at Six Mile Wayside. Mile 10.8, small creek. Mile 43, Logging Cabin Creek. Mile 49.3, West Fork of the Dennison Fork of the Forty Mile River.

Camping/Trails:

Mile 4.9, 1.5 mile trail leads to Four Mile Lake. Mile 9, Track Trail leads 1.5 miles to the 60 Mile Butte area. Mile 6.2, primitive camping area near the spring. Mile 49.3, BLM Forty Mile Campground has 10 campsites.

Food/Lodging:

None.

Roadside Sights:

Mile 33, Mount Fairplay Summit, elevation 3,560 feet/1,085 meters. Mount Fairplay to the east (right) is 5,541 feet/1,689 meters. Mile 35, interpretive sign on Taylor Highway.

ROAD INFORMATION: TAYLOR HIGHWAY

Section 2: Mile 49 (49 Mile Campground)-Mile 96 (Jack Wade Junction)

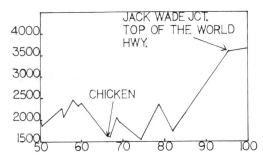

Road Conditions/Terrain:

To Mile 70, the road is hilly, with rises averaging between 200 and 300 feet. (There are also some extreme gains and losses of up to 800 feet.) After Mile 70 the highway continues to be rolling, but climbs about 2,000 feet to 3,600 foot/1,098 meter Jack Wade Junction at Mile 96.

Junctions:

Mile 95.6, Jack Wade Junction. The U.S.-Canada Border is 13.5 miles from the junction. Cyclists travelling to Dawson City continue straight. The road becomes the the Top of the World Highway. Cyclists continuing on the Taylor Highway to Eagle should bear left at the junction.

Water:

Mile 50.5, Taylor Creek. Mile 64.5, Mosquito Fork of the Forty Mile River. Mile 67, Chicken Creek. Mile 75.3, South Fork Forty Mile River. Mile 82, Walker Fork of the Forty Mile River.

Camping:

Mile 82. Walker Fork BLM Campground has 20 campsites.

FOOD/LODGING:

Mile 66.6. The Chicken Cafe, saloon, liquor store and grocery is a short distance off the highway. Chicken, (pop. 35) once a thriving mining town, was given its name in the 1880's when a local at a town meeting suggested the name Ptarmigan. Since only a few could say or spell Ptarmigan, the town was called Chicken.

For many years Chicken was the home of Anne Purdy, who taught in Chicken, Eagle, and Tetlin. She wrote the novels *Tisha* and *Dark Boundary*. Purdy died in 1987, at age 85, at Dot Lake. The Chicken Post Office, established in 1903, is located at Mile 66.3. Zip Code: 99732. The average July temperature in Chicken is 56° F. The average July rainfall is 2.3 inches.

ROADSIDE SIGHTS:

Mile 67. Looking west (left) from the Chicken Creek Bridge, is the Chicken Dredge, in operation from 1959 to 1965. During its peak mining years, the dredge produced about $40,000 worth of gold every two weeks. Mile 86. Jack Wade Dredge was in operation from 1900 to 1942. Originally powered by a wood burning steam engine, the dredge used 10-12 cords of wood daily. By the time the dredge was converted to diesel, most of the area trees had been cut. Mile 96. Just beyond Jack Wade Junction is an interpretive sign on the Taylor Highway.

ROAD INFORMATION: TAYLOR HIGHWAY

SECTION 3: MILE 96 (JACK WADE JCT.)-MILE 163 (EAGLE)

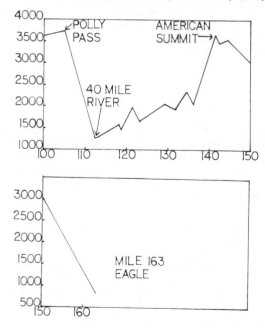

ROAD CONDITIONS/TERRAIN:

The highway climbs over 3,705 foot/1,130 meter Polly Pass and 3,650 foot/1,113 meter American Summit. There are rapid descents to the Forty Mile River (elevation 1,280 feet/390 meter) from Polly Pass, and to the town of Eagle from American Summit. Between the Forty Mile River and the ascent of American Summit are rolling hills.

WATER:

Mile 112.4, Forty Mile River. Mile 13.1, O'Brien Creek. Mile 117, Alder Creek. Mile 119.8, King Creek. Mile 122.4, Glacier Creek. Mile 124.5, Columbia Creek. Mile 131.5, Liberty Creek. Mile 135.9, small creek. Mile 153.5, developed spring.

CAMPING:

Mile 131.4, Liberty Creek BLM Campground. The owners of the Liberty Toy Shop, across the creek, turn off their generator at night. The campground was once an overnight wayside between Chicken and Eagle. The trail between Liberty and Eagle was called "The All American Road." Mile 154, American Creek BLM Wayside. This is one of the most trashed out campgrounds in the state. Since there is no day limit, some people live here all summer. Mile 163, Eagle.

FOOD/LODGING:

Mile 125.5. O'Brien Creek Lodge, built in 1967, is owned by Mickey and Kathy McWilliams. The lodge has a bar and sells snacks. Mile 163, Eagle.

ROADSIDE SIGHTS:

Mile 105.1. Polly Summit, elevation 3,550 feet/1,082 meters. Mile 131.6, Liberty Toys and Gifts. Artist Debbie Burton designs beautiful hand painted wooden toys and puzzles. She will ship. Write: Box 29, Eagle, AK 99738. Mile 141.5, American Summit, elevation 3,650 feet/1,113 meters.

EAGLE

BACKGROUND

Eagle (pop. 194) was at the turn of the century, a busy army and mining town and the first incorporated town in Alaska's Interior. The site, a hunting and fishing camp, was originally a Han Indian village called Jonny's Village. With the Hudson's Bay Company establishment of Fort Yukon in 1847, and Fort Reliance in 1874, the Indians became aggressive traders. This led to the building of a nearby trading post which was moved near the present site of Eagle.

In 1898, 28 miners organized the community of Eagle, naming it after the eagles that nested on the nearby bluffs. Because of Eagle's central location on the Yukon River, and at the end of the Valdez-Eagle Trail, it became the region's supply and judicial center. In 1899, the army established Fort Egbert at Eagle and by 1900, the first link of WAMCATS, the Washington-Alaska Military Cable and Telegraph System, was complete. Messages were sent to Whitehorse, carried overland to Skagway, then sent by ship to Seattle where they were telegraphed to other places in the U.S. Telegraph wires were also run from Eagle to Fort Liscum near Valdez, from Eagle to Fairbanks, and from Eagle to Nome.

Because many of the lines ran through swampy areas, most of the work had to be carried out in the winter. When the men complained about the cold, thermometers were banned. In 1911, the army abandoned Fort Egbert, and left a small Signal Corps detachment to operate the telegraph system, which they did until 1925.

37 buildings, including a 16-bed hospital, a gymnasium, an ice house, a bakery and a 58-stall mule barn were constructed at Fort Egbert. Many of these buildings have been restored by the Bureau of Land Management.

In December 1905, Norwegian Roald Amundsen drove his dogs 1,000 miles from his sloop *GJOA*, iceblocked off Alaska's arctic shore, to Eagle. From Eagle, via telegraph, he announced his successful crossing of the Northwest Passage. Nine months later, the *GJOA* reached Nome. Amundsen's vessel was the first to travel from the Atlantic Ocean, via the Northwest Passage, to the Bering Sea. An aluminum globe, located near the Eagle Post Office, commemorates Amundsen's visit.

The town's economy, which was based on outfitting gold miners, collapsed when World War I began. By the 1940's Eagle's population was nine. Since the completion of the Taylor Highway, the town's population has grown steadily. Eagle remains one of a handful of Alaskan towns accessible by road that has kept its historic appearance and has not yet been overrun by tourists. For further reading on Eagle, see John McPhee's *Coming into the Country* (Farrar, 1977).

Eagle's average July temperature is 60° F. Average July rainfall is 2.1 inches.

Visitors Information

Town Tour:

Weekday town tours, conducted by the Eagle Historical Society, the Bureau of Land Management and the National Park Service, include Judge Wickersham's courthouse, an early church, the Waterfront Customs house, the museum, and Fort Egbert. Meet in front of the courthouse at 10 a.m.

National Park Service:

Eagle is the headquarters of the Yukon-Charlie Rivers National Preserve which lies between the towns of Eagle and Circle. The National Park Service employees are familiar with the area trails and roads. Write: NPS Superintendent, Box 64, Eagle, AK 99738.

Customs Information:

People floating the Yukon River from Canada must report to U.S. Customs agent John Borg. Inquire at the Eagle Post Office.

Traveller's Needs

Medical Services:

Eagle has a public health clinic.

Groceries:

See Lodging.

Lodging/Camping:

The Eagle's Nest and the Eagle Trading Company both sell limited (and expensive) groceries, have cafes, showers, laundromats and cabins.

The best place to camp in Eagle is the BLM campground right outside of town. To reach the campground, turn left on Fourth Avenue while coming into town, pass through historic Fort Egbert, and follow signs to campground. Sarge Waller routinely comes through the campground between 9:30 and 10 a.m. to tell interested campers about the daily historic town tour.

BICYCLES/OUTDOOR STORES:

Eagle has no bicycle store. Boone's Metalwares, Drygoods and Commodities sells general hardware and some camping supplies.

POST OFFICE:

Zip Code: 99738.

LAUNDRY/SHOWERS:

See Lodging.

ALTERNATIVE TRANSPORTATION:

From Eagle, it is possible to either float the Yukon River to Circle or to fly to Dawson City, Tok, Fairbanks, or other locations.

Tatanuk Flying Service has local flights, and rents rafts for $60.00 per day. It is a 3-4 day float trip from Eagle to Circle, and rafts must be mailed back to Eagle. Across the street from the courthouse is a small gift shop with a pay phone. The people inside have airplane and float trip information.

ENTERTAINMENT AND RECREATION

TRAILS:

Information on local roads and the area trails is available from the staff at the headquarters of the Yukon-Charley National Preserve.

MUSEUM/HISTORICAL SIGHTS:

The Eagle Museum and Judge Wickersham's first courthouse are open for viewing during the morning tour at 10 a.m. and later when tour buses arrive in town. The buildings at historic Fort Egbert are also open during the morning tour. There are many interpretive signs on the fort grounds.

Chapter 14: The Haines Highway

Background

The 150 mile/240 kilometer Haines Highway (Alaska Route 7/Yukon Route 3) was built during World War II to provide an escape route in case of Japanese invasion. The highway travels over the Three Guardsman and Chilkat Passes, then descends to Haines Junction and the Alaska Highway.

For centuries the Chilkat Indians used the two passes as a trade route into the Interior. In the 1880's Jack Dalton put in a trail, then controlled access by charging a fee at Three Guardsman Pass. Dalton's trail was preferred over the White Pass or Chilkoot Trails by suppliers with pack animals or cattle. Today, portions of the highway follow Dalton's original trail.

The first forty miles of the highway are within Alaska; the remainder are in Canada's British Columbia and Yukon Territory. Mile, then kilometer posts, run from Haines to Haines Junction.

Information is given in miles up to the border, then in kilometers within Canada.

Road Information: Haines Highway

Section 1: Mile 0 (Haines)-Km 80

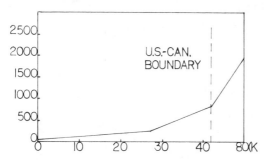

Road Conditions/Terrain:

The highway is paved with a narrow shoulder to the border; in Canada, the highway is paved with a wide shoulder. There's a gradual climb to Mile 27.3, then a moderate climb to Km 80. There is an overall gain of about 2,300 feet/701 meters.

Junctions:

Mile 21.4, road to the Native village of Klukwan. Mile 27.2, road to Mosquito Lake Campground.

Water:

Miles 4-23.8, road parallels the Chilkat River. Mile 23.8, road crosses the Chilkat River. Miles 23.8-40, road parallels the Klehini River. Mile 28.9, Muncaster Creek. Mile 31.6, Little Boulder Creek. Mile 33.8, Big Boulder Creek. Km 72.1, Five Mile Creek.

CAMPING:

Mile 27.2. Mosquito Lake State Recreation Area has 10 campsites and is 2.5 miles from the highway.

FOOD/LODGING:

Mile 10. The Ten Mile Road House, a steak house owned by Ken and Paul Kennedy, is open daily from noon until midnight. Mile 27.2. The Mosquito Lake Store has a limited supply of groceries and also sells sandwiches. Mile 33. The Thirty-Three Mile Roadhouse, owned by Kathi and Jerry Lapp, has hamburgers, homemade pie, and an adjacent small grocery store with canned goods. No shower facilities, but bicyclists may camp here if they ask.

ROADSIDE SIGHTS:

From Miles 8-30, the road parallels the Alaska Chilkat Bald Eagle Preserve. The 49,320 acre undeveloped State Park is the fall gathering point for thousands of bald eagles. A few eagles live year round in the preserve. Mile 42, U.S.-Canada Border. U.S. Customs is open daily from 8 a.m. to 11 p.m. (Alaska time). Mile 42.2/Km 67.7, Canadian Customs is open daily from 8 a.m. to 12 p.m. (Pacific time).

ROAD INFORMATION: HAINES HIGHWAY

SECTION 2: KM 80-KM 160

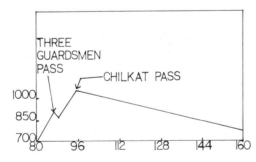

ROAD CONDITIONS/TERRAIN:

The highway continues upward about 213 meters to Km 87.7, Three Guardsman Pass, goes down 61 meters to Km 89.9, then up 516 meters to Km 95.8, Chilkat Pass (elevation 3,493 feet/1,065 meters). From the pass the highway descends about 305 meters to Km 160. The highway is paved and has a wide shoulder. Winds are usually from the southeast; the top of the pass and the adjacent north side are often windy.

WATER:

Km 81.2, Seltat Creek. Km 89.5, Stonehouse Creek. Km 89.8, Clear Creek. Km 101, Chuck Creek. Km 103.2, Nadahini River. Km 110.6, Mule Creek. Km 118, Goat Creek. Km 134, Holum Creek. Km 143.8, Stanley Creek. Km 152, Blanchard River.

Camping:

No official campgrounds in this area.

Food/Lodging:

None.

Roadside Sights:

Km 87.7, Three Guardsmen Pass, elevation 3,038 feet/926 meters. Km 95.8, Chilkat Pass, elevation 3,493 feet/1,065 meters. Km 153.6, British Columbia-Yukon Border.

Road Information: Haines Highway
Section 3: Km 160-Km 240 (Haines Junction)

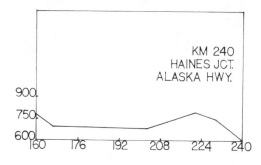

Road Conditions/Terrain:

Pavement with wide shoulder to Km 185.2. Gravel and chipseal to Km 209.2. Pavement with wide shoulder to Haines Junction. The road is mostly down, dropping about 200 meters, except for some rollers along Dezadeash Lake. Strong winds from the southeast may make cycling difficult.

Junctions:

Km 240, Haines Junction. Junction of the Haines and Alaska Highways.

Water:

Km 167, Takhanne River. Km 180.2, Motheral Creek. Km 184.6, Vand Creek. Km 190.5, Klukshu Creek. Kms 203- 218, road parallels Dezadeash Lake. The Chilkat Indians called the lake "Dasar-dee-Ash" or "Dasa dee Arsh," meaning "Lake of the Big Winds." Km 232, Kathleen River. Km 239. Dezadeash River.

Camping:

Km 162.7. Million Dollar Falls Yukon Government Campground has 35 camp sites, eight for tents only. Km 204.9. Dezadeash Lake Yukon Government Campground has no shelter or improved water source. This open area is often very windy. Km

230, Kathleen Lake Kluane National Park Campground is located on a hill above the lake. There are 42 campsites and an enclosed ski shelter with glass windows facing the lakeshore.

FOOD/LODGING:

Km 202, Dezadeash Lake Lodge. In 1988 it was closed and for sale. Km 230.6. Kathleen Lake Lodge has a licensed restaurant and showers. Km 240, Haines Junction. (See Chapter. 15)

ROADSIDE SIGHTS

Km 179.3. Old wagon road to Dalton Post. A few old log cabins remain. Km 192. Gravel road leads to Klukshu, a Native fishing village.

Haines Highway

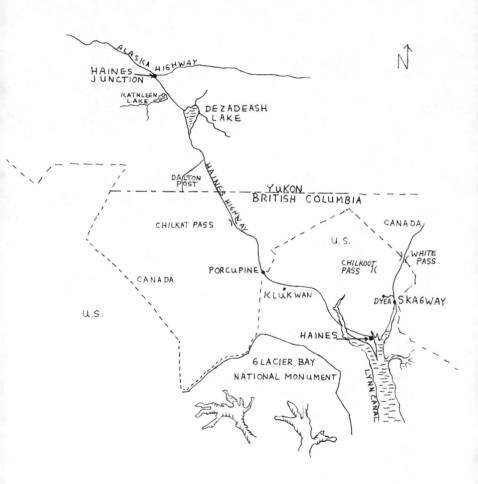

Alaska Highway

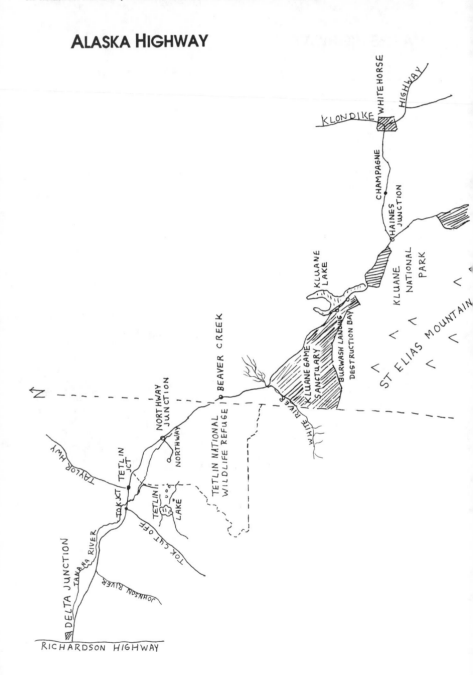

CHAPTER 15: THE ALASKA HIGHWAY

BACKGROUND

The Alaska Highway (Yukon Route 1 and Alaska Route 2) was built in nine months as part of the war effort in 1942. The highway is about 1422 miles (2275 kilometers) from Dawson Creek, British Columbia, to Delta Junction, Alaska. Much of the highway has been widened and straightened since 1942, and work continues to this day. The highway has been straightened so much that it is now approximately 50 miles shorter from Dawson Creek to the border.

This chapter provides information on the Alaska Highway from its junction with the Klondike Highway (just south of Whitehorse) to the end of the highway at Delta Junction. The road information is divided into eleven 50 mile/80 kilometer sections, except for the portion between Beaver Creek and the border, which is 34.4 kilometers, and the last section which is 55.2 miles.

ROAD INFORMATION: ALASKA HIGHWAY

SECTION 1: KM 1459.4 (JCT. KLONDIKE HIGHWAY SOUTH)- KM 1534.4

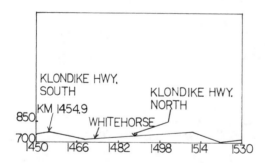

ROAD CONDITIONS/TERRAIN:

This portion of the Alaska Highway has smooth pavement, a wide shoulder, and heavy traffic. The terrain is rolling, with a slight overall gain in elevation.

JUNCTIONS:

Km 1454.9, junction of Klondike Highway South (Yukon Route 2). Km 1469.7, South Access Road to Whitehorse. Approximately 2.4 kilometers to town. Km 1475.1, North Access Road to Whitehorse. Approximately 4 kilometers to town via "Two-Mile Hill." Km 1487.7, junction of Klondike Highway North (Yukon Route 2).

WATER:

Km 1458.6, Wolf Creek. Km 1523.8, Takhini River. Km 1539.6, Stoney Creek.

CAMPING:

Km 1458.6. Wolf Creek Yukon Government Campground has 40 campsites, ten for tents only. There is also a hiking trail and playground.

FOOD/LODGING:

Km 1466.7. Pioneer Trailer Park has a small grocery store, laundromat, and coin operated showers. There are many convenience stores and restaurants along the highway between the South Access Road, Km 1469.7, and the Klondike Highway North, Km 1487.7. For Whitehorse information, see Chapter 16.

ROADSIDE SIGHTS:

Km 1462.4, 135th Meridian. 135 degrees west longitude, approximately 850 miles west of Los Angeles. Miles Canyon viewpoint here. The canyon, as well as the Whitehorse Rapids directly downward, were the most dangerous stretch for stampeders floating from Lake Bennett to Dawson. Km 1510, Takhini Crossing interpretive sign. The old winter road to Dawson crossed the Takhini River at this point. A small settlement with a Royal Canadian Mounted Police post and a roadhouse was located here in 1902.

ROAD INFORMATION: ALASKA HIGHWAY
SECTION 2: KM 1534.9-KM 1614.9

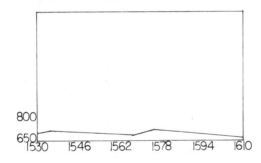

ROAD CONDITIONS/TERRAIN:

This section of the Alaska Highway is a good road with a wide shoulder to Km 1557.3. From here the highway is narrow with a two-foot shoulder, and has occasional sharp turns. The surface is generally asphalt, but in places is chipseal or gravel. The terrain is, for the most part, gradually downhill. There are, however, several steep rolling hills, none longer than one kilometer in length.

JUNCTIONS:

Km 1542.6, Kusawa Lake Road. Km 1602.3, Aishihik Road.

WATER:

Km 1590, Cracker Creek. Km 1604, Aishihik River.

CAMPING:

Km 1542.6. Takhini River Yukon Goverment Campground is located at Km 14.5 Kusawa Lake Road. The campground has eight campsites and no shelter. Located further up Kusawa Lake Road at Km 22.5 is Kusawa Lake Yukon Goverment Campground. Here are 33 campsites, eight for tents only. Km 1602.3. Aishihik Lake Yukon Goverment Campground is located at Km 41.8 Aishihik Road and has 13 campsites, one restricted to tenting. Also along Aishihik Road at Km 30 is the Otter Falls Day Use Area which has a shelter, picnic tables and water.

Food/Lodging:

There's no food or lodging in this section.

Roadside Sights:

Km 1567.2, Champagne. The small settlement was originally a camp on the Dalton Trail, on the way to the gold fields. Later it became a major supply hub for local mines in the area. The settlement earned its name in 1897 when a case of Dawson bound champagne was looted by teamsters to celebrate completing the worst part of the trail. Many of the townspeople moved to Haines Junction in the early 1960s.

Road Information: Alaska Highway

Section 3: Km 1614.9-Km 1694 (Silver Creek)

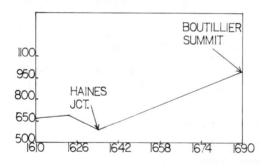

Road Conditions/Terrain:

The road surface is often rough pavement or chipseal with little or no shoulder. The terrain is rolling with an overall elevation gain to Haines Junction. From Haines Junction there are some rollers, but it's mostly uphill with a 600 meter elevation gain to Boutillier Summit. From here, it's down to Silver Creek.

Junctions:

Km 1634.2, Haines Junction. Junction of the Alaska Highway with the Haines Highway (Yukon Route 3/Alaska Route 7).

Water:

Km 1616.8, Marshall Creek. Km 1666, Jarvis Creek. Km 1694, Silver Creek.

Camping:

Km 1628. Pine Lake Yukon Government Campground has 40 somewhat open campsites, seven for tents only. There's a nice view of the lake from here.

Food/Lodging:

Km 1634.2, Haines Junction. Km 1646.6, Mackintosh Lodge, open 24 hours a day, has showers, laundry, sauna, trail rides, a dining room, and a small grocery store.

Roadside Sights:

Km 1622. From the Kluane Viewpoint, there's a view of 15,015 feet/4,577 meter Mount Hubbard on the U.S.-Canada Border. Kms 1660-1662, Kloo Lake to the north of the highway. Km 1690.4. 3,280 feet/999.7 meter Boutillier Summit is the highest point on the Alaska Highway between Whitehorse and Delta Junction.

HAINES JUNCTION (POP. 400)

Medical Services:

Haines Junction has a Health Center. Phone: 634-2213.

Visitor's Center:

Kluane National Park Visitor's Centre. One of Canada's largest national parks, Kluane is 22,015 square kilometers. There are interpretive exhibits, a slide show, and a very helpful staff.

Groceries/Post Office:

Madley's General Store has a complete grocery selection, including fresh produce as well as souvenirs, and hardware items. Madley's is open from 8 a.m. to 8 p.m. Monday through Saturday, and 9 a.m. to 6 p.m. on Sunday. A post office is located in the store. Postal Code: YOB ILO.

Lodging:

There are numerous motels and hotels in Haines Junction.

Eating/Drinking Establishments:

Haines Junction restaurants include Mother's Cozy Corner Cafe.

ROAD INFORMATION: ALASKA HIGHWAY

Section 4: Km 1694 (Silver Creek)-Km 1774

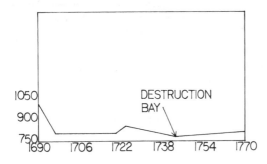

ROAD CONDITIONS/TERRAIN:

The highway is narrow and often winding. There is an initial descent of 200 meters to Kluane Lake. The road is fairly level as it parallels the lake, but becomes rolling.

WATER:

Km 1706.2, Slims River. Km 1722.5, Congdon Creek. Km 1735.6, Nines Creek. Km 1736.2, Mines Creek. Km 1738.8, Bock's Brook. Km 1753.9, Half Breed Creek. Km 1767.9, Duke River.

CAMPING:

Km 1722.7. Congdon Creek Yukon Goverment Campground has 86 campsites, eight for tents only.

FOOD/LODGING:

Km 1711.4, Bayshore Motel and Restaurant. There are no groceries sold here, but the pecan pie comes highly recommended.Km 1742. Destruction Bay was first a highway construction camp. The town got its name when a storm destroyed numerous buildings. The post office is open twice a week. The Talbot Arms Lodge has a restaurant and small grocery store. Phone: 841-4461.

Km 1759.6, Burwash Landing. Burwash Landing Resort has a restaurant, showers for $3.00, and offers glacier flights over the Kluane National Park ice-fields. Also at Burwash Landing is the Kluane Museum of Natural History. Many mounted animals, Indian artifacts and costumes are on exhibit here. Admission: $1.50.

The average July temperature in Burwash Landing is 54° F. The average yearly rainfall is 7.7 inches.

MEDICAL SERVICES:

Km 1742, Destruction Bay Health Centre. Phone: 841-5331.

ROADSIDE SIGHTS:

Km 1707, Soldiers Summit. Kms 1697-1749, the highway parallels Kluane Lake. Km 1707.4, Kluane National Park Sheep Mountain Visitor's Centre. On November 20, 1942 the Alaska Highway was officially opened on this spot. E.L. Bartlett, Alaska's delegate to Congress and later senator, cut a red, white, and blue ribbon while U.S. and Canadian military looked on. Kluane Lake, at 478 square kilometers, is the Yukon's largest lake. The lake lies within a wide flat trench called the Shak Wak Valley and drains through the Yukon River system to the Bering Sea. The lake's unusual color is caused by suspended particles called glacial flour which reflect blue light waves.

ROAD INFORMATION: ALASKA HIGHWAY
SECTION 5: KM 1774-KM 1853.7 (LAKE CREEK)

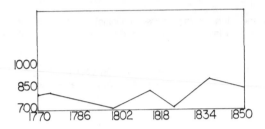

ROAD CONDITIONS/TERRAIN:

Like the preceding section, the road is narrow, winding, and rough in places. The road is hilly, gaining and losing roughly 100 meters at a time, with an overall elevation gain of 60 meters. Between some of the hills are flat stretches.

WATER:

Km 1775.8, Burwash Creek. Km 1783.5, Sakiw Creek. Km 1787.9, Quill Creek. Km 1790.3, Glacier Creek. Km 1799.5, Swede Johnson Creek. Km 1821, Donjek River. Km 1842.8, Edith Creek (good water and fishing). Km 1850.5, Koidern River.

CAMPING:

Km 1853.7, Lake Creek Yukon Government Campground has 17 campsites.

FOOD/LODGING:

Km 1797.2. Kluane Wilderness Village has log cabins, a cafe, grocery store, a laundromat, showers, and an observation tower with a view of 19,516 feet/5,950 meter Mount Logan (Canada's highest peak). Owners are John and Liz Trout. The cafe serves lake trout sandwiches and homemade pie.

Km 1844.2. Pine Valley Motel and Cafe has cabins, camping for $6.00 per site. Showers $1.00 if camping, $2.00 if not. Homemade pies and pastries served in the cafe. No groceries.

ROADSIDE SIGHTS:

Km 1814.6, abandoned lodge, a good foul weather shelter. Km 1815.1, interpretive sign on the Kluane Range icefields.

ROAD INFORMATION: ALASKA HIGHWAY

SECTION 6: KM 1853.7 (LAKE CREEK)-KM 1933.3 (BEAVER CREEK)

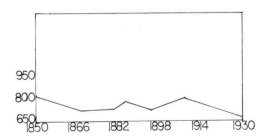

Road Conditions/Terrain:

Narrow winding road with a rough surface. The terrain is rolling, but has many level stretches. There is an overall loss in elevation of about 240 meters.

Water:

Km 1857.6, Longs Creek. Km 1866.1, Reflection Lake (mirrors the Kluane Range). Km 1878.3, White River. Km 1892.3, Sanpete Creek. Km 1897.5, Dry Creek #1. Km 1902, Dry Creek #2. Km 1921, Inger Creek. Km 1929.2, Beaver Creek.

Camping:

Km 1912.8. Snag Junction Yukon Government Campground has 15 campsites.

Food/Lodging:

Km 1877.4. The Koidern River Fishing Lodge is owned by Jim and Dorothy Cook, who built the lodge 20 years ago. In addition to rooms and a cafe, showers cost $2.50 and free tent camping is available. The grocery store claims to have the only fresh produce between Haines Junction and Tok.

Km 1882. White River Lodge has rooms and cabins, a cafe with excellent soup, camping for $4.00, and showers for $5.00. There's a small grocery store.

Km 1934.5. Beaver Creek, (pop. 100) located 34.4 kilometers from the border, and the site of the Canadian Customs, was originally a construction camp. Now it is a major stop for travellers on the Alaska Highway. Several hotels and cafes and a Yukon Goverment Information Centre are located here. Free Yukon maps available. The average July temperature in Beaver Creek is 56° F. The average yearly rainfall is 10.5 inches.

Medical Services:

Km 1934.5, Beaver Creek Health Centre. Phone: 862-7225 or 862-7300.

Road Information: Alaska Highway

Section 7: Km 1933.3 (Beaver Creek)-Km 1965.7 (Canada-U.S. Border)

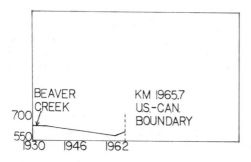

Road Conditions/Terrain:

The section of road between Beaver Creek and the U.S. Border is narrow, rolling, and winding. The road surface is asphalt, but there are gravel sections and many frost heaves. There are no services along this section, nor any at the border. The next grocery store is the 1260 Mile Inn. The Inn is located 38 miles from the border; 81 miles/ 130.9 kilometers from Beaver Creek. There is about a 110 meter loss in elevation from Beaver Creek to the border.

JUNCTIONS:

Km 1936.4, Canadian Customs, open 24 hours. Km 1965.7, U.S. Customs, open 24 hours.

WATER:

Km 1959.4, Little Scottie Creek.

ROADSIDE SIGHTS:

Km 1965.4. Interpretive information about the border and the four foot wide swath which runs along the 141st Meridian from Mount St. Elias to the Arctic Ocean.

ROAD INFORMATION: ALASKA HIGHWAY

SECTION 8: KM 1965.7 / MILE 1221.8 (CANADA-U.S. BORDER)-MILE 1272

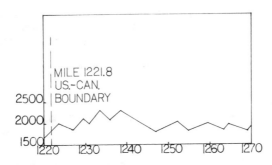

ROAD CONDITIONS/TERRAIN:

Unlike the previous 34 miles, much of the road in this section has been straightened. There is a six foot shoulder. In 1988, some areas were in the process of being widened. Other areas have no shoulder and are winding. Rolling hills with an elevation gain of about 400 feet in the first 40 miles, and a 450 foot drop from Miles 1238.5 to 1246.8. Most elevation gains and losses are between 100 and 200 feet.

JUNCTIONS:

Mile 1264, Northway Road. Northway, (pop. 350) seven miles from the Alaska Highway and within the Tetlin National Wildlife Refuge, is a small Native village and a U.S. small aircraft point of entry. FAA and Customs Service located at airport. For emergency services contact Alaska State Troopers: 788-2245.

WATER:

Mile 1221.8, U.S. Customs restroom. Mile 1223.4, Scotty Creek. Mile 1268.1, Beaver Creek.

CAMPING:

Mile 1249. Deadman Lake State Recreation Site has 16 campsites, but no improved water source. Mile 1256. Lakeview State Recreation Site has eight campsites, but no improved water source.

FOOD/LODGING:

Mile 1222.6. Alaska's First and Last Fuel Service, owned by Dale and Nellie Probert, has candy and sodas. Mile 1260. The 1260 Inn has rooms, a bar, cafe, showers for $2.50, limited groceries, and free tent camping for cyclists. Mile 1261.7. The Wrangell View Motel has cabins, and possibly in 1989, a bunk cabin. Homemade pies and chili are served. Owner Ivor Jones is a very personable fellow who's willing to assist with repairs. He has extra patch kits on hand. Mile 1262, Northway Junction. Owned by the Northway Native Corporation are a grocery store, gift shop, cafe and laundromat. Showers cost $2.00.

ROADSIDE SIGHTS:

The Tetlin National Wildlife Refuge borders the south (left, Alaska bound) side of the Alaska Highway from the border to Mile 1289. Over 150 species of birds and other wildlife may be observed on the Refuge. There are no trails or roads into the Refuge; most access is by plane or boat.

ROAD INFORMATION: ALASKA HIGHWAY

SECTION 9: MILE 1272-MILE 1322 (BLM FORTY MILE RESOURCE HEADQUARTERS)

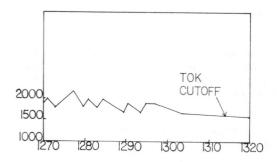

ROAD CONDITIONS/TERRAIN:

Like the preceding section, portions of the road have been widened, have six foot shoulders and a good smooth surface. Portions that have not been improved, have a narrow shoulder and are winding. The first 25 miles are rolling and drop 320 feet in elevation. From the Tanana River it's a gradual descent to Tok.

JUNCTIONS:

Mile 1301.6, Tetlin Junction. Junction of the Alaska Highway with the Taylor Highway. The Taylor Highway (Alaska Route 5) leads north to Eagle on the Yukon River and intersects the Top of the World Highway which leads to Dawson City. Mile 1313.9, Tok Junction. Junction of the Alaska Highway with the Tok Cutoff (Alaska Route 1). The Tok Cutoff Road leads to Valdez via the Richardson Highway, and to Anchorage via the Glenn Highway.

WATER:

Mile 1303.3, Tanana River. This is the first of two crossings, as the Alaska and Richardson Highways parallel this river to Fairbanks. Mile 1309.3, Tok River.

CAMPING:

Mile 1309.3. Tok River State Recreational Site has 50 campsites, a shelter and a hiking trail.

FOOD/LODGING:

Mile 1301.6. Forty Mile Roadhouse is located at the junction of the Alaska and Taylor Highways. Owned by John Nelson since 1946, the roadhouse has cabins and a cafe with ice cream cones and good homemade pie. Showers cost $3.00. Mile 1313.9, Tok.

TOK

BACKGROUND

Located at the Alaska Highway and Tok Cutoff junction, Tok (pop 1,220) is the first and last community road travellers pass through when entering or leaving Alaska. A service center, Tok's economy is tourist oriented.

The average July temperature in Tok is 58° F. The July average rainfall is 2.4 inches.

VISITORS INFORMATION

VISITOR'S CENTER

The Tok Visitor Center and Alaska Public Lands Information Office is located on the north side of the highway just before the junction. Information on state visitor facilities and Alaska recreational lands, as well as a good selection of Alaska natural history books are available. Write: Box 359, Tok, AK 99780.

NATIONAL WILDLIFE REFUGE:

The Tetlin National Wildlife Refuge office is located across the Alaska Highway from the Tok Visitor's Center.

BUREAU OF LAND MANAGEMENT:

The BLM Forty Mile Regional Headquarters is located at Km 1320, Alaska Highway. The office has information on the Forty Mile National Scenic River Canoe Trail and Alaska Lands administered by the BLM. Phone: 883-5121.

TRAVELLER'S NEEDS

MEDICAL SERVICES:

The Tanana Valley Clinic is located 0.2 miles south of the junction on the Tok Cutoff. Dennis Rogers, the Tok Physician Assistant, an avid cyclist, is knowledgeable about burns and bicycle related injuries. Phone: 883-5855.

GROCERIES:

Gateway Food Center, across from the Visitor's Center, has a full selection of groceries and fresh produce.

Bicycling/Outdoor Stores:

Tok has neither.

Lodging/Camping:

There are several hotels near the Tok junction. An AYH Youth Hostel is located eight miles from Tok on Pringle at Mile 1322.5 Alaska Highway. Hostellers stay in a big green wall tent. A wood stove and a cook stove are provided. The houseparents are Wayne Stout and Michelle McDowell. Stay on Pringle Drive for slightly less than 1 mile, and turn right at the hostel sign. The nightly fee for AYH members is $5.50; the fee for non-members is $8.50.

Laundry/Showers:

Showers cost $2.50 at the Northstar Laundry, located at Km 1313.3.

Post Office:

The Tok Post Office is located at the junction. Zip Code: 99780.

ENTERTAINMENT AND RECREATION

Museums/Historical Sites:

The Tok Dog Mushers Museum at Km 1312.6 has daily demonstrations, and equipment on display.

Eating/Drinking Establishments:

Valley Bakery, across from the Visitor Center, has fresh bread and pastries and ice cream. Sourdough Campground, 1.7 miles from the junction on the Tok Cutoff, serves sourdough pancake breakfasts.

ROAD INFORMATION: ALASKA HIGHWAY

Section 10: Mile 1322 (BLM Forty Mile Headquarters)-Mile 1372

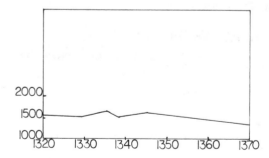

Road Conditions/Terrain:

A paved but bumpy bicycle path parallels the highway from Tok junction to Tanacross junction. The shoulder is wide in places that have recently been upgraded, and nonexistent elsewhere. The terrain is rolling for the first 25 miles, but with little overall change in elevation. The remaining 25 miles drop gradually, losing about 230 feet in elevation.

Junctions:

Mile 1325.8, Tanacross junction. Road leads 1.5 miles to the small village of Tanacross.

Water:

Mile 1333.6, Yerrick Creek (good water). Mile 1338.5, Cathedral Rapids Creek. Mile 1342.2, Sheep Creek. Mile 1347.7, Robertson River. Mile 1357.3, Bear Creek. Mile 1358.6, Chief Creek. Mile 1369, unnamed creek. Mile 1371.2, Berry Creek. Mile 1374.2, Sears Creek. Mile 1378, Dry Creek. Mile 1381.5, Johnson River. Mile 1388.3, Little Gerstle River. Mile 1393, Gerstle River.

Camping:

Mile 1332, Moon Lake State Recreational Site has 15 campsites. Mile 1393, Gerstle River State Wayside has a few sites and a picnic shelter. Unfortunately there is no improved water source here. Camping is also possible at Mile 1371.2, Berry Creek; Mile 1374.2, Sears Creek; and Mile 1388.3, Little Gerstle River.

Food/Lodging:

Mile 1361.3. Dot Lake Lodge, owned by Sandra and George Hasier, has a limited grocery selection, a cafe, and post office. Camping behind the store costs $2.00. The lodge is closed on Sundays.

Mile 1361.4. The Eagle's Rest Motel has a hostel room for $10.00 per person (includes shower). Inquire at Dot Lake Lodge next door.

Mile 1399.2. E.C.'s is located about one mile from the highway (follow signs). Elaine Shannon sells organically grown vegetables (when in season) and everlasting flower arrangements. Will ship arrangements.

Medical Services:

Dot Lake has a Health Clinic. Phone: 882-2695.

ROAD INFORMATION: ALASKA HIGHWAY

Section 11: Mile 1372-Mile 1427.2 (end of Alaska Highway at Delta Junction)

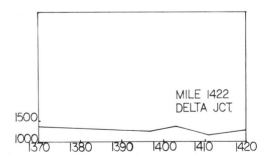

MILE 1422
DELTA JCT.

Road Conditions/Terrain:

No shoulder to Mile 1388, at which point the road widens to a six foot shoulder. Mostly flat with rolling hills toward the end of this section.

Junctions:

Mile 1415, Remington Road. After 5.2 miles this road becomes Jack Warren Road. After eight miles, Jack Warren Road intersects with the Richardson Highway just north of Delta Junction. Mile 1427.2. Delta Junction, junction of the Alaska and Richardson Highways. The junction is Mile 266 of the Richardson Highway which connects Valdez and Fairbanks.

Water:

Mile 1403.8, Sawmill Creek (dry).

Camping:

Clearwater State Recreation Site has 15 campsites. Follow Remington Road (Mile 1415) 5.2 miles to intersection with Jack Warren Road. Turn right and go 3 miles to the campground. Mile 1422, Delta Junction.

Food/Lodging:

Mile 1404.1. The Silver Fox Roadhouse, owned by Dan Splain, contains a limited grocery store, a bar, topographic maps, cabins and the "fourth or fifth purest water in the state."

Mile 1412.4. The Cherokee II Lodge and Restaurant has a cafe, bar, liquor store, laundromat and showers ($2.00). The Cherokee, owned by Kathy Scott, is a meeting place for local farmers. The restaurant opens at 6 a.m. daily. Mile 1427.2, Delta Junction.

Roadside Sights:

Mile 1403, Sawmill Creek Road, agricultural fields. About a mile down this road are the Delta agricultural fields. Farmers, unless they are very busy, will often talk with travellers.

Delta Junction

BACKGROUND

Delta Junction, (pop. 1,207) which began as a construction camp on the Richardson Highway in 1918, was named after the nearby Delta River. It was originally known as Buffalo Center because of the bison that were transplanted to the area in the 1920's. Today the city limits extend eight miles from the edge of Fort Greely on the Richardson Highway to the outskirts of Tok.

Delta has a diverse economic base. Homesteaders, highway construction workers, pipeline workers, business merchants, and military base civilian workers live in the area. The agricultural industry also provides employment. In 1978, 60,000 acres and 22 farms were sold to farmers from all over the U.S. In 1984, more than 22,000 acres were under cultivation. Most of the farmers grew barley, a good all-around livestock feed. But because of several poor growing seasons and problems with loan payments and bison, the Delta Barley Project was short lived. The successful farmers were those who diversified and grew other crops. The July average temperature in Delta is 58° F. The July average rainfall is 26 inches.

VISITORS INFORMATION

VISITOR'S CENTER:

The Delta Visitor's Center is located at the junction of the Richardson and the Alaska Highways. There is a staffed Visitor's Information desk. The center also has books, a dried flower collection, and wildlife displays. Phone: 895-9941.

COOPERATIVE EXTENSION SERVICE:

A branch of the University of Alaska Cooperative Extension Service is located in the Nistler Building, about a mile before the Alaska/ Richardson Highway junction. Don Quarberg, the local cooperative extension agent, can answer questions about Delta agriculture.

TRAVELLER'S NEEDS

MEDICAL SERVICES:

The Delta Rescue Squad headquarters is located at Mile 265.5 Richardson Highway. Phone: 911 or 895-4600.

GROCERIES:

Mile 266.5, Richardson Highway. The Delta Food Store is a full service supermarket with reasonable prices. The store is located 0.5 miles north of the Visitor's Center. Mile 265.5, Richardson Highway. The Alaska Farmers Co-op is a small convenience store just south of the junction.

In the middle of the summer the Delta Farmer's Market has fresh locally grown produce, vegi bags, wildberry jam, cookies, and muffins. The market is located adjacent to the Visitor's Center.

BICYCLE/OUTDOOR STORES:

None here.

LODGING/CAMPING:

The Delta AYH Youth Hostel is located on Main Street USA. There's bunk-style sleeping for ten, and cooking facilities in a multi-windowed tower. Hostellers needing a shower, says houseparent Marsha Fulton, are welcome to use the garden hose. There's no official check-out time, but the Fultons ask hostellers to pick up after themselves. This hostel, because of its relaxed atmosphere and nice country surroundings, is an excellent place to stay. Individual reservations are not required, but large groups should contact the Fultons. No smoking is allowed in the hostel. The nightly charge is $5.00 per member and $6.00-$7.00 for non-members. The hostel is located two miles from both the Delta and Tanana Rivers. To get here, go to Mile 272 on the Richardson Highway. At the junction of Tanana Loop Road, turn right. Follow Tanana Loop Road one mile, and turn right on Tanana Loop Extension and proceed one mile to Main Street USA. Turn left here, and continue one mile to the end of the road. Phone: 895-5074.

Delta State Recreation Area, located north of the junction at Mile 267 Richardson Highway, has 22 campsites.

POST OFFICE:

The Delta Post Office is located across from the shopping center, north of the junction on the Richardson. Zip Code: 99737.

LAUNDRY/SHOWERS:

Bergstad's Travel and Trailer Court is located at Mile 1421.1 Alaska Highway. Coin operated showers and laundry facilities are available.

ENTERTAINMENT AND RECREATION

EATING/DRINKING ESTABLISHMENTS:

Diehl's Delights, a small snack shop, has gourmet candy, ice cream, sodas, and espresso. The shop is open from 10 a.m. to 8 p.m. Monday through Saturday and from 10 a.m. to 7 p.m. Sundays. It is located in the shopping plaza at the junction. The Evergreen, across from the Delta Visitor's Center, has a full breakfast, lunch, and dinner menu and good homemade pie.

FAIRS:

The Deltana Fair is held the first weekend in August. The fair includes livestock exhibits, booths with local art and handicrafts, rides, and displays.

The Bison of Delta Junction

About eight miles outside of Delta Junction on the Alaska Highway, there's a large yellow road sign with a black bison. Since the animals usually cross the highway in the winter, the sign, in the summer, serves to remind visitors that the Delta Junction's claim to fame is its bison.

There are numerous bison related events and businesses in Delta Junction. At Mile 1404.1 is the Silver Fox Roadhouse and its "Buffalo Hall of Fame." On the walls are fading Polaroid snapshots of proud hunters and their bagged bison. In town, in a glass case at the Delta Junction Visitor's Center, is a stuffed bison, shot by eleven year old Gerry Gibson. Delta Junction also has a Buffalo Service Station, and a Buffalo Lodge. And during the summer the town holds the Buffalo Wallow Square dance, and the Buffalo Bar-B-Que. For those who are sports minded, there is also the Buffalo Round Robin Softball Tourney.

The Delta bison have a colorful history. It is believed that bison resided in the Delta area about 500 years ago, and shortly thereafter died out. In 1928, they were re-introduced. Dick Perkins, a Montana cattle wrangler, went to the National Bison Range in Moise, Montana and chose 23 animals. The selected bison were shipped by train to Seattle, loaded onto an Alaskan Steam Company ship bound for Seward, transferred to railroad freight cars for their journey to Fairbanks, then trucked to Delta Junction.

The bison did so well in Delta that portions of the herd were transplanted to Chitina and Farewell. The herd size was well over 500 by the 1950's.

A few members of the free roaming Delta bison herd have became local legends. Old Joe is as famous as Old Grunter, a Kansas bull who was ridden in the 1961 Presidential Inaugural parade. David A. Dary mentions both bulls in *The Buffalo Book* (Avon, 1974). According to Dary, in 1941 when aviator Vern Bookwalter was taking an aircraft up to Fairbanks, he saw numerous buffalo standing in the runway. Some wandered off, but two stood their ground. After Bookwalter buzzed and circled them, they moved so he could land.

Said Bookwalter, "I was glad that the one called Big Joe was not there. He had a reputation for wrecking cars along the Richardson Trail, and he might have got a notion that he didn't like planes either."

Because Old Joe was rather non-descript, it is not known for sure how many cars he crunched. However, one confirmed report states that he did $400 worth of damage to a territorial police car. When he died of natural causes, Old Joe received a fitting obituary. Said an entry on a government report:

"Old Joe passed away at his favorite winter feeding ground, the military garbage dump, where for many years past, he had enjoyed a diet of cardboard boxes, roofing paper, and whatnot. Five buffalo cows, all widowed at a single stroke, mourned at his funeral."

A cohort of Old Joe's, Old Bill, also damaged his share of automobiles. Because he had a broken horn, Old Bill was easily identified, and damages that were attributed to him are probably correct. Old Bill lost his horn in an altercation with a vehicle. One day he led a herd out to graze on the Delta airstrip. Captain James Stewart was planning to take off in his Pan American Airways DC 4 when he saw the animals on the runway. Soldiers in Jeeps were called in to drive the bison away, but didn't leave until after Old Bill had broken his horn on one of their vehicles. In 1950, at age 25, Old Bill was shot by 16-year old Douglas Elbert of Fairbanks, the youngest hunter in the second Alaska bison hunt.

In recent years, there have been farm related bison problems. In the early 1980's farmers began to plant crops, specifically barley, in a designated area off the Alaska Highway. Unfortunately, the land that the state was selling to these farmers has always been considered prime foraging and wallowing land by the bison. Some contend that the bison were responsible for the failure of the Delta Barley Project. Others blamed it on poor farming management and bureaucratic red tape. During this time, a few of the trespassing bison were killed illegally by irate farmers. However the animal deaths did not have an appreciable effect on herd size.

Whatever the reasons for the failure of the Delta Barley Project, there are still free-roaming bison in the Delta Junction area. According to Delta Fish and Game Biologist Steve Dubois, the herd size in November 1988 was about 450 animals, a little on the high side. Usually the herd population is roughly between 275 and 450. To keep the number of bison at a manageable level, a limited number of hunting permits based on herd size are issued yearly. The permits are drawn by lottery.

In addition to being the home of free roaming bison, Delta also has a captive, privately owned herd.

Nick Columbo's front yard looks like any other well-tended residential lawn. There's a vast expanse of close cropped green grass, and a single-story frame dwelling is set well back from the road. But it's the 15 bison at the base of Columbo's front yard that makes his place look a little less suburban.

The bison seemed oblivious to visitors. The large, dark brown animals were shedding patches of lighter brown hair. Wisps of hay clung to their dark brown coats.

Fran Columbo, Nick's wife, stood at the fence and talked about the family owned herd. As she explained, Nick is gradually phasing out of the heavy equipment business and phasing into the livestock business. Nick, who moved to Delta Junction in 1947, had always liked bison. The couple raised their children in close proximity to Delta Junction's free roaming herd. When the opportunity presented itself last spring, he purchased his herd from Berle Mercer of Healy, who sold him nine bulls and six cows. Fran noted that the admiration that Nick and his bison have for one another is mutual. "He's a different person with the animals around." She added, "the bison come running when they see his truck."

However, Nick's love for his bovines does not transcend his practical interests. The Delta Junction resident hopes to sell the bison, which are fed brome hay and whole Delta oats, to local meat markets. He estimates that he could raise between 100-150 head of bison a year "and dispose of them all."

Nick is now trying to develop an elk, moose, bison and reindeer farm. In November 1988, he transported his bison from his front yard in Delta to his farm in the Clearwater area. His plans were to disinfect the bison compound and bring in reindeer. Nick said he wouldn't advertise his home farm because reindeer are skittish, and he doesn't want them to be disturbed by too many visitors. However, he said, bicyclists are welcome to come and see his stock. And at the same time, they can get directions to his other farm.

Those who wish to see the free roaming herd will have to look a little more carefully. From April to mid-May the bison migrate to the Delta River area. The best place to view them is around Mile 225 Richardson Highway at the Black Rapids area, south of Delta Junction. A less prime, but more easily found viewing spot, is the pull-out area and interpretive sign at Mile 241.3 of the Richardson Highway. In the fall the bison migrate to the 3,800 acre state Bison Range, located between Mile 1393 near the Gerstle River and Mile

1408 on the Alaska Highway. The bison can be seen in the fields, about three quarters of a mile off the road.

WHITEHORSE

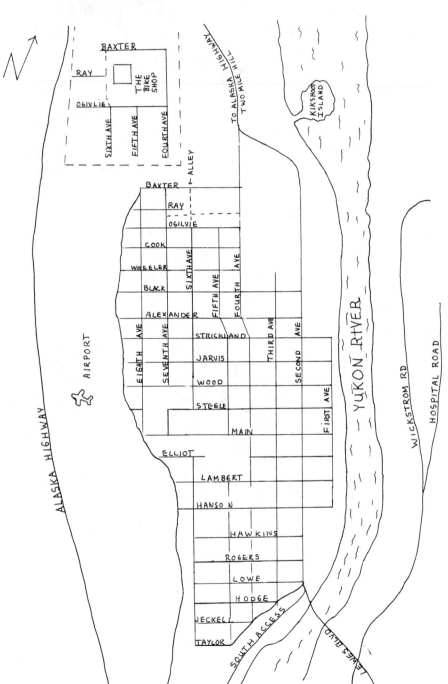

Chapter 16: Whitehorse

Background

Whitehorse (pop. 18,159) was settled in 1897 when Norman Macauley constructed a wooden tramway on the east bank of the Yukon River. The tramway enabled stampeders to portage around Miles Canyon and the White Horse Rapids.

By 1898, over 25,000 individuals who'd hoped to make their fortunes in the Yukon had entered the territory. During break-up that year, 150 boats were wrecked and five men drowned in White Horse Rapids. A small town called White Horse Rapids sprang up at the northern terminus of the Canyon near White Horse Rapids Tramway At the townsite, dubbed "the place where people stopped to wash their socks," miners and speculators rested and prepared to go to Dawson City.

The White Pass and Yukon Railroad from Skagway to White Horse City was completed in 1900. Its terminus was on the west side of the river. During the winter of 1899, residents of White Horse City moved across the river to the new settlement of Closeleigh, at the railhead. When the railroad was complete, Macauley's tramline closed down. The rail terminus was called Closeleigh until the government announced that since White Horse City was already established as the rail terminus in the area, the new townsite would also be called White Horse.

Until World War II, the settlement was the major operational base for the White Pass and Yukon Route Corporation. The corporation provided jobs and attracted other commercial ventures to the community. White Horse outlived the Gold Rush because of the subsequent discovery and development of copper and other mines in the area. The tourist industry was also being developed by the WP&YR.

White Horse was the transportation hub of the Yukon, and headquarters for the U.S. Army during the construction of the Alaska Highway. The population of 350 soared to 23,500 as military and civilian personnel descended upon the town.

The flurry of economic activity diminished following World War II. However, the movement of the Capital from Dawson City to White Horse in 1953 and a world-wide demand for mineral resources allowed Whitehorse to recover from its economic slump. The town name was spelled as two words until 1957.

Prosperity continued until world metal prices declined. Mining has since become secondary to other forms of employment. Most jobs in Whitehorse are now either government or tourist related.

The average July temperature is 57° F. The average July rainfall is 1.2 inches.

Visitors Information

Visitor's Center:

The Whitehorse Visitor's Center, operated by the Whitehorse Chamber of Commerce, is located in the T.C. Richards Building at 302 Steele Street. (Postal Code: Y1A 2C5.) Information on walking tours, river cruises, and local bus service is available as well as maps, brochures and printed material. Hours: 8 a.m. to 8 p.m. daily. Phone: 667-2915.

FOREST SERVICE INFORMATION:

The Whitehorse office of the Yukon Forest Service is located just north of the North Access Road on the Alaska Highway.

TRAVELLER'S NEEDS

MEDICAL SERVICES:

Whitehorse General Hospital provides a full range of treatment and diagnostic services and 24 hour emergency care. There are five health clinics in Whitehorse which are generally open from 9 a.m. to 5 p.m. Phone: 668-9444 or 668-9333. The RCMP telephone number is 667-5555.

GROCERIES:

Whitehorse has numerous supermarkets. There are at least two health food stores in Whitehorse. The Yukon Health Food Center is located at 504 Main Street, and open Monday through Saturday from 11 a.m. to 5:30 p.m. Phone: 667-2306. The Food for Thought Health Food Store has a large bulk food section. Owner Marian Holler says that the produce here is fresh and the trail mixes are homemade. Food for Thought is located at 4133-A Fourth Avenue. Phone: 668-4908.

BICYCLE/OUTDOOR STORES:

The Bicycle Repair Centre, formerly owned by Red Hull, is now owned by Paul Stehelin and managed by Beth Stehelin. The shop has a large selection of quality parts and tires for both mountain and road bikes. Repair work is done here. Trail information is available and guided tours can be arranged. The shop is located at 6210 6th Avenue, behind the Whitehorse Beverage Plant. Hours: Monday through Thursday and Saturday from 10 a.m. to 6 p.m. and Friday from 10 a.m. to 8 p.m. Phone: 667-6501.

Northern Outdoors, owned by Jim Bell, has quality camping gear and outdoor wear including Northface and Velo Face products. The store sells and carries parts and fuels for MSR, Coleman, and Optimus stoves. Northern Outdoors is located at 208-A Main Street. Hours: 9 a.m. to 6 p.m. Monday through Thursday, 9 a.m. to 9 p.m. Friday and 9 a.m. to 6 p.m. Saturday. Phone: 667-4074.

Whitehorse has a bicycle club, the Whitehorse Wheelers. Telephone the Bicycle Repair Centre or Northern Sports for information.

LODGING/CAMPING:

The Yukon Bed and Breakfast Agency is located at 102-302 Steele Street. Phone: 633-4609.

The Fourth Avenue Residence is an inexpensive hotel with laundry, cooking facilities and public showers. The residence has daily, weekly and monthly rates. Shared and private rooms have common bathrooms, a communal kitchen, coin-op laundry facilities and a TV lounge. Showers are available to non-residents for $3.00 with an additional charge if towels are provided. Reservations are recommended. There is limited space for bicycle storage, but bicycles are allowed in customer's rooms. Write: 4051 4th Avenue, Whitehorse, YT Y1A 1H1. Phone: 667-4471.

The Robert Service Municipal Campground is 2 kilometers south of town just off the South Access Road. Tent sites cost $5.00 per night.

POST OFFICE:

The Whitehorse Post Office is located at Third and Main. Postal Code: Y1A 2C5.

LAUNDRY/SHOWERS:

The Porter Creek Laundromat is in the Porter Creek Mall. Hours: 8:30 a.m. to 9:30 p.m. daily. See Public Recreation Facilities for shower information.

ALTERNATIVE TRANSPORTATION:

Greyhound Lines of Canada serves Canada and the Lower 48 from Whitehorse. They are located at 3211-A Third Avenue. Phone: 667-2223. Alaskon Express Motorcoaches provide service to Skagway, Haines, and Fairbanks. Phone: 667-2223.

ENTERTAINMENT AND RECREATION

TRAILS:

"You can ride trails here until you are blue in the face," says Red Hull, the former owner of the Bicycle Repair Centre. The store staff, who know the area very well, are eager to "talk trails." The Old Dawson Road and Black Street Gully trails sound like good rides. They're hoping someone will put out a book with information on the area's mountain bike and ski trails. Any takers?

MUSEUMS/HISTORICAL SITES:

McBride's Museum, at First and Wood Streets, has exhibits on all aspects of Yukon history. On the first floor are photo albums with hundreds of gold rush pictures. On the grounds are old railroad and mining equipment, as well as stagecoaches. Hours: 9 a.m. to 9 p.m. There is an admission charge. Phone: 667-2709.

The Old Log Church is located at Third and Elliot. The Anglican Log Cabin Church was built in 1900 in less than three months by the Rev. R.J. Bowen. There is interpretive information on the life and work of Dr. Hilda Hellaby, who lived from 1898-1983 and Bishop Bompas, the "Apostle of the North." The Old Log Church is open in June from 12 to 5 p.m. Monday through Friday, and closed weekends. July and August hours are from 9 a.m. to 9 p.m. Monday through Saturday, and noon to 4 p.m. Sunday. Admission: $1.50.

The S.S. *Klondike II* was built and modeled after the S.S. *Klondike I* which ran aground in 1936. From 1937 to 1952 the S.S. *Klondike II* was primarily a cargo vessel. Carrying merchandise and passengers, the riverboat could make the downstream run from Whitehorse to Dawson, a distance of 460 miles/740 kilometers, in 36 hours.

In August 1955, the S.S. *Klondike II* made her last run into Whitehorse. Donated to the Canadian Government by the White Pass and Yukon Route, the riverboat is now permanently dry docked on the banks of the Yukon River in Whitehorse. It has been restored by Parks Canada and is a National Historic Site. Guided tours are given every half hour in the summer.

The Heritage Walking Tour leaves 3126 Third Avenue at 10 a.m. and 1 p.m. daily. The tour is offered through the Yukon National Historic Site and Parks. Phone: 667-4704 for more information.

The Whitehorse Public Library, a part of the Yukon Government Building on Second Avenue, has information about the Yukon and Gold Rush eras, art displays and topographic maps. The library is open from 10 a.m. to 9 p.m. weekdays and has shorter weekend hours.

The Yukon Archives Building, next to the library, has holdings dating from 1845, which include government records, private manuscripts, photographs, maps, newspapers, books, pamphlets, and periodicals. The Archives are open from 9 a.m. to 5 p.m. Monday through Friday. Free guided tours of the Yukon Government Building are given daily from 9 a.m. to 4 p.m. The building is located at Second Avenue and Hawkins.

The Yukon Gardens is a 22 acre botanical garden. Fresh produce is available, and Northern-made products are sold in the store. The "only Northern 'show garden' in North America," is located at the top of the South Access Road on the Alaska Highway. Yukon Gardens are open from 9 a.m. to 9 p.m. daily, from early June to mid-September. For additional information, see narrative.

EATING/DRINKING ESTABLISHMENTS:

The Deli has Canadian and imported cheeses, rye and pumpernickel bread, European chocolates, home baking and homemade soup. Food can be eaten here or taken out. The Deli is located at 203 Hanson Street, between the Yukon Territorial Government Building and the Esso Gas Station. Phone: 667-7583.

Rudy's Dining Room at the Airport Inn has over 120 items on three menus. Liz and Rudy, the owners, specialize in German food. A bowl of liver dumpling soup costs $2.50 and a dinner special featuring Ratsherrentopf, $16.50. Phone: 668-4400. Rudy's is open from 6:30 a.m. to 10 p.m.

BOOKSTORES:

Mac's Fireweed, located at 305-B Main Street, specializes in northern books and sells souvenirs. Hours: 7 a.m. to 10 p.m.

MOVIES/PLAYS:

Twin Cinemas is located at Fourth Avenue and Cook Street. Phone: 668-6644.

Atlas Tours/Travel has ticket prices and information on The *Frantic Follies,* a vaudeville review, The Yukon River Cruise on the M.V. *Schwatka*, and the British Columbia and Alaska Marine Highway Systems. The travel agency is located in the Westmark Whitehorse Hotel. Write Box 4340, Whitehorse, YT, Y1A 3T5. Phone: 667-7823

SIDE TRIPS:

The Youcon Cat Riverboat travels between Whitehorse and Lake Laberge. The 2 1/2 hour cruise costs $12.00. Departure is 4 p.m. daily, except Mondays. Phone: 668-2927.

PUBLIC RECREATION:

The Whitehorse Lions Club Pool is located at 4051 Fourth Avenue. There is a sauna, hot tub, weight room, and showers. Admission: $2.50. Phone: 668-7665 for the current pool schedule.

The Yukon Conservation Society offers free guided nature walks on weekdays. Trips range from one to eight hours in length, and guides provide information on local plants, geology and history along the route. The Yukon Conservation Society is located at 302 Hawkins Street. Phone: 668-5678.

The Yukon Gardens

Several years ago, a number of people in Whitehorse thought that Lorne Metropoli was crazy. Now, what was once just a dream of his is the Yukon Gardens, the world's most northerly show gardens, and a major visitor's attraction in the Yukon.

Lorne, believing there should be a large botannical garden in Whitehorse, sought financial backers for his project. This proved to be difficult. Initially there was a lot of paperwork, and said Lorne, "fighting and getting the government to see my dream."

But Lorne, who acquired a mixed farming background on Canada's prairies, ignored his critics and selected a site for his future garden spot. What he wanted, and found was an area with rock cliffs and black soil. The land also fit his specifications because it was near Whitehorse and the Alaska Highway.

The first year Lorne and 22 others cleared a great deal of the area brush and moved soil and rock by hand. After two years of hard work, his 22 acre lot boasted vegetable and fruit gardens and a flora garden with domestic and wild flowers. A bird aviary and a small animal farm came shortly after. The business, which still employs approximately 25 during its peak season, isn't a large money maker but its still growing strong. In 1988, Lorne and his staff planted one quarter of a million annuals and moved 3,000 cubic yards of soil to the site. They also built a hydroponic greenhouse. By late October, the first tomatoes had been harvested.

In August 1988, Lorne and his employees began what he calls "Phase Two." They started building a lake, and began to expand Yukon Gardens.

"We'll have quite a few surprises next year. The garden's going to triple in size. When you see this garden next summer you won't believe it," he said.

In 1989 Lorne plans to keep Yukon Gardens open from April through October. Although the fancy flowers will not last that long, he thinks that the plants, birds and animals will still be of interest to visitors. Lorne is also considering stocking the lake with either rainbow trout or arctic char.

The farmer at heart is eager to be done with the construction aspect of Yukon Gardens. "It's time to step back and stop being a contractor and be a gardener. Now I'd like to enjoy what I've built and make it a business," he said.

Those who were originally skeptical, said Lorne, are now "shocked." However, he still has to convince them that the Yukon Gardens can survive as a business.

"Now they're wondering if I can keep it," he said.

CHAPTER 17: VALDEZ

BACKGROUND

During the 1897-98 Klondike Goldrush, more than 3,000 stampeders endured bad weather and rough terrain as they crossed the glaciers and mountains leading into the Interior. Because it had a deep water, ice-free port, Valdez became an important transportation and fishing center.

Valdez was hard hit during the 1964 Good Friday Earthquake. 33 Valdez residents lost their lives in the quake, which measured about 8.6 on the Richter scale. After, approximately 62 buildings were moved from Valdez to a new townsite, four miles northwest of the original location. The new town was quickly rebuilt and Valdez was voted an All America City in 1965. Valdez won the award again in 1982 for its diversified economic growth. New additions to the town include the world's largest floating dock, a grain terminal, and a multi-million dollar Civic Center.

Valdez (pop. 3,271) is a part of the Prince William Sound area. The Sound's roughly 3,500 plus miles of coastline, its countless bays and hundreds of islands provide excellent exploring, camping and fishing possibilities. Prince William Sound is rich in wildlife. Numerous marine and shore mammals, and all species of Pacific Salmon frequent the area.

The average July temperature in Valdez is 54° F, and the average July rainfall is 4.4 inches.

VISITORS INFORMATION

VISITOR'S CENTER:

The Valdez Visitor Center is located in the Tatitlek Building, 333 Fairbanks Street. The Center provides information on lodging, recreational activities, and local tour information. Hours: Monday through Saturday from 8 a.m. to 8 p.m. and Sunday from 8 a.m. to 6 p.m. Phone: 835-4636. Write: Box 1603-M, Valdez, AK 99686.

The Alyeska Marine Terminal Visitor Center has Alaska Pipeline information. Phone: 835-6283.

FERRY TERMINAL:

There is scheduled Alaska Marine Highway ferry service to Cordova, Whittier, and Seward from the Valdez Ferry Terminal. To get to the Ferry Terminal, stay on the Richardson Highway which becomes Egan Drive, ride to its end, then turn left. The Terminal is approximately a quarter mile down the road. Phone: 835-4436.

FOREST SERVICE INFORMATION:

Numerous USFS rental cabins are located throughout Prince William Sound. Cabin reservations can be made up to six months in advance. The $10.00 nightly fee must be paid when reservations are made. The Anchorage District Ranger Station telephone number is 276-7671.

TRAVELLER'S NEEDS

MEDICAL SERVICES:

The Valdez Community Hospital is located on Meals Avenue. Phone: 835-2249. The emergency number is 911.

GROCERIES:

Foodmart Supermarket has fresh meat, produce, a bakery, and hardware supplies. Hours: 7 a.m. to 11 p.m. daily. Valdez Market is a complete grocery center with fresh produce and meat. Hours: 9 a.m. to 9 p.m. Valdez Market is located at 113 Egan Drive. Valdez Drug and Photo is located at 321 Valdez Drive. Hours: 9 a.m. to 9 p.m. Monday through Friday, Saturday from 9 a.m. to 6 p.m. and Sunday noon to 5 p.m.

BICYCLING/OUTDOOR STORES:

Beaver Sports has Suntour and Shimano parts and does some repairs. They also carry Optimus and Coleman stoves and sell clothing. The store clerks are knowledgable about local trails. Beaver Sports is open from 10 a.m. to 6 p.m. Monday through Saturday and is located at Egan Drive and Chenega Streets. Phone: 833-4727.

Valdez Drug and Photo sells Schwinn bicycles but carries few parts and has no service department.

LODGING/CAMPING:

Valdez does not have a hostel. There are numerous bed and breakfasts and motels in the area.

The Valdez Glacier Campground, which has a $5.00 nightly site fee, has 101 campsites, and a covered picnic shelter. It is located five miles before town, behind the airport on Valdez Airport Road.

POST OFFICE:

The Valdez Post Office is located at Tatitlik Avenue and Galena Streets. Zip Code: 99686.

LAUNDRY/SHOWERS:

Jeff Martens, the facility manager of D&D Laundry, asks that people refrain from throwing dirty, wet and smelly garments in his dryers. A wash costs $2.00, dry is $1.50. See Public Recreation for shower information.

ALTERNATIVE TRANSPORTATION:

The Valdez/Anchorage Bus Lines offers regular service between the two cities, with stops in Glennallen and Palmer. For reservations and information phone: 835-5299 or 337-3425.

Westours Grey Line takes passengers by boat to Whittier. In Whittier passengers board a bus, which rides piggyback on the train to Portage. The bus then proceeds to Anchorage. The total trip cost is slightly more than that of the ferry and lunches are provided. The tour boat also travels closer to the glacier. Bicycles are allowed on a space available basis. Phone: 835-2357.

ENTERTAINMENT AND RECREATION

TRAILS:

The old Valdez Stamp Mill is located seven miles up Mineral Creek Canyon. To reach the mill, turn right off Egan Drive on to Hazelet Avenue, go up to Hanagita, turn left on Hanagita, continue about a block, and take the first right. The hard packed gravel road leads gradually uphill. Portions of the road near the mill might be washed out.

There are two excellent hiking trails in the Valdez area. The historic Goat Trail begins at the wood sign just past Horsetail Falls in Keystone Canyon, at approximately Mile 13.5 Richardson Highway. The trail follows the Lowe River and is only passable for the first five miles. Created in 1963, the somewhat strenuous Solomon Gulch hiking trail ends at Solomon Lake.

MUSEUMS/HISTORICAL SITES:

The central themes of the Valdez Heritage Museum's exhibits are transportation, mining and trapping, women's work in the home, natural history, Valdez social activities, and Alaska Natives. Another exhibit has information and photographs on the 1964 Good Friday Earthquake. An early 19th century Fresnal lighthouse lens, an 1880's hand pump and a 1907 Ahrens steam fire engine, restored by local volunteers, are also on display. The museum also sponsors temporary art, photographic and historical exhibitions. Admission is free, but a $1.00 donation is appreciated. Hours: 10 a.m. to 8 p.m. Phone: 835-2764.

EATING/DRINKING ESTABLISHMENTS:

There are numerous eating and drinking establishments in Valdez. The Visitor's Center has a restaurant listing and sample menus.

BOOKSTORES:

Valdez Drug and Photo has general interest books.

The Valdez Public Library on Fairbanks Street has a magazine swap box for travellers. Hours: from 10 a.m. to 8 p.m. Monday through Thursday, and 10 a.m. to 6:30 p.m. Friday and Saturday.

MOVIES/PLAYS:

Held every August, the Goldrush Days Festival celebrates the history of Valdez. A beard contest, bed races, melodramas, and a parade are featured events.

SIDE TRIPS:

Keystone Adventures offers Keystone Canyon raft trips. Write: Keystone Adventures c/o Mike or Nedra Buck, Box 1486, Valdez, AK 99686. Phone: 835-2606.

The state ferry makes twice-weekly trips to Cordova. Cordova (pop. 1,901) has restaurants, a museum, community facilities, campgrounds, remote cabin rentals, and a bicycle shop. For more information write: Cordova Chamber of Commerce, Box 99, Cordova, AK 99574. For information about the Prince William Sound and Copper River Delta cabins, write: U.S. Forest Service, Box 280, Cordova, AK 99574. The Whiskey Ridge Bicycle Shop phone number is 424-3354. The Copper River Highway ride is scenic, and there is much wildlife along the way. At the end of the 48.1 mile highway is the Million Dollar Bridge at the Copper River.

Construction of the Copper River Highway began in 1945. The highway, built along the abandoned Copper River and Northwestern Railway, was to extend to Chitina and would have linked Cordova with the Richardson Highway.

In the 1964 Good Friday Earthquake, the highway's roadbed and bridges were damaged, and the north span of the Million Dollar Bridge was knocked into the Copper River. The existing highway has been repaired since the earthquake, but only temporary repairs were made to the Million Dollar Bridge.

PUBLIC RECREATION:

The Valdez High School Pool has daily lap swim times. Showers are free if you use the facilities. The Hermon Hutchens Elementary School on Klutina Street has a racquetball court. The Valdez Parks and Recreation 24-hour activity hotline phone number is 835-2555.

Early Fourth of July Parade, Valdez.
Credit: University of Alaska, Fairbanks, Archives

CHAPTER 18: THE RICHARDSON HIGHWAY

BACKGROUND

In 1905 the federal government authorized the Alaska Road Commission to build trails and roads in Alaska, including a road from Valdez to Fairbanks. The road became known as the Richardson Highway, and was named after General Wilds P. Richardson, U.S. Army, president of the Alaska Road Commission from 1905 until 1917.

From Valdez to Fairbanks, numerous roadhouses were constructed by private enterprise to meet the needs of the miners, freighters, mail contractors and other travellers. The roadhouses were built approximately ten miles apart, or roughly as far as one party could travel in a single day. Some were only tent shelters, while others were lavish hotels. Only a few of these roadhouses remain, for the majority either burned or fell into disrepair. The location and history of many of these roadhouses are given throughout this chapter.

Much of the Richardson Highway from its junction with the Glenn Highway south is windy. The wind generally blows from the south to the north. We recommend that cyclists incorporating the Alaska Marine Highway System into their travel plans, consider riding north from Valdez.

ROAD INFORMATION: RICHARDSON HIGHWAY

SECTION 1: MILE 0 (OLD VALDEZ)-MILE 50

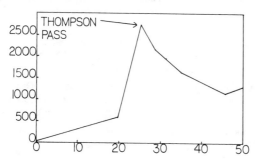

ROAD CONDITIONS/TERRAIN:

Mileposts were placed on this highway long before the 1964 Good Friday Earthquake. The mileposts begin at Old Valdez, four miles north of Valdez. For the first 20 miles, the highway heads gradually upward. The next five miles are tough, as the highway climbs over Thompson Pass, elevation 2,719 feet/829 meters. From the pass, the road drops about 1,350 feet, but its not as steep as the preceding climb. The road is paved and has a wide shoulder.

WATER:

From Mile 0 to Mile 20, the road parallels the Lowe River, crossing it several times. Mile 2.7, Robe River. Mile 5.4, Sheep Creek. Mile 45.6, Stuart Creek. Mile 46.8, Tiekel River. After crossing Thompson Pass, the highway follows the Tsaina, then the Tiekel Rivers.

CAMPING:

Mile 24.1. Blueberry Lake State Recreation Site has 15 campsites, two shelters and a trail. The above treeline campground can be windy and wet. Mile 47.8, Billy Mitchell State Wayside. Shelters and berries here in late summer. Camping is possible along the Lowe River on the Valdez side of Thompson Pass, and along the Tiekel River on the north side of Thompson Pass.

FOOD/LODGING:

Mile 4.2. Rainbow Lodge, owned by Donale, James, and Andy Leitch, has a grocery and liquor store, a laundromat, and showers for $3.00.

ROADSIDE SIGHTS:

Mile 2.7. Salmon spawning viewpoint beside the Robe River. Mile 10. Former site of the Camp Comfort Roadhouse. Mile 13. In 1904-1905 Mr. T.M. Daniels opened the Second Class Roadhouse at the mouth of the Keystone Canyon. Lodging was available, but since most travellers wanted to travel on to Wortman at Mile 18, Daniels mainly served meals.

Mile 13.6. The highway passes first Horsetail then Bridal Veil Falls. These and other area waterfalls are used by ice climbers in the winter. From Miles 14-17 the highway passes through Keystone Canyon. From 1910-16, prospectors searched for gold and copper in the canyon. Two competing companies proposed to build a railroad through the canyon. They fought a gun battle over right of way disputes, but the tracks were never laid. The only sign of either's endeavor is a tunnel drilled through rock at Mile 14.8.

Mile 18.5. Wortman's Roadhouse, built by Bill Wortman, was located at the foot of Thompson Pass, where freight loads were lightened before the climb over the 2,719 foot divide. Wortman's was closed due to lack of business in 1919.

Mile 18.8. The White Roadhouse was also called the White House, Our Roadhouse, and the Wayside Inn. After a fire destroyed Wortman's Roadhouse in 1907, White's was dismantled and the logs and timber were used to rebuild Wortman's.

Mile 20.1. Robert's Roadhouse and Kennedy's Roadhouse were tent roadhouses. Mile 25.1. Thompson Pass, elevation 2,719 feet/829 meters, holds the Alaska snowfall record. In the winter of 1952-53, the pass received 81.2 feet of snow. In addition to snow and rain, the pass is sometimes hit by one hundred mile per hour winds.

Mile 26.1, Summit Roadhouse/Stone House. The original stone roadhouse was located a few hundred feet north of the summit, on the left side of the road. Mile 28.6. Worthington Glacier State Recreation Site has a small shelter and an excellent view of the glacier. Mile 31. The Eureka Roadhouse site can be seen from the Ptarmigan Creek Bridge at Mile 30.7. Mile 32. The Ptarmigan Drop Roadhouse was located on the old trail near the confluence of Ptarmigan Creek and the Tsaina River.

The site, once the crew headquarters for the Alaska Road Commission, is on the west side of the Richardson Highway.

Mile 41. The Beaver Dam Roadhouse, which opened for business in 1903, was built on the old riverside of the Tsaina River. The present highway runs through the area where it once stood. Mile 47.8, interpretive sign on Lieutenant Billy Mitchell and Mount Billy Mitchell.

ROAD INFORMATION: RICHARDSON HIGHWAY

SECTION 2: MILE 50-MILE 100 (COPPER CENTER, OLD RICHARDSON HIGHWAY)

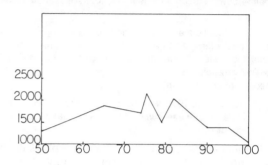

ROAD CONDITIONS/TERRAIN:

After an initial climb of about 700 feet to Mile 81.8, the highway descends with a few rollers. The road is paved with a wide shoulder.

JUNCTIONS:

Mile 82.6, junction with the Edgerton Highway. The highway leads to Chitina, and then through Wrangell-St. Elias National Park and Preserve to McCarthy and the Kennicott Copper Mine. For more information, see Chapter 32. Mile 91.1, Edgerton Highway Cutoff. This gravel road intersects the Edgerton Highway at Mile 7.4. Mile 100, junction with the Old Richardson Highway, leading to Copper Center.

WATER:

Mile 50.7, Tiekel River. Mile 53.8, Squaw Creek. Mile 58.1, Wagon Point Creek. Mile 65.1, Little Tonsina River. Mile 79.1, Tonsina River. Mile 79.6, Squirrel Creek. Miles 88.4-97, road parallels Willow Lake. Mile 90.8, Willow Creek.

CAMPING:

Mile 65, Little Tonsina State Recreation Site has eight campsites. Mile 79.6. Squirrel Creek State Recreation Site has 14 campsites and is often noisy due to proximity of Alaska Pipeline Pump Station #12. Camping is also possible at Mile 53.8, Squaw Creek, and Mile 90.3, Willow Creek.

FOOD/LODGING:

Mile 55.9. The Tiekel River Lodge has cabins, showers for $2.50 and a cafe. The lodge was for sale in 1988.

Mile 79. The Tonsina Lodge has a cafe, coin-operated showers ($1.00), laundry facilities, and the Mangy Moose Saloon and Cantina. Mile 92.7. Grizzly Pizza has a cafe, liquor store and bar, and sells fireworks. Owner Billy Williams is a wrestling coach. Mile 100, Copper Center.

ROADSIDE SIGHTS:

Mile 50.8. The Tiekel Roadhouse is on the west bank of the Tiekel River, about one mile south of Boulder Creek. Mile 57.5. The Tacoma Roadhouse, now preserved as a historic site, opened for business in 1907. Mile 62. The Ernestine Roadhouse, built in 1904 was located where the State Highway Maintenance Buildings now stand. Mile 64.7, Alaska Pipeline pump station #12. Mile 71, Kings Roadhouse/Glacier House.

Mile 79. The Upper Tonsina Roadhouse, built around 1903, was originally located near a telegraph station, post office, and general store. The original roadhouse burned in 1928. The rebuilt lodge is still standing. Current owner is Robert Hamilton. Mile 88.4. Alaska Pipeline viewpoint and interpretive sign and Wrangell-St. Elias National Park and Preserve interpretive sign.

Mile 89. The Wayside Inn, built around 1909, was located on the west side of the Old Trail. Paul Hansel, the original roadhouse owner, was a sign-maker, and so the roadhouse and grounds were full of signs.

Mile 90.9, Willow Creek Roadhouse/Bingham's. The farm property of F.J. Bingham was situated on a section which touched on the southern boundary of the baseline of the Copper River Meridian. This was problematic in later years when the Edgerton Cutoff Route was established, for Bingham had the right-of-way fenced off.

COPPER CENTER

BACKGROUND

Copper Center (pop. 229) is the first white settlement in the Copper River Basin and dates to the establishment of a trading post in 1896. In 1899 the U.S. Army telegraph line trail, which connected Fort Liscum in Valdez with Fort Egbert in Eagle, and later with Fairbanks, was established.

The miners were unaware of Keystone Canyon and Thompson Pass, so they followed a precarious route over the Valdez and Klutina Glaciers before they descended into the Copper River Basin. Many of the men built cabins and spent the winter in a place dubbed "Rapid City," near Klutina Lake. Others reached the small but growing settlement of Copper Center before building small cabins for the winter.

About 800 men spent the winter in Copper Center, where Andrew Holman set up a trading post and later built a hotel, now known as the Copper Center Lodge. That winter the men at Klutina Lake and Copper Center lived in small, poorly ventilated cabins and subsisted on sourdough pancakes, salt fish and whiskey. Suffering from scurvy, malnutrition, and in some cases frostbite, many of the would-be miners dreams of fortunes ended about a thousand miles from their destination, Dawson City.

Because of Copper Center's location on the Valdez-Fairbanks Trail and Telegraph line, it, unlike so many other gold rush settlements, continued to prosper. In 1901 the town's first post office was opened and for many years was the region's main supply center.

During the summer of 1988, a bypass route was built on the hills west of town. To reach Copper Center, exit the highway at either the south (Mile 100) or north (Mile 106) junction of the Old Richardson Highway.

The average July temperature in Copper Center is 59° F. The average July rainfall 2 inches.

Medical Services:

Phone 911 or 822-3203 for emergencies. The nearest hospital is in Glennallen.

Visitor's Center:

Wrangell-St. Elias National Park and Preserve Headquarters and Visitor's Center has information on the roads leading into the park and is located near the northern junction of the Old Richardson Highway.

Groceries:

The Copper River Cash Store is part of the original Copper Center Trading Post established in 1896. Owners Bob and Jeannie Sunder sell groceries, fresh produce, and some hardware items. Hours: 9 a.m. to 7 p.m. six days a week.

Lodging/Camping:

There are no hostels in Copper Center.

Copper Center Lodge, open from 7 a.m. to 9 p.m. serves sourdough pancakes, homemade bread and pies. The Lodge was named by former Governor Hickel as a State Historic Site. A private campground is located next to the Klutina River just before the south junction on the Old Richardson Highway.

Post Office:

The Copper Center Post Office hours are 8:30 a.m. to 5 p.m. Monday through Friday and from 9 a.m. to noon Saturdays. Zip Code: 99573.

Laundry/Showers:

The Safe Water Laundromat, located near the north junction of the Old Richardson Highway, is a clean, community owned and operated laundromat with coin operated showers.

Museum/Historical Sites:

The George Ashby Memorial Museum, located next to the Copper Center Lodge, was once a log bunkhouse. There are many artifacts and photographs of the Copper River Basin area, many of which date to the 1898 Klondike Gold Rush. Hours: 1 to 4 p.m. Wednesday, Thursday, and Friday.

The Chapel on the Hill is the oldest surviving log chapel in the Copper River Basin. It was built during World War II with the help of military personnel stationed at Dry Creek. The chapel was built with spruce logs and the pews were made of wooden boxes and rough lumber.

Gift Shops:

The Old Post Office Gallery sells Native crafts, gold pan art and Alaskan books.

Road Information: Richardson Highway

Section 3: Mile 100 (Copper Center, Old Richardson Highway)-Mile 147.5 (Sourdough)

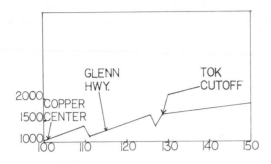

Road Conditions/Terrain:

The road ascends gradually, climbing about 1,000 feet, with a few rolling hills. It is paved with a wide shoulder to Big Timber Junction (Mile 128.6). The highway was upgraded from the junction to Sourdough in 1988. It has a temporary chipseal surface and a wide shoulder.

Junctions:

Mile 106. North junction of the Old Richardson Highway, leading into Copper Center. Mile 115. Junction with the Glenn Highway leading to Anchorage and the Parks Highway. Mile 128.6, Big Timber Junction. Junction with the Tok Cutoff leading to Tok and the Alaska Highway.

Water:

Mile 110.7, Tazlina River. Mile 126.9, Gulkana River. The highway parallels the river for about 40 miles to Paxson Lake. Mile 136.4, Coleman Creek. Mile 138.1, Poplar Grove Creek. Mile 147.5, Sourdough Creek.

Camping:

Mile 117.5. Dry Creek State Recreation Site has 58 campsites, four of which are for tenters and are located along a creek-side trail. Mile 147.5, Sourdough BLM Campground has 18 campsites. 13 are next to Sourdough Creek, and five are by the Gulkana River. There is a trail paralleling Sourdough Creek.

Food/Lodging:

Mile 115. The Hub, a 24-hour convenience grocery store, has limited groceries. (A full service supermarket is located a mile down the hill in Glennallen; see Chapter 26.

Mile 128.5. Gakona Junction Village, owned by Alan and Shirley LeMaster, has a restaurant and a limited grocery store, the Little Alaska Cache. Fresh produce is available. The lodge is known as "Bunnies" because rabbits were imported here from Anchorage. Iditarod posters by John Van Zyle and prints by Copper Center artist Gail Niebrugge are on display and for sale. Also here is the "best water in the valley."

Mile 147.5. The Sourdough Roadhouse is the oldest operating roadhouse along the Richardson Highway. It was placed on the *National Register of Historic Places* in 1974. A $5.00 breakfast includes two eggs, sausage or bacon, and unlimited sourdough pancakes.

ROADSIDE SIGHTS:

Mile 101.1. In 1898 Andrew Holman established a temporary lodge near the Klutina and Copper Rivers. The Hotel Holman provided shelter for prospectors on their way to the goldfields. After numerous management and building changes, Florence Barnes, the Copper Center postmaster, bought the facility in 1923 and renamed the establishment the Copper Center Roadhouse and Trading Post. In 1948, Mr. and Mrs. George Ashby purchased the property, and named it the Copper Center Lodge. In 1967, it was named a State Historic Site.

Mile 101.5. Homesteader John McCreary constructed the McCreary Roadhouse in 1902. When the roadhouse was destroyed by fire in 1909, he built the Copper Center Hotel, which had 21 private rooms. In later years, it too was destroyed by fire.

Mile 110. Bundy and Porter built the Tazlina Roadhouse in 1902 on the north side of the treacherous Tazlina River. Bundy, who operated the river ferry, drowned in 1903. In 1906 "Tazlina Billy," a German farmer, took over the roadhouse. In the next 20 years several bridges were built over the Tazlina. In 1927, Tazlina Billy's livestock was on the other side of the river when the bridge was washed out. Billy attempted to cross by boat, was marooned and subsequently died of exposure. The site of the roadhouse is at least 0.5 miles below the present bridge.

Mile 115, junction with Glenn Highway. The Copper Basin Visitor's Center has information on local accommodations, fishing, and history. Mile 117.5. The Dry Creek Roadhouse, built in 1906, later fell into disrepair.

Mile 126.9. The Gulkana Roadhouse has had numerous owners and name changes during its 39 year existence. The lodge, which was advertised as the "largest and best equipped on the trail from Valdez to Fairbanks," burned in 1948.

Mile 130.6. The Gakona Roadhouse, built in 1902, was later acquired by the Valdez Transportation Company, which made the roadhouse their principle Interior station. It was at the junction of the Valdez/Eagle Trail and the winter trail to Fairbanks. The roadhouse did a brisk business until the fall of 1906 when the Alaska Road Commission established an all season road, which diverted Fairbanks traffic. The Gakona Lodge and Trading Post, now at Mile 1.8 Tok Cutoff, is listed in the *National Register of Historic Places*.

Mile 137.8. All that remains of the Poplar Grove Roadhouse, built in 1906, are two old cabins on the left-hand side of the highway.

Mile 147.5. The Sourdough Roadhouse was built by trapper John Hart in 1906 when a road survey crew told him that the new road would pass by his front door. The present business is housed in the original log structure. In October 1974, the Sourdough Roadhouse was placed on the *National Register*.

The average July temperature at Sourdough is 54° F, the average July rainfall 3.9 inches.

ROAD INFORMATION: RICHARDSON HIGHWAY

Section 4: Mile 147.5 (Sourdough)-Mile 200.5 (Fielding Lake Road)

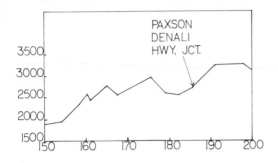

Road Conditions/Terrain:

The highway has some rolling hills, but is mostly a gradual climb, with an overall elevation gain of about 1,300 feet. The road is paved with a narrow shoulder.

Junctions:

Mile 185.5, junction with the Denali Highway (Alaska Route 8). The highway leads to the Parks Highway near Denali National Park. Mile 200.5, junction with Fielding Lake Road.

Water:

Miles 165.5 and 166.5, two small lakes. Mile 170.1, Meier Lake. Mile 173.4, Dick Lake, access by gravel road to the east. Miles 175-186, road parallels Paxson Lake. Mile 184.7, One Mile Creek. Miles 189-195, road parallels Summit Lake. Mile 196.4, Gunn Creek.

Camping/Picnic Areas:

Mile 175, Paxson Lake BLM Campground has 20 campsites. Mile 181, Paxson Lake BLM Wayside Picnic Area. Miles 188.5 and 190.5, State Rest areas with picnic tables. Mile 200.5. Fielding Lake State Recreation Area, located two miles downhill off a gravel road, has seven unsheltered campsites.

Food/Lodging:

Mile 150.9, 151 Mile Liquor Store. Joe Chimielowski has sold liquor, beer, wine, candy, and soda here since 1985.

Mile 185.5. Paxson Lodge, owned by Stan Brown, is open from 6 a.m. to midnight. In addition to a post office, (Zip Code: 99737) the lodge has a cafe, a bar and sells some groceries.

Mile 194.9. Summit Lake Lodge, owned by John Wallner and Buzz Jackozich, has been open since the 1940's. The Lodge has a cafe, bar, showers for $3.00, and sells groceries out of the kitchen.

Roadside Sights:

Mile 160.9. Our Home/McGee's was constructed in 1906-07. Around 1924 the buildings were dismantled and taken to Glennallen. Mile 168, Abbot's Roadhouse.

Mile 170. Meier's Roadhouse was located four miles southeast of Paxson Lake, on the left side of the road. At an altitude of 2,750 feet/838 meters, building owner Charles Meier raised vegetables. The building was destroyed by fire in 1925, and rebuilt. A second roadhouse was destroyed by fire in 1950. An old barn remains on the site.

Mile 185.5. Alfred J. Paxson built a log style roadhouse and a large barn on the right side of the road, three miles southeast of Summit Lake. Situated in the timber, the roadhouse was sheltered from the severe winds of Isabel Pass. After a number of owners and fires, John Windust and Boots Newland built a new roadhouse in 1958. What was left of the original building burned in 1976.

Mile 197.6. Interpretive sign and monument honor General Wilds P. Richardson, first president of the Alaska Road Commission. Richardson put in much of the original trail.

Mile 198, Isabel Pass (elevation 3,284 feet/1,001 meters). Water north of this pass empties into the Bering Sea via the Yukon Drainage System. Water south of the pass empties into the Pacific Ocean via the Copper River Drainage System.

ROAD INFORMATION: RICHARDSON HIGHWAY

SECTION 5: MILE 200.5 (FIELDING LAKE ROAD)-MILE 250

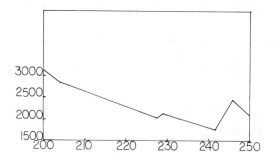

ROAD CONDITIONS/TERRAIN:

The highway is mostly downhill 1,240 feet to Mile 242, where there is a moderate 700 foot climb to Mile 246. The road is paved, the shoulder narrow.

WATER:

Mile 201.4, Phelan Creek. Mile 202.3, McCullum Creek. Mile 203.8, developed spring, good water here. Miles 206.8, 206.9, small creeks. Mile 216.7, Lower Miller Creek. Mile 217.1, Castner Creek. Mile 218.7, Trims Creek. Mile 219.8, Michael Creek. Mile 220.8, Flood Creek. Mile 222.9, Whistler Creek. Mile 223.7, Boulder Creek. Mile 224.4, Lower Suzi Q. Creek. Mile 224.8, Upper Suzi Q. Creek. Mile 226.8, Gunnysack Creek. Mile 228.2, One Mile Creek. Mile 231, Darling Creek. Mile 233.3, Bear Creek. Mile 234.7, Ruby Creek. Mile 238, Donnelly Creek. Mile 246, unnamed creek.

CAMPING/PICNIC AREAS:

Mile 214, state rest area with picnic table. Mile 225.5, state rest area with viewpoint and picnic tables. Mile 238. Donnelly Creek State Recreation Site has 12 campsites.

FOOD/LODGING:

Mile 227.4. Black Rapids Lodge, built in 1903 as a roadhouse along the Valdez-Fairbanks Trail, is presently owned by Gerald and Wanda McMillan. Breakfast is served all day. Hours: 8 a.m. to 10 p.m. daily.

ROADSIDE SIGHTS:

Mile 203. Yost's Roadhouse, built in 1905, was located at an altitude of 2,897 feet/883 meters in the Alaska Range and was subject to severe winter storms. In bad weather travellers found their way across the Delta River by means of a two-strand wire fence that was placed there by the Alaska Road Commission. By 1984, no buildings remained.

Mile 212.5, Casey's Cache/McKinley's Roadhouse. Mile 214, Miller's Roadhouse/McDavitt's. No evidence of this roadhouse remains. Mile 225.5. Interpretive sign explains how the Black Rapids Glacier surged more than three miles during the winter of 1936-37, and almost reached the Richardson Highway. Mile 227.4. Black Rapids Roadhouse/Black Rapids Hunting Lodge, was built in 1902-03.

Mile 238. Built in 1906, the Donnelly Roadhouse was washed out by the Delta River in 1914 and 1926. Another roadhouse, Donnelly's Inn, was established back from the river at Mile 237.7.

Mile 241.3. A view of the Alaska Range and the Delta River, and an interpretive sign on the Delta bison, which spend their summers on the far side of the Delta River. Mile 246. Road passes by Donnelly Dome, west of highway (elevation 3,910 feet/1,192 meters).

ROAD INFORMATION: RICHARDSON HIGHWAY

SECTION 6: MILE 250-MILE 300

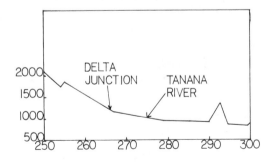

ROAD CONDITIONS/TERRAIN:

The highway is downhill, dropping about 1,300 feet (some areas are almost level) to Mile 275.2, where a series of rolling hills begin. The road is paved with a narrow shoulder to the Alaska Highway junction (Mile 266) where there's a six-foot shoulder.

JUNCTIONS:

Mile 261.1. Main Gate of Fort Greely. The highway cuts through the fort from Mile 258.7 to Mile 265.9; access into the woods on either side of the highway is restricted. Mile 266, Delta Junction. The Alaska Highway ends here, at the junction of the Richardson Highway.

WATER:

Mile 265.8, Jarvis Creek. Mile 275.1, Tanana River. Mile 286.5, Shaw Creek. Mile 295.5, Banner Creek (muddy).

CAMPING/PICNIC AREAS:

Mile 252.8, state rest area with tables. Mile 267, Delta State Recreation Site has 22 campsites. Mile 277.8, Quartz Lake State Recreation Area. There are 16 campsites at Quartz Lake, and eight campsites at nearby Lost Lake. Lost Lake is a nicer campground, but its a short walk, via a trail, to the other campground for water.

FOOD/LODGING:

Mile 266, Delta Junction. See Chapter 15.

Mile 274. Tom's Bar, owned by Tom and Shirley Smith, was built by Tom in 1953 and is the oldest bar on the highway with its original owners. The Smiths have a book exchange, and cyclists are welcome to eat their lunches inside. Ask to see Shirley's hand-made Native dolls.

Mile 274.5, the Big D Bar has been owned by Clarence Brunt since 1964. It has a twenty foot shuffleboard, one of only three in the state. Clarence claims to have the best water in town.

Mile 275, Rika's Roadhouse. Presently the White Stone Community, a multi-denominational Christian group, has a contract with the state to run the refurbished roadhouse. The Community maintains the lodge and food concession. A garden, a gift shop and an old blacksmith shop (now a museum) are on the premises.

Mile 295, Richardson Roadhouse. Owner John Konichak runs a small liquor store and sells snacks, soda, sandwiches, and ice cream.

ROADSIDE SIGHTS:

Mile 257. Beale's Cache Roadhouse was abandoned in 1928. Mile 266. Junction with the Alaska Highway. This is the end of the 1422 mile/2275 kilometer Alaska Highway. Interpretive sign and Visitor's Center at the junction.

Mile 275. Big Delta State Historic Park, the site of Rika's Roadhouse, originally known as Bennett's. When the roadhouse was called McCarthy's, it was a transportation hub and a trading post. Sternwheelers came from as far away as Tanana, and prospectors and miners stocked up on supplies. In 1923 John Hajdukovich gave the property to Rika Wallen for back wages. In 1943-44 a high truss steel bridge was built across the Tanana at Big Delta, eliminating the need for a ferry. The Richardson Highway then passed the roadhouse, eliminating a lot of business. In the early 50's, Rika built and moved into a new frame house a short distance northwest of the old roadhouse.

Mile 295. The original Richardson Roadhouse, built in 1909, burned in 1981. It was moved in 1922 from the town of Richardson, which was being washed away by the Tanana River.

ROAD INFORMATION: RICHARDSON HIGHWAY
SECTION 7: MILE 300-363 (FAIRBANKS)

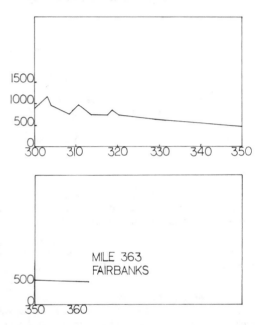

ROAD CONDITIONS/TERRAIN:

The first twenty-five miles of road are rolling and followed by a gradual downhill slope. The road is paved and has a wide shoulder. At Mile 340.6, the highway widens to four lanes and traffic increases. Much of the property adjacent to the highway is privately owned. To reach Fairbanks, take the Old Richardson Highway exit at Mile 361. Beyond Mile 361, bicycles are prohibited.

JUNCTIONS:

Mile 321.4. Harding Lake Road leads 1.4 miles to Harding Lake Campground. Mile 340.6, main gate of Eielson Air Force Base. Mile 346.7. Laurance Road leads 2.2 miles to Chena Lakes North Star Borough Recreation Area. Mile 349, exit for the town of North Pole. Mile 361, the Old Richardson Highway. Bicycles must exit here. Mile 363, Airport Road, the end of the Richardson Highway, and the beginning of the Steese Highway.

WATER:

Mile 306, Birch Lake. Mile 323.1, Salcha River. Mile 324, Clear Creek. Mile 325.5, Munson's Slough. Mile 328.4, Little Salcha River. Mile 344.8, Moose Creek.

Camping:

Mile 321.5. Harding Lake State Recreation Area, located 1.4 miles from the highway has 89 campsites including a tenting section located about 100 yards down a trail. A State Parks Ranger Office, a shelter, and a trail are here. Mile 323.3. Salcha State Recreation Site, on the banks of the Salcha River, has 25 campsites. Mile 346.7, Chena Lakes North Star Borough Recreation Area has two campgrounds.

Food/Lodging:

Mile 315. Midway Lodge has a bar, cafe, and showers for $1.00. Mile 319.4. Tryphs Texico and General Store has a limited supply of groceries and showers for $1.00. Mile 323. The Sno-Shu Inn, owned by Deborah Mutchler, was built in 1949.

Mile 323.3. The Salchaket Homestead, owned by Brian and Nenette Tumbleson, has a cafe, rooms, used books and showers for $2.00. Mile 328.6. The Salcha Store and Service Station, established in 1958 and owned by Lynx and Linda Balch, has a limited supply of groceries. Mile 331. The Boondox Bar, Liquor Store and Laundromat is owned by Anne Burnett. Mile 343.7. The Moose Creek General Store is located about 200 yards off the highway and sells some groceries.

Mile 249, North Pole.

Roadside Sights:

Between Miles 311.5 and 313.4 the road closely parallels the Tanana River. On clear days there's a view of the Alaska Range.

Mile 312. The Overland Roadhouse, built in 1909, was destroyed by fire in 1945. Mile 325. Salchacket/Munson's was built in 1904 and destroyed by fire in 1925. Mile 349, North Pole.

North Pole

Background

North Pole, (pop. 1,640) a bedroom community of Fairbanks and Eielson Air Force Base, is located in the Tanana Valley. It has professional services, schools, and a mall. North Pole became a first class city in 1961. The town was settled in 1944 when Bon and Bernice Davis homesteaded a 160 acre parcel at 15 mile Old Richardson Highway.

The area was named North Pole by subdividers Dahl and Gaske, in the hope that a toy manufacturer would establish a factory and sell toys made at the North Pole.

Visitor's Center:

The North Pole Visitor's Center is at Mile 348.8 Richardson Highway. Hours: 9 a.m. to 4:30 p.m.

Groceries:

In the North Pole Mall at the junctions of the Richardson Highway and Santa Claus Lane is a Super Valu Supermarket and a pharmacy.

Lodging/Camping:

North Pole has no hostels. North Pole Park, at Fifth Avenue, has nine spaces for tents only, with restrooms and water. According to a city employee, this is a nice place to camp.

EATING/DRINKING ESTABLISHMENTS:

The North Country Inn, on Santa Claus Lane, next to Santa's Suds, has breakfast, sandwiches, lunch and dinner specials.

POST OFFICE:

The North Pole Post Office is located at 500 East Fifth Avenue. If requested, letters will be hand stamped. Zip Code: 99705.

LAUNDRY/SHOWERS:

Santa's Suds, on Santa Claus Lane, next to the North Country Inn, has a modern coin-operated laundry. Hours: 8 a.m. to 10 p.m. daily.

PUBLIC RECREATION:

The North Pole High School has a swimming pool. Phone 448-9401 for information.

RICHARDSON HIGHWAY

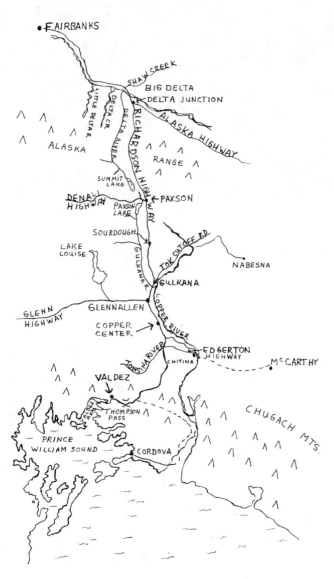

FAIRBANKS

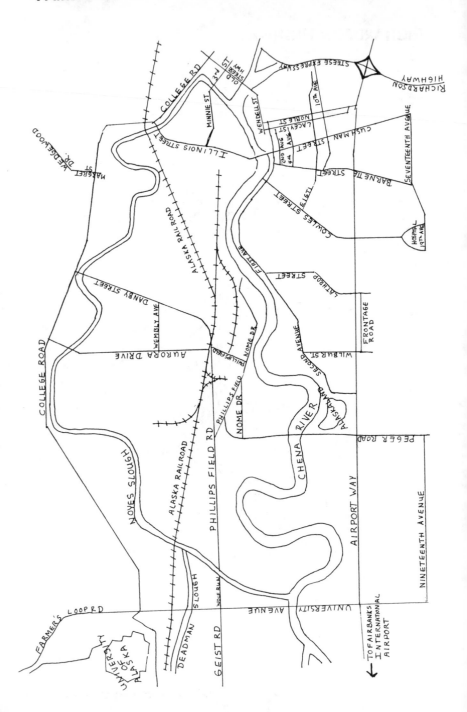

CHAPTER 19: FAIRBANKS

BACKGROUND

Fairbanks (pop. 28,000) was originally a supply point for area mining activities. In the summer of 1901, Captain E.T. Barnette boarded the steamer *Lavelle Young* intending to establish a trading post where the Valdez-Eagle Trail crossed the Tanana River. Fairbanks became this site when local prospector Felix Pedro informed Barnette of area gold prospects.

By the fall of 1904, Judge James Wickersham had moved his third judicial district courthouse from Eagle to the already larger mining district in Fairbanks. At Wickersham's suggestion, the new town was named Fairbanks after Senator Charles Fairbanks of Indiana, who was later Theodore Roosevelt's Vice President.

With the completion of the Alaska Railroad in 1923, a dependable year round transportation link was established, and large scale mining began. Though the rest of the country suffered during the Depression, gold mining was profitable for the area settlers and Fairbanks grew steadily. Soon the town gave rise to theatres, office buildings, and apartments.

During World War II, some Fairbanks residents, concerned about a Japanese invasion, left for the Lower 48. However, Congress funded the construction of two military bases near Fairbanks, causing another growth spurt. Unlike many of the bases in the U.S. which closed after the war, the ones near Fairbanks remained active, and are still important to the area economy.

The University of Alaska, Fairbanks (UAF) is the town's major employer. Created in 1917 by the Territorial Legislature, the Alaska Agricultural College and School of Mines opened in 1922 with six faculty members and six students. In 1935, the name was changed to the University of Alaska.

Though local government is a larger employer than the mining industry, there are still many active mines in the area. Some of these mines are located just outside of the Fairbanks city limits, while others are north of town in the Circle mining district.

VISITORS INFORMATION

VISITOR'S CENTER:

The Fairbanks Convention and Visitor's Bureau Log Cabin, located at 550 First Avenue, near Cushman Street, has a staffed information desk and brochures on lodging, food establishments, adventure opportunities, recreational activities, guided walking and driving tours, local bus lines, and camping. Hours: 8 a.m. to 6:30 p.m. daily. Phone: 456-5774.

PUBLIC LANDS OFFICE:

The Alaska Public Lands Information Center at 250 Cushman Street is located on the lower level of the Courthouse Square building, with its main entrance on Third Avenue. The APLIC has information and films on Alaska's natural and cultural history. The Alaska Natural History Association sells slides, books and maps, including the Parks Highway Road and Recreation Map. Hours: 8:30 a.m. to 9 p.m. daily.

NATIONAL PARK SERVICE:

Fairbanks is the headquarters for the Gates of the Arctic National Park and Preserve. The office is located in the Federal Building at 101 12th Avenue. For information, write: Superintendent, Gates of the Arctic National Park and Preserve, Box 74680, Fairbanks, AK 99707.

MAP INFORMATION:

Topographical maps are available at the Alaska Distribution Section of the USGS, Room 126, Federal Building, 101 12th Avenue. Hours: 9 a.m. to 4:30 p.m. Monday through Friday. Phone: 456-0244. Write: Box 12, Fairbanks, AK 99701. The University Library has an extensive collection of Alaska topographic maps.

COOPERATIVE EXTENSION SERVICE:

The Tanana District Office of the CES is located in Room 303, 1514 South Cushman Street, in the Sportsman's Mall. The office has brochures on everything from sourdough preparation to cabin building. Hours: Monday through Friday during regular business hours. Phone: 452-1530.

UNIVERSITY TOURS:

UAF offers guided tours during the summer months. Phone: 474-7581.

TRAVELLER'S NEEDS

MEDICAL SERVICES:

The emergency phone number of the Fairbanks Memorial Hospital, at 1650 Cowles Street, is 451-3567. The Fairbanks Fire and Police Department emergency telephone number is 911.

GROCERIES:

Fairbanks has four major malls, and each has a supermarket. At the Bentley Mall, at College Road and Old Steese is a Safeway Supermarket and a pharmacy. There is also a Safeway Supermarket and a pharmacy at the University Center Mall at Airport Way and University Avenue.The Gavora Mall, at Third Street between Old Steese and the Steese Expressway has a Super Valu Supermarket. Shopper's Forum at Airport Way and Cowles also has a Super Valu Supermarket. Foodland Supermarket, at Gaffney Street and Cushman, just off Airport Road, has a health food section and a pharmacy. These supermarkets are open 24 hours a day.

Whole Earth Grocery and Delicatessen, at College Road and Deborah Streets, near UAF, has food for cyclists and backpackers, including trail mixes, dried fruits and nuts, juices, instant dinners, herbs and teas. Hours: 10 a.m. to 7 p.m. Monday through Saturday. Phone: 479-2052.

BICYCLE/OUTDOOR STORES:

Campbell's Sports, at 609 Third Street, carries Shimano and Suntour components, tools, tires and tubes, and some backpacking and camping equipment. Repair work is done here. Boxes are available for $5.00. Campbell Sports is owned by long time

Fairbanks residents George and Donna Campbell. Hours: 9 a.m. to 7 p.m. weekdays, 9 a.m. to 6 p.m. Saturday and noon to 4 p.m. Sunday. Phone: 452-4672.

Beaver Sports, on College Road, near the UAF campus, carries Shimano, Suntour and some Campagnelo components and has a wide selection of tires and tubes. Beaver Sports sells backpacking and camping equipment, clothing, and rents canoes. Free bike boxes for airline travel are available. Beaver Sports is owned by James Whisenhant and the bicycle store manager is Barbara Kelly. Hours: Monday through Friday, 9 a.m. to 7 p.m. Saturday, 9 a.m. to 6 p.m. Phone: 479-2494 or 479-0876.

The Bike Route is located at 1018 College Road, next to Creamer's Field. Owner Bob Hawkins does repairs and has some components for sale. The Bike Route is often closed, so phone 456-1110 before visiting.

Victor Mimken makes custom mountain bike frames, does repairs and sells componentry. Phone: 479-7213 or write: Box 80710, Fairbanks, AK 99708.

Bicycle mechanic Simon Rakower builds wheels, repairs frames and sells quality equipment, including rims and hubs. Accommodations are sometimes available. Phone: 457-2995.

Clem's Backpacking Sport, owned by Clemens Rawert, sells high quality backpacking items, including stoves and sleeping bags. Hours: 10 a.m. to 6 p.m., Tuesday through Saturday. Phone: 456-6314.

Apocalypse Design, at 101 College Road, sells custom made outdoor gear, including rain overbooties, front and rear panniers, and insulated handlebar hand covers. They also do emergency repairs. Apocalypse Design is owned by Richard Faharty and Sherry Steffens. Hours: 9 a.m. to 6 p.m. weekdays, 10 a.m. to 4 p.m. Saturday. Phone: 478-7555.

LODGING/CAMPING:

The Fairbanks AYH Youth Hostel is located on College Road, in a quonset hut next to the fairgrounds. Says former houseparent Sean O'Neil, the hostel is "quite rustic, and the atmosphere's nice." The hostel sleeps 18, and has separate facilities for men and women. Sleeping bags required. Water, showers, and inexpensive laundry facilities are in an adjacent fairgrounds building. Cooking facilities will be available in 1989. The nightly charge for hostel members is $6.25. For more information write: Sean O'Neil, P.O. Box 2196, Fairbanks, AK 99707.

The John Alphonsi Sr. Memorial Campground, on the University's West Ridge, is open to university students. The campsite fee is $2.00 a night or $10.00 per week. The campground has restrooms and a dumpster, but the water's unfit for drinking. Laundry and showers are available at UAF's Wood Center.

The Chena River State Campground on University Avenue, near Airport Road, has 51 campsites, is noisy and has a five-day limit. The nightly site fee is $10.00.

The Goldhill RV Park, at Mile 355.2 Parks Highway, has a nightly $5.00 per tent site fee. Showers cost $1.00 for campers, and laundry facilities are available.

The Chena Pump Wayside is located at 4.5 Mile Chena Pump Road. The campground, on the banks of the Tanana River has no established campsites.

Privately owned Norlite Campground at 1660 Peger Road, near Alaskaland, has over 200 campsites. The nightly fee is $6.50. A restaurant, showers, laundry, limited groceries, tour tickets and information on area attractions available.

The Tanana Valley Campground, next to the Tanana Valley Fairgrounds has 31 campsites, showers, laundry, and picnic tables. The nightly site fee is $9.00.

POST OFFICE:

The downtown Fairbanks Post Office is at 315 Barnette Street. Zip Code: 99701. The College branch Post Office is at 4025 Geist Road. Zip Code: 99707. The UAF branch Post Office is in Constitution Hall. Zip Code: 99708.

LAUNDRY/SHOWERS:

Free shower and laundry facilities at UAF's Wood Center are available to students with a current I.D. It costs $1.00 to do a wash, and .75 to dry.

For $3.00, non-students may use the UAF Patty Athletic Center facilities. The fee includes showers, the use of both weight rooms, the basketball and racquetball courts, the swimming pool and the sauna.

The B&C Laundromat at 3677 College Road, around the corner from Hot Licks Ice Cream, has showers for $2.50. To do a load of wash costs $1.75, to dry costs 25 cents. Hours: 8 a.m. to 11 p.m. daily.

ALTERNATIVE TRANSPORTATION:

The Fairbanks International Airport is located at the end of Airport Road, on the west side of town.

The Gray Line of Alaska bus line offers tours out of Fairbanks, Anchorage, Skagway and Haines. Alaskon Express Motor Coaches provides regular non-tour service between Fairbanks, Whitehorse, Skagway and Haines. Phone: 456-7741.

The Fairbanks office of the Alaska Railroad is located at 280 North Cushman Street, near the Fairbanks Daily News-Miner building. There is regular train service to Denali National Park and Anchorage. For more information, see the Introduction. Phone: 456-4155.

ENTERTAINMENT AND RECREATION

TRAILS:

The Creamer's Field Migratory Wildlife Refuge and Nature Path two mile loop trail is a good place to view area vegetation, geology and wildlife. The Interior's oldest surviving farm buildings are on the Creamer's Field property. In 1903 Charles Hinckley arrived from Nome with his family and three of his best cows. By the end of the summer he had built the Creamer's Field dairy, his third log barn in Fairbanks. In 1927, Hinckley sold the operation to his brother-in-law, Charles Creamer, who with his wife Annie ran the farm until her death in 1969.

In 1969 the State purchased the fields, and in 1981 the buildings. An interpretive brochure is available at the beginning of the trail, or at the nearby Deparment of Fish and Game office.

There are approximately 25 kilometers of well-marked trails in the 460 acre Birch Hill Recreation Area, located at Mile 2.3 Steese Highway. Bicycling in the park is permitted in the summer. The park is maintained by the Fairbanks North Star Borough.

A new map of the Birch Hill ski trails, designed by Nicole McCulloch, Special Projects Planner, Department of Community Planning, is available from the Fairbanks Parks and Recreation Department. The office is located at 19th and Lathrop, on the second floor of the Big Dipper building. Phone: 456-4218.

MUSEUMS/HISTORICAL SITES:

The University of Alaska Museum, located on the West Ridge of the UAF campus, has Alaska history exhibits, wildlife displays, Alaska's largest gold collection, a Birds of the Wetland exhibit, and a display case containing Blue Babe, a restored prehistoric bison. The museum and adjacent gift shop are open from 9 a.m. to 9 p.m. Admission is $3.00.

Alaskaland has a public picnic area, a Native village, a pioneer museum, the Fairbanks Civic Center, art galleries, the President Harding railroad car, the Riverboat *Nenana*, a salmon bake and shops. The Northern Inua Show, a slide show of the World Native Eskimo and Indian Olympics, is presented at 8 p.m. daily. Admission is $5.00. Alaskaland is located at Airport and Peger Roads. There is no admission charge to Alaskaland.

The Alaska Dog Mushers Museum, at Mile 4 Farmer's Loop Road, has mushing exhibits, demonstrations, and shows race videos. Hours: 9:30 a.m. to 4:30 p.m. (admission: $2.00). There is an 8 p.m. evening show. (Admission: $6.00).

The UAF Institute of Arctic Biology Large Animal Research Station (Muskox Farm) is located behind the campus on Yankovich Road. Either turn right off Miller Hill Road, or left off Ballaine Road. Guided tours from June until August are given at 1:30 and 3 p.m. Tuesdays and Saturdays and also in September at 1:30 on Saturday. Meet at the front gate near the viewing platform. Phone: 474-7207.

Riverboat *Discovery*, off Airport Way, near the airport, offers scenic five-hour narrated riverboat cruises aboard an authentic sternwheeler. The riverboat stops at an Indian river village and at the home of an area dog musher. The cost is $25, and reservations are requested. Departure times are 8:45 a.m. and 2 p.m. daily. Phone: 479-6673.

ALASKA PIONEER'S HOME:

The Alaska Pioneer's Home, a state-run nursing home welcomes visitors. The Pioneer's Home is located at 2221 Egan Drive. Phone: 456-4372.

EATING/DRINKING ESTABLISHMENTS:

At A Moveable Feast Restaurant, the food's good, but the portions are small. The restaurant has outdoor seating and live music in the summer. A Moveable Feast is located next to Baker and Baker Books in the Northgate Mall. Hours: 11 a.m. to 9 p.m. Monday through Saturday.

Claudio's Restaurant serves good Italian food, and fine pastries. Claudios is open daily except Sundays. Although Claudio's is difficult to find, it is one the nicest eating establishments in Fairbanks. Claudio's is located on Second Street and Graehl, next to the Steese Expressway, and can be reached by following Second Street east of the Old Steese Highway. Second Street north of the Chena River should not be confused with Second Avenue south of the Chena River.

Hot Licks Ice Cream, located at 3549 College Road, has good homemade ice cream, soups and beverages, and is open daily. The Blue Marlin, at 3412 College Road, has pizza, lunch and dinner menus and serves beverages.

The Pump House Restaurant and Saloon, at 1.3 Mile Chena Pump Road, serves lunches, dinners and Sunday brunches. Seating is indoors or on the banks of the Chena River.

The Royal Fork Buffet Restaurant, an all you can eat cafeteria, is located at 414 Third Street, next to the Steese Expressway. Hours: Monday through Thursday, 11 a.m. to 8:30 p.m., Friday and Saturday, 11 a.m. to 9 p.m., and Sundays from 9 a.m. to 8 p.m.

The Wood Center Cafeteria, located on the UAF campus, has cafeteria style food.

BOOKSTORES:

Both Gulliver's used bookstores have a good selection of used and some new general interest books. The first store is located next to Hot Licks Ice Cream, at 3535 College Road. Phone: 474-9574. Another Gulliver's is located in the Shopper's Forum Mall at the Corner of Airport Road and Cowles Street. Phone: 456-3657.

Baker and Baker sells new books and has a good selection of Alaska titles. They'll mail to "just about anywhere" and are located in the Northgate Square, at 330 Old Steese Highway. Phone: 456-2278. UAF's Elmer E. Rasmusson Library, open to the public, is the largest library in Alaska. The library also houses the northernmost federal depository library in the U.S. Book Cache is located at the University Mall. Waldenbooks is located at the Bentlley Mall.

FAIRS:

The Tanana Valley Fair, the oldest fair in the state, is the official Alaska State Fair in even numbered years. The fair is usually held in mid-August, on the Fairgrounds, off College Road.

MOVIES/PLAYS:

The Palace Theatre, on the Alaskaland grounds, presents "Good as Gold," a nightly historical, musical review of Fairbanks. Admission is $6.00. Admission to the Jim Bell after hours show, an adult comedy, is $4.00. Reservations are requested. Phone: 456-5960.

The Goldstream Cinema (phone: 456-5113) and The Center (479-0008) are both located on Airport Road.

The Fairbanks Summer Arts Festival starts in late July, and includes two weeks of workshops, and classes in music, dance, theater and the visual arts. Reservations recommended. Write: Fairbanks Summer Arts Festival, Box 80845, Fairbanks, AK 99708. Phone: 479-6778.

SIDE TRIPS:

Fairbanks is a major jumping off point for explorations in the Interior and Arctic. Check at the Visitor's Center or phone travel agents.

PUBLIC RECREATION:

The Mary Siah Recreation Center, at 1025 14th Avenue, has a pool and showers. Phone 456-6119 for current hours and prices. The Hamme Pool is located at 901

Airport Way. Phone: 456-2969 or 456-2960. The Big Dipper Arena, at 19th and Lathrop Streets, has an indoor skating arena and a running track. Showers cost $2.00.

Car Camping

In early June, about 450 miles into our trip, Pete felt ill, so we took a room at the Eagle's Nest Motel outside of Dot Lake. That evening, I cooked dinner. Since there was no table nearby, I made one by lying two boards across two sawhorses. My cooking area was a little unsteady, but I thought, very functional.

Even though Pete was sick the next morning, we decided to ride to Tok. As I stuffed the sleeping bags into their sacks, Pete began to prepare breakfast. A few minutes after lighting his Svea stove, he sat on the edge of my makeshift table. When he crossed his legs, the pot of boiling water flew up into the air and landed on his foot. The water was absorbed by his sweats and sock. Pete ran to the bathroom and immersed his foot in cold water. Then, he crawled back in bed.

The following day, Pete bandaged his foot, which he said didn't hurt much, and we left for Tok, stopping first at the Dot Lake Health Clinic, which was only 800 yards from the motel. There, Joyce McNutt, the primary community health nurse and E.M.T. Judy Lowe examined Pete's burn. Under the clinic's florescent light, the injury looked far worse than it had in the dimly lit motel room. Shaped like Antarctica, it extended from the top of Pete's foot clear around to his ankle.

Joyce suggested that Dennis Rogers, the Tok Physician's Assistant examine Pete. Knowing he couldn't ride the 50 miles to Tok, and headed there herself, Joyce offered to drive us to the clinic. Her husband and I put our bicycles and gear in his van. At this point, I choked back tears. Now we were going to Tok the easy way. In my mind, this was cheating. A hard-core cyclist, who never accepted rides, I vowed that if we continued the trip, I'd return to Dot Lake and ride back to Tok.

In the Tanana Valley Clinic examining room, Dennis donned a light green surgical mask and tended to the burn. When he asked where we were planning to stay, Pete replied we'd probably go to the Tok River campground, which was five miles distant. Fortunately, Dennis, who'd worked in a burn care unit in Iowa, had an idea of the extent of the injury, and suggested that we stay at his place. We accepted his offer.

After a night's rest, Pete and I, with Dennis's help, made some tentative plans. Dennis said the foot would require daily scrubbing and needed to be kept elevated. He added that Pete wouldn't be able to ride for a few weeks, but he'd be able to drive in about a week. I volunteered to hitchhike back to Fairbanks, and get my truck. This way, when Pete felt up to it, we could continue to Haines. I'd ride and he'd drive.

I didn't want to use a support vehicle, but I knew that if we didn't, we'd have to go back to Fairbanks. And if we did that, we might not finish our trip. I returned to Tok with my truck, and additional gear which included a large water jug, a dutch oven, the tape player, tapes, our tool boxes, an axe, extra bicycle tires, more clothes, blankets, and food and ice chests. The truck was nearly full, but I didn't think too long about what I took. At the time, I still thought we'd bring the Toyota and extra gear back to Fairbanks, and continue without it.

After three nights on Dennis's floor, Pete felt well enough to camp. We drove from his place armed with miles of gauze, bottles of Betadine, and plenty of Tylenol. In camp, I re-packed everything neatly in the back of the truck. Of course, after two days, nothing was where I'd put it. Unable to find my windbreaker, I got very irritated. When Pete asked what was wrong, I snapped, "We're not cyclists any more. We're car campers!"

The day before we left for Haines, Pete drove me back to Dot Lake. As I rode back to Tok, I thought about what had happened. In less than a week, we'd become different kinds of travellers. We were no longer touring cyclists. Now we were car campers, or more specifically, sag wagon users. To me, the terms presented two different images. Touring cyclists usually carried tents, sleeping bags, ground pads, and food and cooking supplies on their bicycles. They were proof that a person could travel comfortably for an extended length of time with a minimal amount of gear. If the wok, pillow, caribou antlers, radio, or extra tires made their load too heavy or cumbersome, they either ditched it or mailed it home. A sag wagon user, or car camper, rode and used a car or truck as a support vehicle. I figured, if you couldn't carry it on your bike, you didn't need it. The use of a vehicle was a waste of gas. Now, much to my dismay, I was to become a sag wagon user. I just hoped it wouldn't be for long.

On the road Pete and I established a routine. After I left in the morning, Pete heated water, then scrubbed and dressed his foot. When done, he'd meet me, and we'd pull out the ice chest, make lunch and eat. Afterwards, he'd drive on ahead. When I caught up with him in the afternoon he'd usually be sleeping, with his bandaged foot propped up on the dashboard.

By the time we arrived in Haines we were both exhausted. For myself, even without gear, riding was hard. I'd been averaging between 50 and 70 miles a day and taking most of the road notes. Although Pete was over the flu, his foot was still swollen and sore. We both needed a place to rest. My only contact in Haines was Deb Smith, a former housemate. I hesitated to call her because we wouldn't be arriving at her house with our gear strapped neatly to our bikes. Rather, we'd greet her with a truck full of odds and ends. In the Toyota's cab, maps, brochures, receipts, road notes, tapes, first aid supplies and notebooks were mixed up with letters, candy bar wrappers, and loose change. Pete had picked up a plastic Tesoro litter bag, which he'd hung on the cigarette lighter knob. This was still empty when we got to Haines. In the rear of the truck was two weeks worth of dirty laundry and all our other earthly possessions.

I wondered what my friend Deb, who'd spent a year bicycling in Europe would think about our lack of organization. After all, she'd carried all her gear. But I swallowed my pride and phoned. After I told her what had happened, she invited us to stay at her place. For the next week, we shared Deb's tiny basement apartment with her adopted two year old son Dylan. I tried to keep our gear in order, but it was difficult. The contents of our truck slowly became the contents of her living room. Fortunately, Deb, who has always been meticulous, but easy going, didn't seem to mind. When I apologized, she just laughed. Looking back, I still think that if we'd made her home base camp for more than a week, we would have worn out our welcome.

By the time we got to Price of Wales Island, Pete was riding again. Here, and in the other Southeast towns we visited, Pete carried his first aid supplies in a pale blue dishpan, which he strapped to the rear of his bicycle. I was pleased. I thought we wouldn't need to use the truck any more.

When we arrived in Skagway, it was July, and we still had over 3,000 miles left to ride. For this reason, we continued to use the vehicle. To maximize our vehicle use, we devised a system of leapfrogging, which doubled our daily road mileage from 40 to 80 miles a day, and allowed us to stop at most of the restaurants, campgrounds and points of interest along the way. In the morning, one of us drove the vehicle to a predetermined point approximately 20 miles distant. The other person rode their bicycle to the vehicle, put their bicycle in the rear of the truck, and drove 20 miles further. The rider took notes.

Pete adapted much better to this system than I did. Driving, I always felt like I was going too fast and might miss something. And being in a car, I was less apt to stop if I did see something unusual. On the other hand, Pete didn't mind driving. After he put his bike in the truck, he put a tape in the box and headed happily up the road.

In August, when we returned to Fairbanks, we picked up a 25 pound sacks of beans, flour, rice, oatmeal, and a bag of dog food. To make room for the dog, we left the tape box and tapes behind. To make room for the food, we built a rack so that a bicycle could be strapped to the back of the truck. At this point, I resigned myself to car camping. The summer was nearly over, and we still had a good number of roads left to ride. I tried as hard as I could to enjoy the benefits of a support vehicle. Because we had the dutch oven, Pete baked cookies, and brownies directly in the campfire. And having an axe and shovel, he chopped fire wood and dug a pit, so he could cook his baked goods in a "stove."

The use of the truck had also enabled us to do side trips. Because we covered the main roads so quickly, we had time to ride the Dempster Highway and the Denali Park Road. We also leapfrogged our way to Eagle, Nabesna, and McCarthy. These sideroads were the most memorable portion of the trip, so now I guess I must grudgingly admit that having a support vehicle did have its advantages.

GREATER FAIRBANKS

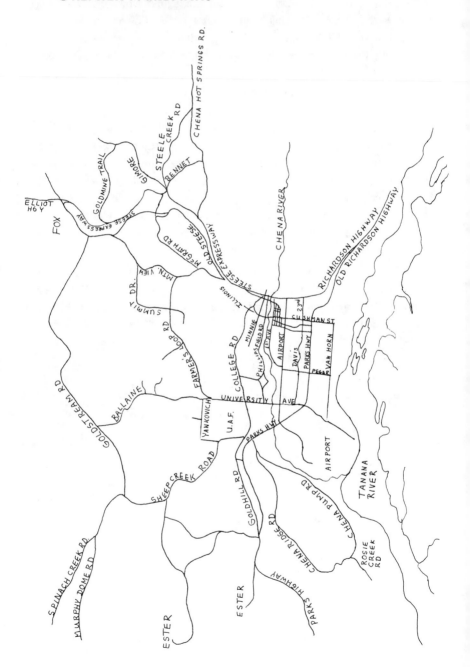

III: THE THREE HOT SPRINGS RIDES

THE THREE HOT SPRINGS ROADS

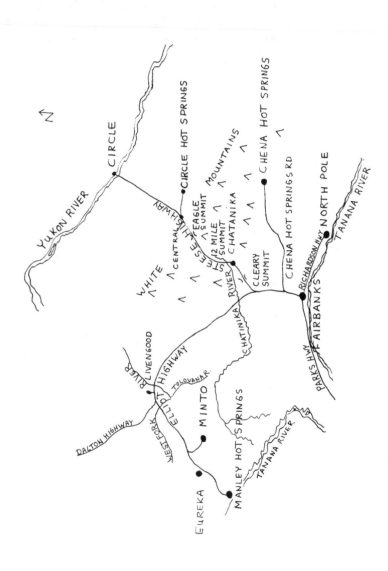

CHAPTER 20: CHENA HOT SPRINGS ROAD

BACKGROUND

Chena Hot Springs Road leads to Chena Hot Springs Resort. Chena Hot Springs were supposedly found in 1905 by prospector Felix Pedro, who started the Fairbanks Gold Rush. But officially credit for the discovery of Chena Hot Springs goes to a 1907 U.S. Geological Survey team.

The springs are in the center of an area of about 40 square miles that has been classified as "an area of geothermal resources." However no one knows the true thermal capabilities of Chena Hot Springs.

The hot springs have a historical reputation as being medicinal. Says *Descriptive of Alaska* (Fairbanks Commercial Club, 1918): Of the highly medicated quality of the springs there is no question, and many who have sought relief from various ailments have returned well pleased with the results achieved.

ROAD INFORMATION: CHENA HOT SPRINGS ROAD

SECTION 1: MILE 0 (OLD STEESE HIGHWAY) - MILE 56.5 (CHENA HOT SPRINGS)

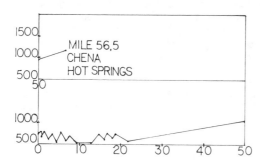

ROAD CONDITIONS/TERRAIN:

Chena Hot Springs Road leaves the Old Steese Highway at Mile 4.6. The paved road lacks a shoulder, but the Alaska Department of Transportation is planning to widen the first 6.4 miles to Nordale Road, construct four lanes and put in a shoulder.

The first 10 miles of Chena Hot Springs Road have a series of steeply rolling hills, with elevation gains and losses ranging between 100 and 200 feet. A few moderate climbs to about Mile 13 follow. There is a gradual uphill climb to the road's end, with an overall elevation gain of about 600 feet.

JUNCTIONS:

Mile 6.4. Nordale Road leads to Badger Road and North Pole.

WATER:

Mile 11.9, Little Chena River. Mile 19.5, Jenny M Creek. Mile 26.5, Flat Creek. Mile 31.3, Colorado Creek. North of the creek is a trail which leads to a few cabins built in the 1920's as an overnight stop midway to the hot springs. Mile 33.9, Four Mile Creek. Mile 37.8, the first of many crossings over the North Fork Chena River. Mile 39.6, North Fork Chena River. Mile 44.1, North Fork Chena River. Mile 49, North Fork Chena River. Mile 49.7, Angel Creek. Mile 52.3, West Fork Chena River. Mile 55.2, North Fork Chena River. Mile 56.5, Monument Creek.

CAMPING/PICNIC AREAS/TRAILS:

The Chena River State Recreation Area begins at Mile 26, and continues beyond the road's end. The recreation area has two campgrounds and one picnic area. Mile 27, Rosehip Campground has 38 campsites. Mile 39.5, North Fork Campground has 18 campsites. Mile 43, Red Squirrel Picnic Area has a shelter. Mile 39.4, Granite Tors Trail. Mile 49, the Lower Chena Dome Trail. Mile 50.5, the Upper Chena Dome Trail.

FOOD/LODGING:

Mile 9.3. Anders' Cache, carries liquor, limited groceries, and fresh produce. Hours: 7 a.m. to 11 p.m. daily. Mile 23.4. Valley Center General Store carries similar items and is also owned by Martha and Ed Anders. Mile 23.5. Tack's General Store and Greenhouse Cafe, owned by Steve and Cindy Tack, sells fresh produce, bulk foods, hardware and great homemade pie. Mile 49.6. The Angel Creek Lodge has a bar, cafe, cabins and a liquor store. Staff can be rather rude. Mile 56.5. Chena Hot Springs Resort is owned by a 32 member partnership and is managed by Bird Curtis. A soak in the hot springs costs $5.50. There are two indoor pools. One is a small hot pool where the temperature is roughly 108° F and the other is a larger pool with 90° F water. The resort permits camping for $6.00, and has a restaurant, bar and cabins for rent, three of which were built in the 1920's.

ROADSIDE SIGHTS:

Mile 22.5. Pleasant Valley Animal Park has game animals, horseback riding, fishing and canoe trips. Hours: 9 a.m. to 8 p.m. daily. Admission is $5.00 for adults, $3.00 for children.

CHAPTER 21: THE STEESE HIGHWAY

BACKGROUND

The 163 mile Steese Highway (Alaska Route 6) connects Fairbanks with the town of Circle on the Yukon River. The highway begins at an elevation of 434 feet/132 meters and ends at 598 feet/182 meters. Between are three summits, the highest being Eagle Summit at 3,880 feet/1,183 meters.

Throughout the Goldstream Valley, on the first portion of this ride, are piles of washed rock, or tailings, which were left behind by gold dredges. The machines scooped up the dirt and rock, and the gold was sifted out with screens. The gravel was then washed through the dredge and deposited, by means of a conveyor belt, behind it.

The first 44 miles of the highway are paved. The rest of the road has a hard packed surface, and is often dusty. The Twelve Mile and Eagle Summit climbs, because of steep terrain and strong headwinds, are among the toughest climbs in the state.

A historic profile of the Steese Highway was drawn for the War Department and Alaska Road Commission by Donald MacDonald in 1928. Original copies of this map, printed on rag paper, are on display at the Miracle Mile Lodge at Mile 66 and at Circle Hot Springs Lodge.

ROAD INFORMATION: STEESE HIGHWAY

SECTION 1: MILE 0 (FAIRBANKS, AIRPORT ROAD)-MILE 50

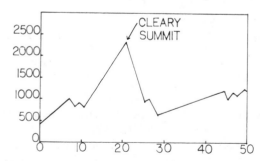

ROAD CONDITIONS/TERRAIN:

The first 11 miles of the Steese Highway, the Steese Expressway, is a four-lane highway which replaced the narrow and winding Old Steese Highway that still parallels it. Cyclists may follow either the New Steese or the Old Steese for 11 miles to the town of Fox. The expressway has an eight foot shoulder, and a bike path for the first two miles. It is illegal to ride on the shoulder for the first two miles, although this is being contested locally. The Old Steese and the New Steese join at Mile 11.

At this junction, the New Steese becomes the Elliot Highway leading to Manley and the Dalton Highway, and the Old Steese Highway becomes the Steese Highway.

There's a more scenic, shorter way to get to Fox. If you are on the west end of town, near the University of Alaska, it is shorter to ride up through the Goldstream Valley. Goldstream Road, paved and rolling, meets the Old Steese Highway just before Fox. Turn left on the Old Steese to reach the junction just described. To reach Goldstream Road, ride up Farmer's Loop Road (University Avenue becomes Farmer's Loop Road) to Ballaine Road, at the golf course. Ballaine ends at Goldstream Road. (Turn right onto Goldstream Road.)

Whichever road is followed, there is a 1,867 foot climb to Mile 20.6, Cleary Summit. The road drops 1,630 feet in the next eight miles, then leads upward to Mile 40 where it begins to climb moderately. The road is paved, and following Mile 11, has a narrow shoulder to Mile 44. From where the pavement ends, the road surface is gravel, often hard packed, and dusty.

JUNCTIONS:

Mile 1, College Road (west, left) leads to the University of Alaska campus. Mile 2.8, Farmer's Loop Road (west, left) and the Old Steese Highway, about 100 yards from this junction. To the east (right) is Fairview Road which leads 2.5 miles to the Birch Hill Ski Trails (see Fairbanks Trails). Mile 4.6, Chena Hot Springs Road. Mile 11, junction of the Old Steese Highway, the Steese Expressway and the Elliot Highway.

WATER:

Mile 0.7, Chena River. Mile 32.3, Captain Creek. Mile 37.3, Kokomo Creek. Mile 39, Chatanika River. Mile 40.4, Crooked Creek. Mile 41.5, Belle Creek. Mile 42.7, McKay Creek. Mile 45.1, Long Creek. Mile 43.5, Boston Creek. Mile 47.1, Camp Creek. Mile 49.6, Moose Creek.

CAMPING/TRAILS:

Mile 39, Upper Chatanika River State Recreation Site has 25 campsites.

The 58 mile Circle-Fairbanks Historic Trail parallels the highway on the ridges to the east. The trail begins on the gravel road at Cleary Summit, (follow the road four miles to the trailhead) and ends at Twelve Mile Summit at Milepost 86. Parts of the trail are rocky and may be difficult to ride.

FOOD/LODGING:

Mile 11. The Fox Store, owned by Larry and Janice Wilce, has limited groceries and is located at the junction of the Steese and Elliot Highways.

Mile 27.5. The Old F.E. Company Gold Camp. Built in 1921 by the Fairbanks Exploration Company, the mining camp fed and housed 200 miners for over 30 years. In 1977 the facility was opened as a lodge. On weekends the lodge serves an unlimited sourdough pancake breakfast which is cooked on a ten foot coal cook stove. The lodge opens at 9 a.m. and has no set closing time.

Mile 28.6. The Chatinika Lodge, rebuilt after the original building burned in 1975, has showers for $2.50, and a bar. Mile 41.8. Miner Ed's Trading Post, owned by Ed Ebber, carries limited groceries, beer and souvenirs. Excellent well water.

ROADSIDE SIGHTS:

Mile 9. The Old Steese Highway is the location of Gold Dredge Number 8. On the *National Register*, the dredge building is 250 feet long and five stories high. Retired in 1959, the building is now a restaurant and a museum. Tours are available. Phone: 457-6058. Mile 9.5. At the intersections of Goldstream Road and the New Steese Highway is a permafrost tunnel. Dug by the U.S. Army to test methods of tunneling in frozen silt and gravel, the 360-foot long tunnel penetrates through a 40,000 year old accumulation of soil, gravel, ice, and wood. The tunnel is used by the federal Cold Regions Research and Engineering Laboratory as an underground lab for conducting experiments related to the permafrost environment.

Mile 11.5. Fox (pop. 150), was named because of its location on the right bank of Fox Creek. Fox was established in 1905 as a mining camp in the Goldstream Valley by Frank Cleary, the brother-in-law of E.T. Barnette. In 1907, with a population of 500, Fox had several bawdy houses and saloons. As the gold production declined, so did the population. By 1935, Fox had only 35 residents.

Mile 13.5, Satellite Tracking Station. Large receiving stations, 85 feet in diameter, gather information from polar orbiting weather satellites. Computers transmit the data to world wide subscribers. Phone: 452-1155 for tour information. Mile 16.6. Interpretive sign and monument honor prospector Felix Pedro, who discovered gold in 1902, and subsequently started the Fairbanks Goldrush. Mile 20.6, Cleary Summit (elevation 2,301 feet/701 meters). Mile 28.6. Trail across the road from Chatanika Lodge leads over tailings to an old gold dredge.

ROAD INFORMATION: STEESE HIGHWAY

SECTION 2: MILE 50-MILE 101 (101 MILE LODGE)

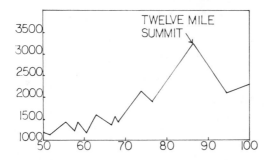

ROAD CONDITIONS/TERRAIN:

There are a few rollers, but mostly a 2,000 foot climb to Mile 85.6, Twelve Mile Summit. From the summit the road descends 1,100 feet to Mile 90, then rolls upwards.

WATER:

Mile 51.5, Grouse Creek. Mile 53.5, Ptarmigan Creek. Mile 57.3, U.S. or Nome Creek. Mile 58.8, Lost Creek. Mile 60.3, Cripple Creek. Mile 64.1, Caribou Creek. Mile 65.7, No Name Creek. Mile 66.1, Sourdough Creek. Mile 68, Tough Luck Creek. Mile 68.9, Faith Creek. Mile 76.1, Little Little Idaho Creek. Mile 77.2, Little Idaho

Creek. Mile 78.6, Idaho Creek. Mile 81, Montana Creek. Mile 81.3, DOT developed spring. Mile 86, Drift Creek. Mile 89.6, Reed Creek. Mile 94.2, North Fork Twelve Mile Creek. Mile 95.6, Willow Creek. Mile 97.4, Snider Creek. Mile 98.2, Bear Creek. Mile 99.5, Fish Creek.

CAMPING/TRAILS:

Mile 60.5. Cripple Creek BLM Campground has 15 campsites (five walk-in). There are two shelters; one is in the walk-in area. This is one of the nicest campgrounds in Alaska. Camping is also possible on the grass behind the 101 Mile Lodge. Camping along one of the above-mentioned creeks may be difficult due to steep terrain.

The Pinnel Mountain Trail connects the Twelve Mile and Eagle Summits. The trail is said to be rideable, but is rough and windy.

FOOD/LODGING:

Mile 66. Miracle Mile Lodge has a small cafe, bar, cabins and showers for $2.50. Mile 101. The 101 Mile Lodge, owned by Digger Dick, was once owned by the late Fairbanks State Senator Don Bennett. In the early 1970's, an arsonist burned down the roadhouse; he served 12 years in prison. A small shack remains from which Digger sells liquor, junk food and sandwiches. Digger says the area is mosquito free because the wind blows 5-10 MPH 24 hours a day. Cyclists may camp here for free.

ROADSIDE SIGHTS:

Mile 57.3, Davidson Ditch. In 1925 the Fairbanks Exploration Company developed a series of ditches and inverted siphons to transfer water to Fox and the surrounding area where it was used to float gold dredges. The system was capable of carrying 56,100 gallons of water per minute. Mile 85.6, Twelve Mile Summit (elevation 3,225 feet/983 meters).

ROAD INFORMATION: STEESE HIGHWAY

SECTION 3: MILE 101 (101 MILE LODGE) - MILE 163 (CIRCLE)

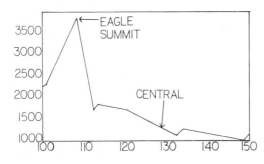

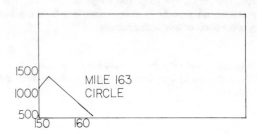

ROAD CONDITIONS/TERRAIN:

From Mile 101, its a hard 1,500 foot climb to Mile 108.3, Eagle Summit (elevation 3,880 feet/1,183 meters). There are often strong headwinds coming from the northeast. From the summit it is mostly downhill, (a loss of 3,382 feet) with some gradually rolling hills to Circle.

JUNCTIONS:

Mile 127.8, junction with Circle Hot Springs Road. It is eight fairly level miles to Circle Hot Springs.

WATER:

Mile 119.5, Bedrock Creek. Mile 117.5, Mammoth Creek. Mile 118.2, Stack Pup Creek. Mile 128.9, Crooked Creek. Mile 132.1, Albert Creek. Mile 135.3, Big Mosquito Creek. Mile 139.1, Quartz Creek. Mile 140.5, Jump Off Creek. Mile 145.6, Six Mile Creek. Mile 148.4, Birch Creek. Mile 149.7, Bolgen Creek. Circle Hot Springs Road crosses over Mile 2.9, Deadwood Creek, and Mile 5.7, Ketchem Creek.

CAMPING:

Mile 119.5, Bedrock Creek BLM Campground has eight campsites. There is no developed water source. The creek may or may not be suitable for drinking depending on upstream mining activity. Mile 163. Circle Campground. See Circle at the end of this chapter . Mile 148.4, Birch Creek, camping possible.

At Mile 5.7 Circle Hot Springs Road is Ketchem Creek BLM Campground, which has six campsites.

FOOD/LODGING:

Mile 127.8, Central. Mile 8, Circle Hot Springs Road, Circle Hot Springs. Mile 163, Circle.

ROADSIDE SIGHTS:

Mile 108.3. Eagle Summit (elevation 3,880 feet/1,183 meters) is a popular spot for celebrating the summer solstice.

CENTRAL

BACKGROUND

Mile 127.8. The small mining town of Central (pop. 100 winter, 400 summer) has two lodges, a post office, a museum, an airport and in the summer, a BLM fire-fighting crew. The town celebrates the Fourth of July with a parade.

FOOD/LODGING:

Central Motor Inn, owned by Bob Le Ruche, has a restaurant, bar, laundromat and showers. Crabs Corner Cafe, owned by Jim Crab, serves big sandwiches. Some groceries, a bar and showers here.

POST OFFICE:

Zip Code: 99730.

MUSEUMS/HISTORICAL SITES:

The Circle District Museum contains old mining equipment and artifacts. Hours: noon to 5 p.m. daily. Just beyond Central, on the other side of Crooked Creek, is the old Central Roadhouse. First reported by the U.S. Geological Survey in 1896, this roadhouse is one of the oldest in Alaska.

CIRCLE HOT SPRINGS

BACKGROUND

The Circle Hot Springs Lodge is located at Mile 8 Circle Hot Springs Road. The 139° F water, which flows from the springs at 386 gallons per minute, fills an Olympic sized pool, jacuzzis and hot tubs which are located on each hotel floor. The lodge, built by Frank and Emma Leach, is owned by Bobby Miller. Much of the materials used to construct the large three story frame building were brought overland 60 miles by wagon from the Yukon River at Circle. The lodge has a restaurant, bar, cabins, laundromat and a limited grocery which sells ice cream cones.

The average July temperature in Circle Hot Springs is 60° F. The average July rainfall is 2 inches.

CIRCLE

BACKGROUND

Circle (pop. 94) is Interior Alaska's oldest major mining camp. Circle began as a mining supply town when Jack McQuesten established a trading post here in 1887. The town was named Circle because it was thought to be on the Arctic Circle.

In addition to supplying the miners of the Circle Mining District, Circle was a stopping point along the Yukon River Trail from Dawson City to Nome. A handful of wheelmen once bicycled the frozen river trail after a herd of stampeders packed it firm. For fifty years, Circle was the farthest north point of the connected U.S. highway system. The average July temperature in Circle is 62° F, the average July rainfall is 1.4 inches.

GROCERIES:

H. C. Company Store, owned by Dick and Earla Hutchinson, carries groceries. The Trading Post has a general grocery store, cafe, bar and liquor store.

LODGING/CAMPING:

The Riverview Motel has rooms and hostel rooms, a laundromat and showers for $5.00. Circle has a community campground next to the river, but it is very open and offers little shelter or privacy.

ALTERNATIVE TRANSPORTATION:

Dale Boone will take up to seven people, their bicycles, and gear to Eagle or Dawson City. It's a two day trip up river through the Yukon Charlie National Preserve to Eagle. In 1988 Boone charged $275 to Eagle and $400 for a trip to Dawson. Those interested should contact Dale. Write: Box 28, Circle, AK 99733 or leave a message for him at the Riverview Motel. Phone: 474-0518.

Forty Mile Air brings the mail to Circle every weekday. The type of aircraft varies with the number of passengers. Cyclists wanting to fly out of Circle should contact Forty Mile Air. Phone: 474-0518. The 1988 price was 80 cents a pound for bicycles and 40 cents a pound for baggage. The charge per passenger is $50 one way to Fairbanks.

CHAPTER 22: THE ELLIOT HIGHWAY

BACKGROUND

The 152 mile Elliot Highway (Alaska Route 2) leads from the old mining town of Fox, at Mile 11 Steese Highway, to the village of Manley. The first 73 miles of the road connect Fairbanks with the Dalton Highway, the principle overland route to the North Slope oil fields. When the Dalton was built in the early '70's, the Elliot was upgraded and widened to accommodate the oil company truck traffic. The rolling road, which leads to the Dalton Highway has a lot of truck traffic, but isn't as heavily travelled as in previous years. Past the Dalton Highway junction, the Elliot Highway is narrower, more hard packed and a pleasure to ride. The road climbs above treeline, then descends to boreal spruce, muskeg, tiaga and birch forests, before arriving at Manley.

ROAD INFORMATION: ELLIOT HIGHWAY

SECTION 1: MILE 0 (STEESE - ELLIOT JCT. AT FOX) - MILE 50 (LEMONADE STAND)

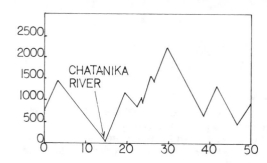

ROAD CONDITIONS/TERRAIN:

The first 28 miles of the Elliot Highway are paved and have a narrow shoulder; the remainder of the highway has a gravel surface. The terrain is rolling with some major hills. There are overall elevation gains and losses of over 500 feet.

WATER:

Mile 0.3, Fox Spring. Source of drinking water for many Fairbanks residents. Mile 11, Chatanika River. Mile 13.9, Willow Creek. Mile 18.3, Washington Creek. Mile 20.3, Cushman Creek. Mile 29.8, developed spring. Mile 37, Globe Creek. Mile 44.8, Tatalina River. There are small unnamed creeks at Miles 31, 34.8, 41 and 46.1.

CAMPING/TRAILS:

Mile 11. Chatanika State Recreation Area Whitefish Campground has 15 campsites and a shelter. Camping is also possible by the creeks at Miles 31 and 34.8, at Globe Creek at Mile 37, and at the Tatalina River Wayside at Mile 44.8.

The BLM White Mountain Summer Trail begins at Mile 28. The trail leads 28 miles to Borealis Le Fevre Cabin, available for $15.00 per night. Phone the Fairbanks BLM Office for cabin reservations (474-2200).

FOOD/LODGING:

Mile 5.3. The Hilltop Cafe truck stop serves large home-cooked meals. Mile 50. The Wildwood General Store and Lemonade stand carries limited groceries and snacks.

ROAD INFORMATION: ELLIOT HIGHWAY

SECTION 2: MILE 50 (LEMONADE STAND)-MILE 94.6 (TOP OF HILL)

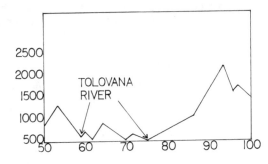

ROAD CONDITIONS/TERRAIN:

The first portion of this section is much like the last. The highway first climbs 440 feet, then is rolling with an overall loss of about 900 feet to the second crossing of the Tolovana River at Mile 75. For the next 20 miles, there is a 1,800 foot climb. The highway is wide and heavily trafficked to the Dalton Highway junction at Mile 72.8. Here the road narrows and is less travelled.

JUNCTIONS:

Mile 70.7, Livengood Road. Mile 72.8, junction with the Dalton Highway. For Dalton Highway information, see Chapter 34.

WATER:

Mile 57, Tolovana River. Mile 70.1. Livengood Creek, water unsuitable for drinking. Mile 74.9, Tolovana River. Small unnamed creeks, some of which may be dry in midsummer, at Miles 82.6, 84.4, 89.9 and 90.7.

CAMPING:

Mile 57. Tolovana River BLM Campground has seven campsites and is close to the road. Mile 74.9, Tolovana River. The open area beside the river is a popular camping spot. Mile 76.4. The road leads a short ways to the Tolovana River.

FOOD/LODGING:

Livengood, located two miles off the Elliot Highway at the end of the Livengood Access Road, was founded in the winter of 1914-15, when hundreds of people arrived at the newly formed mining district. Livengood was named after Jay Livengood, who in July 1914, along with N.R. Hudson discovered gold in Livengood Creek. Livengood's largest employer is the Alaska Department of Transportation Maintenance Station.

Grandpa's Enterprises, a gift shop which sells wooden toys, and John's Likkerbox, are both located in Livengood. John sells beer, liquor and Koala sodas. According to John, Livengood may soon have a general store. Livengood's average July temperature is 59° F. The average July rainfall is 2.3 inches.

ROADSIDE SIGHTS:

Mile 94.6, the highest point on the Elliot Highway (elevation 2,221 feet/677 meters). The view is excellent when the weather's clear.

ROAD INFORMATION: ELLIOT HIGHWAY

SECTION 3: MILE 94.6 (TOP OF HILL) - MILE 152 (MANLEY HOT SPRINGS)

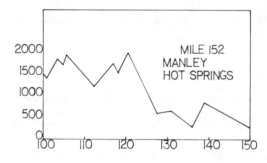

ROAD CONDITIONS/TERRAIN:

After dropping about 800 feet in the first six miles, the road becomes rolling, with occasional flat stretches. Manley's elevation is 270 feet.

JUNCTIONS:

Mile 109.2, Minto Spur Road. The road leads 12.2 miles, mostly down hill, (a 1,163 foot drop) to the Native village of Minto. Mile 130.8, the road leads to the almost abandoned mining town of Eureka. Mile 151, Tofty Road leads 16 miles to the Tofty mining camp. Mile 152. The Elliot Highway becomes Manley's Main Street, then ends two miles further at the Tanana River.

WATER:

Mile 119.5, small creek. Mile 113.5, West Fork of Hutlitakwa Creek. Mile 129.3, Hutlinana Creek. Mile 137.6, Baker Creek.

CAMPING:

There are no official campgrounds within this section. Camping is possible at Mile 129.3, Hutlinana Creek and at Mile 137.6, Baker Creek.

FOOD/LODGING:

There are no facilities until Manley.

MANLEY HOT SPRINGS

BACKGROUND

Mile 152, Manley Hot Springs. In 1902 J.F. Karshner established a homestead at about the same time that the Army Signal Corps built the WAMCATS telegraph station nearby. The hot springs were originally named Baker Hot Springs, after nearby Baker Creek. Then in 1907, Frank Manley built a four-story resort hotel, and a post office was established. By 1910 the village population was 101 and the town was the principle supply center for the nearby mining districts. Since then, the number of residents has fluctuated: the present year-round population is 88. In 1957, the town's name was changed from Baker to Manley. Manley's July average temperature is 59° F. The average July rainfall is 2.6 inches.

The two principle hot springs are the property of Manley resident Chuck Dart. The springs generate approximately 208,800 gallons of water every twenty four hours.

GROCERIES/POST OFFICE:

The Manley Trading Post sells liquor, general groceries and is the site of the town post office. Zip Code: 99756.

LODGING/CAMPING:

Manley Hot Springs Resort, located on the highway just before town, is owned by Jules and Elise Wright. A few years ago, the Wrights were walking on their property when they spotted a small amount of lukewarm water bubbling out of the ground. Drilling produced hot water. Their log cabin was converted into a restaurant, bar and kitchen, a pool was dug, and cabins were constructed. To enjoy a soak costs $4.00 per day.

Manley Roadhouse, located next to the hot springs slough at the town entrance, has been in business since 1910. The roadhouse has a bar, rooms and serves food.

Across the road from the Manley Road House is a community campground. It is however in the open, and offers little privacy.

The Ride to Chena Hot Springs

The last ride of the season is to the end of Chena Hot Springs Road. I leave my driveway, turn right and ride up the first of several steep hills. Between my place and the road's end are frozen creeks, deserted campgrounds, leafless trees and a few general stores. As I push uphill, my thoughts turn inward. This particular tour began with trips to Manley and Circle Hot Springs, and is now, in mid-October, 1988, ending with a ride to Chena Hot Springs.

When Pete and I rode to Manley Hot Springs and Circle in early May, it was that undefined season between winter and spring. Now, it is the undefined season between fall and winter. Again, there is a nip in the air, and splotches of snow decorate the landscape. And the tourists, who before were headed northward, have now headed south. The same is true of the geese and sandhill cranes.

As I ride, I first think about the ride to Circle. I see again, a curled up piece of tire, a tin can being tossed about by the wind, a bird flying overhead. Last fall's leaves rustle, are blown around the road in circles. Snow rims the banks of the Chatanika River, which twists and winds its way west. The hills at first are rolling, but ahead are a few passes. There is little traffic on this road. In 20 miles, five cars, all coming from Circle, pass and leave me choking in their dust. I remember later what was then vague: a stiff tailwind, the sun on my back, the cold spring air.

At Miner Ed's store, Ed Ebber shows me some of the lamps, tables, coat racks, jewelry trees, and canes that he's made out of burled wood.

Ed says it takes him about a day to make a cane. When I ask him if he can picture what his final products look like, he scratches his grey beard, nods, and says yes. When he adds that locals often bring him wood—but only one of seven pieces can be turned into anything of worth, I realize that even burled wood carving, which has always seemed a little tacky to me, is an art form.

Ed hands me a piece of willow. The former miner, tall, and square shouldered, wears a John Deer hat and a yellow shirt. My eyes focus on his hands and what they hold. His fingers are large, bony, gnarled and full of imperfections. Looking at wood, I see knots, whorls, dark spots, indentations. I wonder how Ed will be able to turn it into an art object.

On the store wall is a post card of three cyclists, all smiling and standing near a sign in Spanish. Ed tells me the three guys had bicycled from Circle to Tierra Del Fuego in 1985-1986. This makes my little jaunt seem very unimpressive, so when he asks where I'm headed, I just say "up the road." Touching my head, I realize that I'm wearing my helmet and I feel quite foolish. Hastily saying good-bye, I head outside. Ed follows. Before leaving, I ask him if I can take a photo. When he agrees, I pull my camera out of my panniers and take a picture of Ed next to "Charley," a figure he made of burled wood pieces.

Old timers—later, at Circle Hot Springs Resort, after a soak, I talk with Henry Hughes, who is sitting in the hotel lobby, watching late night TV.

Henry, with little prompting, begins to tell stories.

When he first came to Alaska, Henry worked on a sternwheel which ran between Fort Yukon and Fairbanks. Before he was 21 he had 22 motorcycles, and never had to have any of them repaired.

"I had Flying Merkels, Indians, Harleys, but I never had a Japanese one," he says, lighting his pipe, the base of which he cradles in his right hand. In the following years Henry travelled extensively around Alaska, Canada and across the Pacific. The latter he did "with a tape recorder and a $2,000 camera outfit." Many of the photos, he says, are now in the Alaska State Archives.

In 1964, Henry testified before Congress and helped secure funding for the Fairbanks Correctional Facility, the Fairbanks Pioneer's Home and Alaskaland.

At age 72 he built a log cabin in Eagle.

Henry is now working as a night time handy person at the resort. On his own time he works on his '75 Ford pick-up.

Says Henry, "Two fellows from Cantwell once broke into my place. They got four months apiece and assessed damages. I hunted them up and found out where they all were. I lined them up and put them on a freighter. They didn't break into my place ever again."

Henry, whose impatient nature can be seen in the quick movements of his hands, lit his pipe again. "If vigilantes use legal means its OK because the law is crooked."

Riding along Chena Hot Springs Road, I smile, thinking about Henry. It doesn't seem strange to me that this man, in his 80's, isn't spending time in the nursing home which he helped establish. Rather, it seems in character for him to be living comfortably in a resort, a glorified nursing home. Here, for the exchange of labor, his frugal needs for food, friendship and board are being met.

At the top of a hill, my thoughts are interrupted by the sight of a car that's slid off the icy road. I stop to take notes, and see what's going on. Two women, one with her arm around another who is holding her hand to her forehead, walk downhill. The windshield of a blue Subaru is cracked. One of three guys standing by the car removes a cardboard Beck's beer case from the rear of the car and glances nervously at me. As I leave the scene behind, it takes its place among other car related accident memories.

Further down the road, birch trees, open space, and bales of snow covered hay remind me of the ride to Manley Hot Springs. The stands of budding birch make me feel like I'm back in New England. Scattered spruce trees, silhouetted by the late afternoon sun, remind me that I'm not. The road, in places, runs along ridge tops, where there are views of snow-capped mountains. It ends in Manley, where Chuck Dart lives. Pete and I discover Chuck in our search for the Manley Public Baths. When we see a lawn with patches of bright green grass and a house which has a front covered with Visqueen, we know we're in the right area. When the door opens, we introduce ourselves to the owner of the house, lawn, and Manley bath house. When asked, Chuck explains that the front of his house doesn't have any insulation or walls because it doesn't need it. Heat from hot springs water, piped through the house, keeps his place warm.

Since we're interested, Chuck shows us his greenhouse. Inside, it is humid. Outside, the rain beats down on the greenhouse roof. What he is growing, he says, in a soft, almost inaudible voice, are Dombellos, a hybrid greenhouse indeterminate. These, I learn, are tomatoes that are grown year round. As he talks, he walks, with knife in hand, up and down the rows, pruning, cutting and tying up plants.

"You have to be stubborn and a little dumb to grow tomatoes," he says, grinning, and winding a plant around a piece of twine. Although tomatoes are his principal crop, Chuck has also grown cucumbers, bok choy, egg plants and peppers. He says he tried to grow strawberries, but found that, because the sweetness of the berry is determined by the soil temperature, they don't do well in the greenhouse. His degree, from the University of Alaska is in biology, but says Chuck, "I didn't study horticulture. I guess I should have."

Chuck, who purchased his property in 1955, built his house, the bathhouse and the 150 foot by 36 foot greenhouse shortly after. The greenhouse, like his house, is heated with piped-in hot springs water.

Our conversation with this short balding man twists and turns, and like a river, goes in several different directions. We talk for an hour about people we have in common, greenhouse management and travelling.

Recently Chuck went to Japan, with the intention of checking out the spas. "They're called jungle baths," he said. "One place had 150 baths. They had both men's and women's sides. The women could go on the men's sides, but the men couldn't go on the women's sides."

Wanting to travel more, Chuck is now thinking about going to Africa.

Mentioning that we'd seen horse walkers in an area dog musher's front yard turns the conversation to mushing. Knowing that Pete and I would like to meet a local musher, Chuck hands us a few cucumbers to give one he knows. We thank him, and go to see her, but she's not at home. We do however, talk at length to Amy Wright, her summer handler, and meet the distance musher's lead dog, Granite.

At the end of the Chena Hot Springs, I compare the hot springs themselves. Chuck Dart's public bath house, concrete tubs situated in a greenhouse, among overgrown mustard plants, is the most informal. Circle, with its large outdoor pool and historic hotel, is the most posh, and seems like it is a part of another era. And the Chena Hot Springs pool, although in need of paint, is after a cold ride, at least warm.

Although the thought of a good hot soak kept me going on these three somewhat chilly rides, the hot springs weren't the best part of the ride. By bike, I was able to go slowly, take in the scenery, and think about the unusual people I'd met along the way. And so, at the end of the day, it does not seem like I'm saying enough, when I write about the first twenty miles of the Chena Hot Springs ride, "This road has a series of steep rolling hills, which gradually flatten out, and for the next ten miles or so, become fairly level."

IV: INTERIOR AND SOUTHCENTRAL ALASKA

Parks Highway

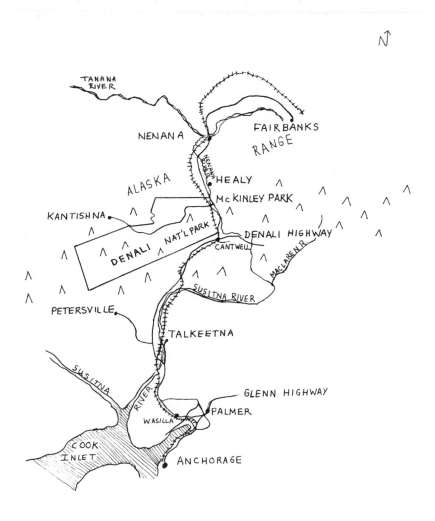

Chapter 23: The Parks Highway

Background

The 362 mile George Parks Highway (Alaska Route 3) begins at Mile 35.1, the junction of the Glenn Highway, and ends at Mile 362.2 where it intersects the Richardson Highway. The road incorporates parts of the Glenn, Denali, and Nenana Highways. After its completion in 1971, the highway was named the Anchorage-Fairbanks Highway. In 1975 it was renamed the Parks Highway after George Parks (1883-1984), Alaska's territorial governor from 1925 to 1933. The Parks Highway is paved and for most of its length has a wide shoulder. Between short expanses of wilderness are roadside businesses.

Road Information: Parks Highway

Section 1: Mile 35.1 (Junction with the Glenn Highway)-Mile 83.3 (Kashwitna River)

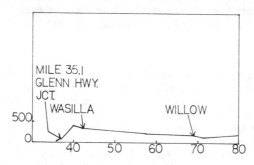

Road Conditions/Terrain:

The Parks Highway begins at Mile 35.1 of the Glenn Highway. The highway mileposts show the distance from the beginning of the Glenn Highway in Anchorage. Thus, one mile after the highway begins is Mile 36.1. The highway is paved, and has a wide shoulder. Through Wasilla, the traffic increases and for about a mile the road has four lanes. The terrain is rolling for the first 40 miles, then flat for the remaining ten.

Junctions:

Mile 35.1, junction with the Glenn Highway (Alaska Route 1). Mile 35.8. Trunk Road leads east (right) to University of Alaska Experimental Farm. Mile 38. The Fairview Loop Road leads southwest (left) to join the Knik-Goose Bay Road which rejoins the Parks Highway at Wasilla. The Knik-Goose Bay Road leads 13.5 miles from Wasilla to the town of Knik on the Knik Arm. Mile 41.1. The Palmer-Wasilla Highway connects the towns of Wasilla and Palmer. Mile 42.2. Downtown Wasilla, junction with Knik-Goose Bay Road west (left) and Wasilla Fishhook Road to the east (right). The latter connects with Schrock, Lakeview and Hatcher Pass roads. (These roads are not included in this book.) Mile 44.4, Church Road, connects with Schrock Road. Mile 48.8. Pittman Road connects with Schrock Road. Mile 52.3, Big Lake Road leads to three state campgrounds and Burma Road. Mile 67.2. Nancy Lake Parkway (gravel) leads to Nancy Lake State Recreation Area. Mile 71.2, Hatcher Pass Road. Mile 69.5. Road leads to Willow Post Office and Willow Trading Post.

WATER:

Mile 37.7, Wasilla Creek. Mile 57, Little Susitna River. Mile 71.4, Willow Creek. Mile 74.7, Little Willow Creek. (Excellent salmon fishing in both Willow Creeks.) Mile 76.4, Kashwitna Lake to the west (left) of highway. Mile 82.6. Side road leads west (left) one mile to the Susitna River. Mile 83.3, Kashwitna River.

CAMPING:

Mile 52.3. Big Lake Road leads to the town of Big Lake and three state recreation sites. At Mile 3.5 Big Lake Road is Rocky Lake State Recreation Site with 10 campsites. At Mile 5 North Big Lake Road is Big Lake North State Recreation Site, with six campsites and a shelter. At Mile 5.2 Big Lake Road is Big Lake South Recreation Site, with 13 campsites. Mile 57.4. Houston Municipal Campground has 30 campsites and a shelter. Mile 66.5. Nancy Lake State Recreation Site has 30 campsites and a shelter. Mile 67.2, South Rolly Lake State Recreation Area is located at Mile 6.5 Nancy Lake Parkway. The campground has 98 campsites, a shelter, and a trail.

FOOD/LODGING:

Mile 39.9. The Tundra Chocolate Factory, located in the Cottonwood Shopping Center, is owned by Barbara Heikes and John Wilson. Candy is sold in bulk or by the piece. Mile 41. Jacobson's Greenhouse sells fresh produce after August 1. Mile 42.2, Wasilla. Mile 50. The Silver Fox Inn has a cafe, bar, and rooms with kitchenettes. Mile 52.3. Little Kobuk, at Mile 2.6 Big Lake Road, serves breakfast all day. The owners contend that their milkshakes, which contain soybean milk, are good for cyclists and stroke victims. Mile 57.5. Miller's Market, owned by Gary Miller, has a cafe, limited groceries, and showers for $3.00. Mile 69, Willow (pop. 494). Although Willow was selected by voters for the new state capital in 1976, they defeated funding for the move in 1982. Located here are the Willow Hardware Store, the Mat-Su Credit Union and the Willow Creek Grocery. Mile 69.5, Willow Post Office. Zip Code: 99688.

ROADSIDE SIGHTS:

Mile 2.2, Knik Goose Bay Road. The Iditarod sled dog race headquarters.

WASILLA

BACKGROUND

Wasilla (pop. 3,977) gets its name from nearby Wasilla Creek, which was reportedly named by miners after Knik Indian Chief Wasilla. In 1916 the Alaska Railroad established a station here, and in 1917 a post office was built. Until 1935, Wasilla was the major supply center for the Matanuska-Susitna Valley's miners and farmers.

With the move of the Alaska Rural Rehabilitation Corporation to Palmer, and development of the nearby agricultural Matanuska Colony in 1935, Wasilla's economy suffered, but recovered in the 1950's when World War II veterans homesteaded here.

Construction of the Parks Highway in the 1960's and improvements on the Glenn Highway resulted in a rapid population increase in Wasilla, for many of Wasilla's newcomers could commute to work in Anchorage. Wasilla has large shopping centers, supermarkets, and except for a bicycle shop, all the modern conveniences one would expect in a first class city.

VISITORS INFORMATION

VISITOR'S CENTER:

The Wasilla Visitor's Center, located in the museum just up from the Parks Highway on Main Street, has information and brochures on Wasilla and the Matanuska-Susitna Valley. Phone: 376-1299.

TRAVELLER'S NEEDS

MEDICAL SERVICES:

The nearest clinic is the Valley Hospital in Palmer. Dial 911 for emergencies. A doctor's office is located in the Arctic Insta-Care Land Co. building on the Parks Highway. Phone: 376-0122.

GROCERIES:

Shop-Rite Supermarket is in the large Wasilla Shopping Center north of Main Street on the Parks Highway. Carrs Shopping Center, just south of Main Street on the Parks Highway, also has a supermarket.

BICYCLING/OUTDOOR STORES:

Wasilla has no bicycle stores. A sporting goods store located north of Main Street in the Wasilla Shopping center carries Svea, MSR and Coleman stoves, and dehydrated foods.

LODGING/CAMPING:

There are no hostels in Wasilla. There are numerous lodges, hotels, and bed and breakfast establishments. For camping information, see the camping section under Road Information.

POST OFFICE:

The Wasilla Post Office is located on Main Street and Swanson Avenue. Zip Code: 99687.

LAUNDRY/SHOWERS:

The laundromat in the Wasilla Shopping Center (north of Main Street) has showers for $3.50.

ENTERTAINMENT AND RECREATION

MUSEUMS/HISTORICAL SITES:

The Wasilla Museum has displays on pioneer life. In the basement is a mining exhibit and a mock display of the office of Dr. Lee L. McKinley, the flying dentist. Located behind the building is Frontier Village, a collection of Wasilla's old and historic buildings. The museum is operated by the Wasilla-Knik Willow Creek Historical Society and is located on Main Street in the old community hall. Book Cache and Waldenbooks are both located on the Parks Highway.

Public Recreation:

Wasilla High School has a swimming pool. Check at the Wasilla Visitor's Center for hours.

Road Information: Parks Highway

Section 2: Mile 83.3 (Kashwitna River)- Mile 135.2 (Denali Viewpoint)

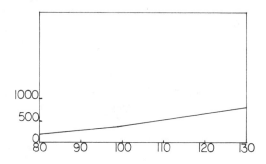

Road Conditions/Terrain:

The road has a wide shoulder and is flat with a few mild rollers to Mile 117. From here to the Denali Viewpoint, the terrain is hilly with approximately a 400 foot elevation gain.

Junction:

Mile 98.9, Talkeetna Spur Road. A paved road with gently rolling hills travels 15 miles to the town of Talkeetna. Mile 115, Petersville Road leads 30 miles to the abandoned mining camp of Petersville.

Water:

Mile 88.6, Sheep Creek. Mile 91.2, Goose Creek. Mile 93.5, Caswell Creek. Mile 96.7, Montana Creek. Mile 104.2, Big Susitna River. Mile 115.6, Trapper Creek. Mile 132.8, Chulitna River. Mile 133, small creek. Mile 134.6, Small plank bridge leads across a ditch to a developed spring.

Camping:

Mile 96.5. Montana Creek State Recreation Site is a large gravel parking lot for RVs. Camping is possible in the woods alongside the creek. Mile 104. Big Susitna River State Wayside has water and tables, but no developed campsites. Mile 121.7, rest area. A good place to camp, but no water is available.

Food/Lodging:

Mile 88.2. Sheep Creek Lodge has a bar and a cafe. Breakfast is served from 7 a.m. to 1 p.m. Mile 90.8, Cache Country General Store carries some groceries, has a laundromat and showers for $3.00. Mile 96.5. Montana Creek Lodge has a store, bar, cafe and liquor store. The bar often has live music on weekends. Mile 98.9, Talkeetna. Mile 99.4. The H&H Cafe is open 24 hours a day and has a grocery store. Mile 104. Big Su Lodge has a bar, cafe, and liquor store and is open 24 hours a day. Mile 115. Trapper's Creek Lodge has fresh produce, a laundromat and cabins.

ROADSIDE SIGHTS:

Mile 98.9, 1 Mile Talkeetna Spur Road. Mary Carey's Fiddlehead Fern Farm. Mary Carey sells locally grown fiddlehead ferns and recipes. An author and journalist, Carey has written eight books including *Amazing Alaska*, a book of Alaska facts and records and *How Long Must I Hide*, (Tex-Alaska Press) which is about her two year marriage to a fugitive on the Ten Most Wanted Criminals List. Mile 108.5, view of Mount McKinley. Mile 132, southern border of Denali State Park. Mile 135.2, Denali viewpoint. Outhouses and interpretive signs.

TALKEETNA

BACKGROUND

Talkeetna is a Tanana Indian word loosely meaning "River of Plenty." The village was once a supply center for the miners working the lower reaches of the Susitna River. By 1910, riverboats were using the site as a landing. In 1915, with the arrival of the Alaska Railroad, Talkeetna was saved from becoming just another mining town.

Today Talkeetna (pop. 269) is the jumping-off point for individuals planning Alaska Range expeditions. The climbers and the numerous Alpine hunting and fishing guides who reside and operate out of Talkeetna are a mainstay of the village's economy.

VISITORS INFORMATION

VISITOR'S CENTER:

Talkeetna Gifts and Collectables, on the corner of Main Street and the Talkeetna Spur Road, has brochures on area businesses.

NATIONAL PARK SERVICE:

Denali National Park Talkeetna Ranger Station, located just off Main Street, has climbing information. Mt. Foraker and Mount McKinley climbers must register with the NPS prior to climbing. The station has mountaineering publications and a comfortable reading area.

TRAVELLER'S NEEDS

MEDICAL SERVICES:

The Talkeetna emergency phone number is 911.

GROCERIES:

Denali Dry Goods, on Main Street, carries bulk foods, herb teas, and some clothes. B&K Trading Post on Main Street has some groceries, including fresh produce, and sells liquor. The Trading Post has a small museum, which has historical newspaper clippings.

LODGING/CAMPING:

There are presently no hostels in Talkeetna. Check with the Visitor's Center for information on local hotels and lodges.

There are three campgrounds in the Talkeetna area. Climbers camp in the Talkeetna River Park at the end of Main Street in May and June. The Talkeetna Chamber of Commerce Campground is located next to the boat launch. A nightly $4.00 site fee is charged at the park entrance gate. Christianson Lake Road Campground is located off the Talkeetna Spur Road before town. Follow paved Comsat Road (unmarked) at Mile 14, 0.8 miles to Christianson Lake Road. Ride 0.7 miles on the gravel road until reaching a sign which says "Float Planes." Turn right on the gravel road which leads downhill to the campground and lake. There are six campsites between two sections and shelters.

POST OFFICE:

The Talkeenta Post Office is located on the Talkeetna Spur Road just before town. Zip Code: 99676.

LAUNDRY/SHOWERS:

Talkeenta Tesoro, just before town on the Talkeetna Spur Road, has an eclectic assortment of non-coin operated machines. Showers cost $2.00.

ALTERNATIVE TRANSPORTATION:

The Alaska Railroad runs a self-propelled rail diesel car between Anchorage and Hurricane Gulch. The flag stop service runs between June 11 and August 27. The units leave Anchorage at 9:30 a.m. on Wednesday, Saturday and Sunday. Bicycles carried on a space-available basis.

ENTERTAINMENT AND RECREATION

TRAILS:

Talkeetna has a network of ski trails, which are also used by mountain bikers. A summer race is sponsored by the Arctic Bicycling Club of Anchorage. Phone: 346-1117. For trail information, see Rose Jenne at Twister Fuels or consult the large map at the Latitude 62 Lodge on the Talkeetna Spur Road.

MUSEUMS/HISTORICAL SITES:

The Talkeenta Historical Society was formed in 1972. In 1974 the society acquired and restored the Little Red Schoolhouse, which was built in 1936, and later turned into a museum. The museum has pioneer and mining artifacts, as well as displays on Mount McKinley mountain climber Ray Genet, and the legendary Alaskan bush pilot Don Sheldon. The museum also has archival photos and a large plaster of paris model of Mount McKinley.

SIDE TRIPS:

Area flightseeing companies offer a variety of trips. For information, check at the Visitor's Center.

ROAD INFORMATION: PARKS HIGHWAY

SECTION 3: MILE 135.2 (DENALI VIEWPOINT)-MILE 185.1 (EAST FORK CHULITNA RIVER)

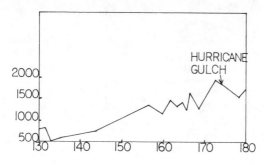

ROAD CONDITIONS/TERRAIN:

The rolling road climbs approximately 1,300 feet to Mile 172.5, then descends 425 feet to Honolulu Creek. The road then climbs 400 feet to Mile 181.3, then descends 136 feet to the East Fork Chulitna River. This section has a wide shoulder.

WATER:

Mile 136.7, Lower Troublesome Creek. Mile 143.9, Byers Creek. Mile 159.9, Horsehoe Creek. Mile 163.3, Little Coal Creek. Mile 178.1, Honolulu Creek. Mile 185.1, East Fork Chulitna River. Unnamed creeks at Miles 165.6, 172.2, and 178.1.

CAMPING/TRAILS:

Mile 137.2, Lower Troublesome Creek, Denali State Park Trailhead has ten campsites and a shelter. The trail leads 15.2 miles to Byers Lake Campground. Mile 137.6, Upper Troublesome Creek Trail leads 36.2 miles to Little Coal Creek Trailhead, located at Mile 163.9. Mile 147, Byers Lake Denali State Park Campground. 61 campsites located off the highway in a lush forest setting.

FOOD/LODGING:

Mile 156.2. Chulitna River Lodge and Cafe is owned by Steve and Jackie Hanson. The lodge rents cabins, and serves large sweet rolls and homemade soup. Mile 134.5. Mt. Haus Motel and Cafe, once owned by Mary Carey, was closed and for sale in the summer of 1988. Excellent view of Denali and the Alaska Range.

ROADSIDE SIGHTS:

On a clear day there are many good views of the Alaska Range for roughly 20 miles. This includes Miles 147.1, 158.1 and 162.3. Mile 147.2. The Alaska Veterans Memorial, a rest stop honoring Alaska's veterans, has picnic tables, outhouses and water. Mile 174, Hurricane Gulch. The bridge span is 550 feet and is 260 feet above Hurricane Creek.

ROAD INFORMATION: PARKS HIGHWAY

SECTION 4: MILE 185 (EAST FORK CHULITNA RIVER)- MILE 237.3 (DENALI NATIONAL PARK ENTRANCE)

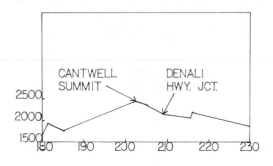

ROAD CONDITIONS/TERRAIN:

There's a wide shoulder except for a small stretch between Miles 230-231.3, where the road is narrow and winding. This section is rolling, with an overall elevation gain of 650 feet to Cantwell Summit at Mile 202.7. From the summit, the highway descends 720 feet to the Denali National Park and Preserve entrance at Mile 237.3.

JUNCTIONS:

Mile 209.9, junction with Denali Highway (Alaska Route 8). Mile 237.3, Denali National Park Entrance.

WATER:

Mile 194.5, Middle Fork Chulitna River. Mile 208.9, Pass Creek. Mile 209.5, Jack River. Mile 215.8, Nenana River. Mile 220, unnamed creek. Mile 224, Carlo Creek. Mile 231.3, Nenana River. Mile 237.5, Riley Creek.

CAMPING:

There are no official campgrounds until Denali Park at Mile 237.3. For information on Denali National Park, see Chapter 30. Camping possible at Mile 220, by the creek, and at Mile 234.8, by a small pond.

FOOD/LODGING:

Food and lodging are expensive in the Denali National Park area. It is not uncommon to charge $100 for a night's lodging. For information and reservations for the Denali area hotels, contact: Central Reservations, Box 200984, Anchorage, AK 99520. Phone: 274-5661. Mile 188.5. Sam McCloud's Igloo Service, sells snacks, sodas, and for 50 cents, a boneless chicken dinner. The giant igloo, next to the store, was an unfinished 48 room hotel in 1988. McCloud's "Eskimo Hatchery," should be open next year. Mile 209.5. Reindeer Mountain Lodge, owned by Jack and Jan Lawson, has a cafe and showers for $2.00. Mile 209.9. Tesesya Service Station, located at the junction of the Parks and Denali Highways, has limited groceries. Mile 224, McKinley Cabins bed and breakfast is owned by Ran Bitzer. Mile 229. Denali Cabins has a small grocery store, horseshoe pit, volleyball court and hot tubs. Mile 231.1. Grizzly Bear Cabins and Campground has a limited grocery, liquor store and coin-operated showers. ($1.00 for two and a half minutes.) Mile 231.2, McKinley Village Hotel.

SIDE TRIPS:

Osprey Expeditions, owned and operated by Aaron Underwood and Julie Boselli, leads state-wide wilderness river trips. Cyclists can meet the outfitters at the put-in spot on the river, float downriver, and have their bicycles transported to a predetermined take-out spot. For instance, cyclists may bicycle to McCarthy or Chitina, then float the Copper River to Cordova, where they can pick up their bicycles and take the ferry to Valdez or Whittier. Osprey Expeditions is known for their high quality food and itinerary flexibility. Reservations recommended. Write: Osprey Expeditions, Box 209, Denali National Park, AK 99755. Phone: 683-2734. Underwood and Boselli own Nenana Boat Works, and sell kayaking and rafting supplies, camping gear and Counter Assault, a non-lethal bear repellent. Other outdoor adventure operators are located along the Parks Highway near Denali National Park.

ROAD INFORMATION: PARKS HIGHWAY

SECTION 5: MILE 237.3 (DENALI NATIONAL PARK)-MILE 296.7 (FISH CREEK)

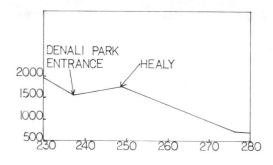

ROAD CONDITIONS/TERRAIN:

The road is rolling, but climbs 200 feet to the town of Healy at Mile 248.7. The rollers continue but the road descends about 1,100 feet to Mile 275.8, where it is level. The highway has a wide shoulder to Mile 263.1, then a narrow shoulder to Nenana.

JUNCTIONS:

Mile 248.7, road leads to Healy (pop. 414). Mile 283.5. Spur road to Clear Air Force Base and the small community of Anderson.

WATER:

Mile 238, Nenana River. Mile 238.4, Kingfisher Creek. Mile 240, Ice Worm Gulch. Mile 240.2, Hornet Creek. Mile 242.4, Dragonfly Creek. Mile 248.9, Nenana River. Mile 243.6, Bison Gulch. Mile 244.6, Antler Creek. Mile 249.9, Dry Creek. Mile 252.5. Panguingue Creek, named for a Phillipine card game. Mile 264.4, Bear Creek. Mile 275.8, Nenana River. Mile 285.7, Julius Creek. Mile 296.7, Fish Creek.

CAMPING:

Mile 269.1, state wayside and shelter. Camping is possible at Mile 241.7, along the Nenana River; Mile 242.1, Dragonfly Creek; Mile 243.6, Bison Creek; Mile 252.5, Panguingue Creek; and Mile 275.8, the Nenana River.

FOOD/LODGING:

Mile 238.6. In the area are a salmon bake, two hotels, and a pizza parlor. Mile 245. The Healy Roadhouse, owned by Wendell Neff, has a restaurant and bar. Mile 248.7. Brannen's Grocery and Liquor Store, at the junction of the Healy cutoff, sells limited groceries and fresh produce. Mile 280. The Hop, owned by Irene Gonzales, has been in operation since 1975. The Hop sells limited groceries, burritos, tacos, chicken and hamburgers. Hours: 10 a.m. to 11 p.m. Mile 280. Clear Sky Lodge has a bar and liquor store. Mile 283.5. Anderson, at the end of a six mile paved road, has a bar and restaurant (The Do Drop Inn), a grocery store, a campground with a shelter and a post office. Zip Code: 99790.

ROADSIDE SIGHTS:

Mile 250.8. Berle Mercer's bison graze in the distant fields.

ROAD INFORMATION: PARKS HIGHWAY

SECTION 6: MILE 296.7 (FISH CREEK)-MILE 362.2 (JCT. WITH THE RICHARDSON HIGHWAY AT FAIRBANKS)

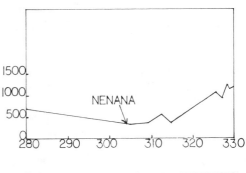

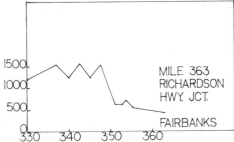

ROAD CONDITIONS/TERRAIN:

The highway has a narrow shoulder to Mile 305, Nenana. After crossing the Tanana River at Nenana, the road runs along the ridge tops, climbing about 1,200 feet to its highest point, elevation 1,598 feet/487 meters at Mile 342.8. From here it continues to roll, but descends 963 feet to the Old Nenana Highway junction at Mile 351.2. After one more hill, it is flat from this junction to the highway's end at Mile 362.2.

Unfortunately, cyclists wishing to bypass Fairbanks by remaining on the wide shouldered Parks Highway are unable to do so. The highway is closed to cyclists at Geist Road, Mile 356.8. Presently Geist Road leads as far as University Avenue. In the future, this road will lead to downtown Fairbanks and the Steese Highway on the east end of town. A bicycle path leads 1.5 miles from Geist Road to Airport Road.

JUNCTIONS:

Mile 304.7, Nenana. Mile 351.2. The Old Nenana Highway leads 0.5 miles into the mining town of Ester. Mile 355.8. Tanana Road leads to Sheep Creek Road, and a half mile further, the UAF campus. Mile 356.8, Geist Road leads to University Avenue, and eventually will lead to downtown Fairbanks. Mile 358, Airport Road. To the left, the road leads to the south end of downtown Fairbanks. To the right, Airport Road leads to Fairbanks International Airport.

WATER:

Mile 305.1, Tanana River. Mile 314.8, Little Goldstream Creek. Mile 357.7, Chena River.

CAMPING:

Mile 304.7. Camping in the past has been permitted on the Nenana Visitor Center grounds. This camping area has little privacy and is noisy. Water and bathroom facilities on the premises. A fee campground may be opened in Nenana at which time the the present roadside campground will be closed.

Free camping permitted at the Monderosa, Mile 308.9, and Skinny Dick's Halfway Inn at Mile 328.

FOOD/LODGING:

Mile 304.7, Nenana. Mile 308.9. The Monderosa, owned by Nick and Carol Monroe, is claimed by many to be the home of the best hamburger in Alaska. Mile 328. Skinny Dick's Halfway Inn, owned by "Skinny" Dick Hiland, has a bar and pool table. No food served here. Mile 351.2, Ester, (pop. 285) located off the Old Nenana Highway, is the site of an old mining camp. The Golden Eagle Saloon, a neighborhood bar, and the Cripple Creek Resort are in downtown Ester. All you can eat dinners are served in a former mining camp mess hall. In the evenings there is a live goldrush show in the Malemute Saloon, which was once an old machine shop. Mile 353.5, Goldhill Liquor sells limited groceries.

ROADSIDE SIGHTS:

Miles 319-324.8. View of the Alaska Range on a clear day. Mile 344.2. Monument honoring George Alexander Parks, Alaska territorial governor.

NENANA

BACKGROUND

The name Nenana (pop. 574) comes from the Athabascan word "Nenashna" which means "Point of Camping at Two Rivers." Nenana was established in 1903 when the Army Signal Corps set up a station running telegraph lines from St. Michaels to Eagle. On July 15, 1923, President Warren G. Harding hammered in a gold spike, signifying the completion of the Alaska Railroad. Nenana grew because of the railroad, and was incorporated in 1921.

The town population was roughly 5,000 when it was the headquarters for the northern terminus of the Alaska Railroad.

The town's claim to fame is the Nenana Ice Classic. In 1917, railroad engineers bet $800 guessing at what time the river would break up. Every year since, a large black and white log tripod has been imbedded in the middle of the frozen Tanana River between the highway and railroad bridges. The earliest recorded break-up was April 20, 1940 at 3:27 p.m. and the latest, May 24, 1964 at 11:41 a.m. Ice Classic Tickets, which cost $2.00, may be purchased at the Nenana Visitor's Center.

In addition to income from the ice classic, many Nenana residents are employed by the Yutana Barge Lines, which move supplies to the Yukon River villages. Some area residents also supplement their income by trapping.

The largest expansion bridge on rollers ever built can be seen when entering town.

VISITOR'S CENTER:

The Nenana Visitor's Center is located at the junction of the Parks Highway and the spur road into town.

GROCERIES:

Coghill's General Merchandise carries a complete selection of groceries, as well as some hardware items. Hours: 9 a.m. to 6 p.m. Monday through Saturday.

EATING/DRINKING ESTABLISHMENTS:

A good place to eat breakfast is at the Nenana Inn, on Main Street. Vernice Reid and daughter Jackie Suckling serve an excellent sourdough pancake breakfast which includes homemade wildberry syrup, reindeer sausage, and an egg. The restaurant opens at 8 a.m. Bed and breakfast accommodations are sometimes available.

Bike Touring, Mt. McKinley National Park.
Credit: University of Alaska, Fairbanks, Archives

Denali Highway

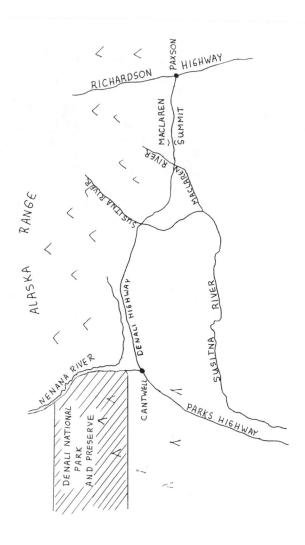

Chapter 24: The Denali Highway

Background

The 136 mile Denali Highway (Alaska Route 8) was opened in 1957 and, until 1972, with the completion of the Parks Highway, was the only road access to Denali National Park and Preserve. The highway leads from Paxson at Mile 185.5 on the Richardson Highway to Cantwell at Mile 210 on the Parks Highway, and is mostly above treeline.

Though a short ride, the Denali Highway is not to be rushed. The scenery is like that of Denali National Park, but minus the crowds. Glaciers and mountains can be seen from the roadside. Bears, moose, caribou, and wolves live in the area.

Road Information: Denali Highway

Section 1: Mile 0 (Paxson)-Mile 42 (Maclaren River)

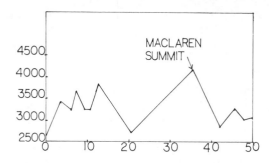

Road Conditions/Terrain:

The road is mostly uphill, gaining about 1,000 feet to Mile 13.1, drops 800 feet to Mile 20.6, then climbs 1,280 feet to Maclaren Summit at Mile 35.2. From the summit, the highway drops 1,211 feet to the Maclaren River. The first 20.5 miles are paved, and the road was resurfaced in 1988. The rest of the road is narrow and has a hard packed gravel surface.

Water:

Mile 0.2, Gulkana River. Mile 6.8, road leads to Seven Mile Lake. Mile 21.4, Tangle River. Mile 21.5, Tangle Lakes. Mile 21.7, well water at wayside. Mile 24.8, Rock Creek. Mile 35.2, small creek. Mile 42, Maclaren River.

Camping:

Mile 21.5. Tangle Lakes BLM Campground has 13 campsites and is a short distance from the highway. Mile 21.7. Tangle River Boat Launch BLM Campground, near the roadside, has seven campsites.

Food/Lodging:

Mile 20. The Tangle River Inn has been owned by Jack and Nadine Johnson since 1971. The Inn contains a bunkhouse and cafe. Canoes are available for rent. Mile 22. Sleeping Lady Lodge, owned by Fred and Marie Drew, was named for the mountain due west of the lodge. Cabins are available, and good homemade pie is served in the cafe.

Roadside Sights:

Mile 3.6. Excellent view of the Gakona Glacier to the northeast. Icefall Peak is at the west end of the glacier. The mountains to the north, visible for the next fifty miles or so, are from left to right: Mount Deborah, elevation 12,339 feet/3,762 meters; Mount Hess, elevation 11,940 feet/3,640 meters; and Mount Hayes, elevation 13,832 feet/4,217 meters. Mile 20.6 Maclaren Pass. Elevation 1,280 feet. Mile 21. The Nelchina caribou herd travels through this area in the fall.

Road Information: Denali Highway

Section 2: Mile 42 (Maclaren River)-Mile 88

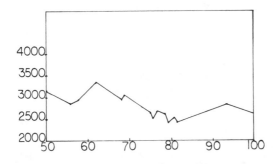

Road Conditions/Terrain:

The highway is rolling with gains and losses in elevation of about 100 to 200 feet. At Mile 68.6, the road drops 400 feet to Mile 75. The road continues to be rolling, but with less extreme elevation differences.

Water:

Mile 43.4, road leads to the Maclaren River. Mile 55.9, Clearwater Creek. Mile 65.7, Waterfall Creek. Mile 69.1, Raft Creek. Mile 72.2, Nowater Creek. Mile 73.5, Swampbuggy Lake. Mile 79.3, Susitna River.

Camping:

Mile 55.9. BLM Clearwater Creek Campground is a small, non-secluded roadside camping area. Camping is also possible at Mile 65.7, Fall Creek, and at Mile 70.8, Swampbuggy Lake, via a small road.

Food/Lodging:

Mile 42.1. Maclaren River Lodge is owned by Ken and Emily Jennings. The lodge was built by Whitey who sold it to Red Cooney. When Whitey sold the place to

Cooney, an agreement was made that Whitey could live out his days in the old log cabin on the property. Supposedly the cabin is now haunted by two female ghosts. The lodge has a bar and a cafe, and turkey is served here on Sundays. Cabins for rent include Whitey's. Mile 82. Gracious House, a lodge, has a cafe, bar, and cabins for rent. Many recreational activities including river boat trips to the glacier, gold panning, fly-in fishing, and horseback riding are available.

ROADSIDE SIGHTS:

Mile 45.7, Crazy Notch Gap (elevation 3,258 feet/993 meters.) Mile 78.9, gravel road leads to the Valdez Creek Mine. In 1988, this was the second most productive mine in Alaska. The mine is near the old Denali Mining Camp, established in 1907.

ROAD INFORMATION: DENALI HIGHWAY

SECTION 3: MILE 88-MILE 133.7 (JCT. WITH THE PARKS HIGHWAY)

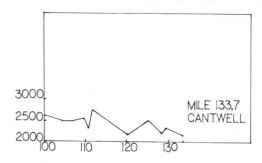

ROAD CONDITIONS/TERRAIN:

The highway continues to roll, but with overall elevation changes of between 200 and 400 feet. There is an overall loss in elevation of about 700 feet.

JUNCTIONS:

Mile 133.7. End of the Denali Highway at junction with the Parks Highway (Alaska Route 3).

WATER:

Mile 94.8, Cabin Creek. Mile 104.4, Brushkana River. Mile 107.1, Stixkwan Creek. Mile 110.9, Seattle Creek. Mile 111.9, Lily Creek. Mile 128.2, Fish Creek. There are small unnamed creeks at Miles 111.2, 114.4, 117.4, and 121.4

CAMPING:

Mile 104.4. Brushkana River BLM campground has 12 campsites and a nice shelter. It is necessary to travel a distance to find firewood. It is also possible to camp along the Nenana River, which the road parallels after Mile 117.1

FOOD/LODGING:

Mile 99.6. Adventures Unlimited is owned by Jim and Vonnie Grimes. The pair homesteaded the land in 1966 and opened the lodge in 1972. The lodge has a small cafe and is near excellent bird viewing areas. In 1988 the lodge was for sale.

ROADSIDE SIGHTS:

Mile 95.6, highway crosses watershed divide. To the east, water drains through the Susitna River into Cook Inlet. To the west, water drains via the Nenana and Tanana Rivers into the Yukon River which empties into the Bering Sea. Mile 92.6. Great view of the West Fork Glacier which advances 60 feet per year. Mile 133. At the power lines, a trail leads to the top of Reindeer Mountain, offering a view of the Alaska Range.

CHAPTER 25: THE TOK CUTOFF

BACKGROUND

The 125 mile Tok Cutoff (Alaska Route 1), built in 1942, connects the Alaska Highway with the Richardson and Glenn Highways. The road generally follows the old Valdez-Eagle Trail, first blazed in 1885 by Lt. Henry Allen. Presently the Tok Cutoff Road is narrow, winding and has numerous frost heaves, gravel patches and roughly paved sections. In the next few years the Tok Cutoff will be widened and realigned.

The average temperature in July along the road is 56° F. The average July rainfall is 2.5 inches.

ROAD INFORMATION: TOK CUTOFF

SECTION 1: MILE 0 (GAKONA JCT.)-MILE 60 (NABESNA ROAD)

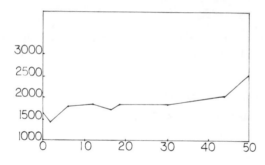

ROAD CONDITIONS/TERRAIN:

The highway is rolling and climbs 1,294 feet to Mile 55, then drops roughly 500 feet to the Nabesna Road. The Tok Cutoff is paved with a narrow shoulder.

JUNCTIONS:

Mile 0. Big Timber Junction, beginning of Tok Cutoff at Mile 128.6 of the Richardson Highway. Mile 59.9, Nabesna Road leads 46 miles through Wrangell-St. Elias National Park and Preserve to the old Nabesna Gold Mine. For more information on this road, see Chapter 31.

WATER:

Mile 1.7. The Gakona River gets its name from an Indian word first reported in 1885 as being "Ga Ka Tna," or "Rabbit River." Mile 17.8, Tulsona Creek. Mile 34.5, Sinona Creek. Mile 35.6, Chistochina River #1. Mile 35.8, Chistochina River #2. Mile 43.7, Indian River. Mile 49.9, small creek.

CAMPING/PICNIC AREAS/TRAILS:

There are no official campgrounds within this section. There are picnic areas and possible camping at Mile 17.9, beside Tulsona Creek and at Mile 43.7, beside the Indian River. Camping is also possible near the two Chistochina River crossings at Miles 35.6 and 35.8 and at the rest area, Mile 24.5, where a path leads to the Copper River.

Mile 35.5. The Chistochina River Trail follows the west fork of the Chistochina River. Mile 44.8, Eagle River trailhead. Both trails are said to be muddy where they traverse muskeg.

FOOD/LODGING/POST OFFICE:

Mile 1.9. Gakona Lodge and Trading Post, built in 1904, was placed on the *National Register of Historic Places* in 1977. The roadhouse, at the junction of the Valdez-Fairbanks-Eagle trails, was an important stop for travellers. Says its current owner, "Bikers are a hell of a lot more intelligent than...truck drivers." The roadhouse has a grocery store, restaurant, bar and showers for $3.00. Mile 32.8, the Chistochina Lodge and Trading Post, built in 1921, was originally a roadhouse. The lodge has a cafe, small grocery, and a public sauna. Tent camping is free. Mile 44.8. Posty's Trading Post sells Native gifts, snacks, and liquor. There are clean restrooms. Tent camping is $4.00 per night.

ROADSIDE SIGHTS:

Mile 20. Views of 12,010 foot/3,661 meter Mount Drum to the south, and 16,237 foot/4,950 meter Mount Sanford to the southeast. Mile 28.2, interpretive sign on the Alaska Road Commission.

ROAD INFORMATION: TOK CUTOFF

SECTION 2: MILE 60 (NABESNA ROAD)-MILE 125 (TOK)

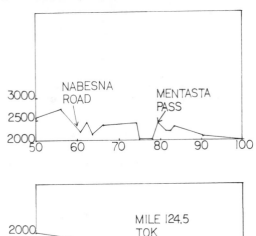

Road Conditions/Terrain:

The highway is rolling with elevation gains and losses ranging between 100 and 300 feet. From Mentasta Pass, elevation 2,450 feet/747 meters at Mile 79.5, the road descends to Tok, elevation 1,632 feet/498 meters. The road is paved and has a narrow shoulder until just outside of Tok.

Junctions:

Mile 81. Road to the Native village of Mentasta Lake. Mile 124.5, end of the Tok Cutoff. Junction with the Alaska Highway (Alaska Route 2) at Tok Junction.

Water:

Mile 60.8, Ahtel Creek. Mile 64.3, Porcupine Creek. Mile 67.9, Carlson Creek. Mile 75.6, Slana River. Mile 75.8, Slana Slough. Mile 76.3, Mable Creek. Mile 83.4, Bartell Creek. Mile 91, Little Tok River. Mile 103.8, Tok River. Mile 109.6, Clearwater Creek. There are small, unnamed creeks at Miles 73.4, 78.5, 85.7, 89, and 104.5.

Camping/Trails:

Mile 64.3. Porcupine Creek State Recreation Site has 14 campsites, many suitable for tenting. Mile 109.5. Eagle Trail State Recreation Site has 40 campsites and a shelter. The Old Eagle Trail from Valdez to Eagle passed through the campground; parts of the trail are still suitable for hiking. Another trail leaves the campground and follows the creek above treeline.

Food/Lodging:

Mile 62.7. Duffy's, established in the 1940's, is currently owned by Bill Ellis. Duffy's has a bar, cafe, and sells limited groceries. Mile 72.1. The Mentasta Mountain AYH Home Hostel is managed by Coy Brown. The hostel sleeps four; the nightly fee is $5.00. From Mile 72.1 on Tok Cutoff Road, hike up the Suslositna Valley following the marked trail for six miles to hostel. Reservations required. Write: Mentasta Home Hostel, Box 950, Slana, AK 99586. Mile 78. Mentasta Lodge has a cafe, bar, limited groceries, a laundromat and showers ($2.00.) Free tent camping.

Roadside Sights:

Mile 63. Viewpoint and interpretive sign about the Wrangell-St. Elias National Park and Preserve. In addition a marker indicates 8,174 foot Noyes Mountain, named for Brig. General John Rutherford Noyes, a former Alaska Territorial Road Commissioner.

GLENN HIGHWAY AND TOK CUTOFF

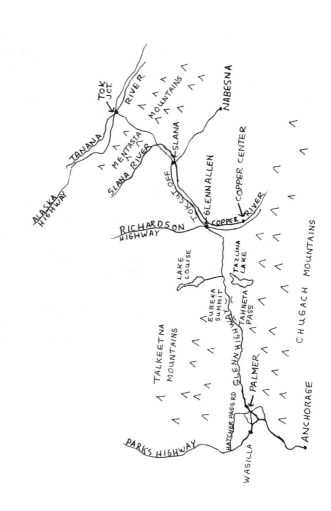

CHAPTER 26: THE GLENN HIGHWAY

BACKGROUND

The Glenn Highway (Alaska Route 1) connects the Richardson Highway and Anchorage. The scenery and terrain of the 189 mile highway is varied. On the Anchorage side, spruce and rocky terrain predominate. On the Richardson Highway side, the land is more alpine; the trees are sparse and the air's dryer. The highway has several steep passes, but becomes less rolling towards Glennallen, and for the last few miles, is downhill. The Glenn Highway, which parallels the Denali Highway, has more roadside businesses than its counterpart, and because it is paved, is more heavily travelled. The highway has little or no shoulder, but the Alaska Department of Transportation plans to widen it in the near future.

ROAD INFORMATION: GLENN HIGHWAY

SECTION 1: MILE 0 (ANCHORAGE)-MILE 54.4 (MOOSE CREEK CAMPGROUND)

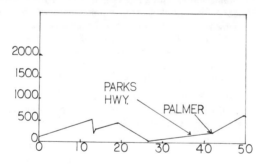

ROAD CONDITIONS/TERRAIN:

Except for a few short hills, the first fifty or so miles of the Glenn Highway travel gradually up to Palmer. At Palmer the highway climbs before dropping steeply to Moose Creek. For the first 21 miles to Peters Creek, cyclists are required to stay off the four lane highway's smooth eight foot shoulder and ride on the rougher and hillier bike path. The divided four lane highway ends at Mile 27.3. Except for four bridge crossings there is a six foot shoulder to Palmer. At Mile 48.1, the shoulder ends, the road narrows and becomes more winding.

Though Moose Creek is at Milepost 54.4, the actual road length is about 49 miles. The Old Glenn Highway which departs from the new Glenn Highway at Mile 29.5 and ends in Palmer, is roughly 18.6 miles long. The newer highway from the junction to Palmer is about 12.5 miles. When the new highway crosses the old highway in Palmer, the Glenn Highway again follows the original mileposts. Instead of being Mile 42, it is actually Mile 48.

JUNCTIONS:

Mile 2.8, Boniface Parkway. Mile 4.5, Muldoon Road. Recommended Anchorage bypass route. Follow Muldoon Road south to Tudor Road, then west to the Seward Highway. Mile 12.6, Hiland Road. Mile 13. The bike path passes through Eagle River, a suburb. Mile 26.5, Eklutna Road. Mile 29.5, junction with the Old Glenn Highway. This scenic, but narrow road leads 18.6 miles to Palmer. Mile 35.2. Junction with the Parks Highway (Alaska Route 3), leading to Denali National Park and Fairbanks. Mile 41.2, Palmer South Exit. Mile 41.6. West Evergreen Avenue to the right leads into Palmer. The Palmer-Wasilla Highway (left) leads to Wasilla and the Parks Highway.

WATER:

Mile 13, Eagle River. Mile 21.3, Peters Creek. Miles 29.8, 30.5, and 30.8, highway crosses the Knik River. Mile 31.4, Matanuska River.

CAMPING/PICNIC AREAS:

Mile 36.4. Kepler-Bradley State Recreation Area has picnic sites. Mile 54.4. Moose Creek State Recreation Site has 14 campsites including two good tent sites along a trail, a shelter and spring water.

FOOD/LODGING:

There are many shops, restaurants and stores along the highway leaving Anchorage, including Muldoon Supermarket about a half a mile from the Glenn Highway on Muldoon Road. Mile 13. Eagle River has a shopping center, numerous business establishments and a post office. Zip Code: 99577. Mile 38.6. The Pole-Lock Farm Bar and Liquor Store, owned by Lloyd and Ruth Rebischke, was established in 1971. Ask to see the "Pole-Lock Trailer," or buy a round for the house and receive a certificate. Inexpensive rooms are available.

Mile 37.6, Self-Serve Vegetable Stand. Help yourself: consult the price list on the wall, and deposit money in "bank." Bags provided. Mile 38. The Matanuska Farm Market is open from 10 a.m. to 6 p.m. daily, and sells locally grown produce. Mile 42, Palmer. See the end of this section.

ROADSIDE SIGHTS:

Mile 50.1, Muskox Farm. Daily tours begin at 9:30 A.M. The farm is home to over 109 muskox. Interpretive displays on site. Admission: $3.00. Mile 51.7, Wolf Country USA. What looks like a sled dog yard, is actually a yard full of hybrid wolf/dog crosses. Puppies for sale.

PALMER

BACKGROUND

The Matanuska Valley's agricultural potential was recognized in 1898 when Captain Edwin Forbes Glenn led a company of soldiers to explore and map a trail from the coast to Alaska's isolated Interior. Accompanying Glenn on this trip was Walter C. Mendenhall. A civilian employee with the U.S. Geological Survey, Mendenhall reported that the area had agricultural possibilities, and that there were extensive coal fields in the Matanuska Valley.

After the railroad was built, a spur line was laid to the Matanuska coal fields. In 1915, just one year after the railroad's arrival, all available homestead land had been staked. But with the coming of World War I, many farms were abandoned. Then during the Depression, the Federal Government established a farming colony in the Matanuska Valley to aid drought stricken Midwest farmers.

203 families were transplanted to the Matanuska Valley in May 1935. Shortly after, Palmer displaced Wasilla as the area's principal supply center. Palmer's average July temperature is 57° F. The average July rainfall is 2.5 inches.

VISITORS INFORMATION

VISITOR'S CENTER:

The Palmer Visitor's Center is located across the railroad tracks from where South Alaska Street and South Colony Way merge. A staffed information desk has printed material available on Palmer (pop. 3,116) and the Matanuska Valley. There is also a small museum in the building's basement and an outdoor show garden. In addition, the Visitor's Center has a fleet of old clunker bicycles available for sight-seeing.

TRAVELLER'S NEEDS

MEDICAL SERVICES:

Valley Hospital is located at 515 E. Dahlia Way. Phone: 745-4813.

GROCERIES:

Carrs Supermarket is located in Pioneer Square on the corner of the Glenn and Palmer-Wasilla Highways.

BICYCLE/OUTDOOR STORES:

Palmer has no bicycle stores.

LODGING/CAMPING:

Mile 113.5 Glenn Highway. The Sheep Mountain Lodge AYH Hostel sleeps 12. The houseparents are Diane Schneider and David Cohen. The nightly fee for members is $8.00. No kitchen facilities available. There are mountain bike trails in the area. Write Sheep Mountain Lodge AYH, Box 8490, Palmer, AK 99645. Phone: 745-5121. There are also a few hotels around Palmer. See Road Information for campground information.

POST OFFICE:

The Palmer Post Office is located at 211 West Elmwood. Zip Code: 99645.

LAUNDRY/SHOWERS:

The Old Town Laundromat, at 127 South Alaska Street, near West Arctic Avenue, has single showers for $3.00, and "buddy showers" for $4.00.

ALTERNATIVE TRANSPORTATION:

The Palmer Airport is located at the southeast end of town on Airport Road.

ENTERTAINMENT AND RECREATION

MUSEUMS/HISTORICAL SITES:

Mile 40.2. Palmer is the current home of the Alaska Museum of Transportation and Industry. Early farm machinery, airplanes, boats, bulldozers and mining equipment are on display. There is also an Alaska Railroad exhibit. The museum is located next to the Alaska State Fairgrounds. A new museum site is under development at Mile 42, Parks Highway, Wasilla. Hours: Tuesday through Saturday from 8 a.m. to 4 p.m. Admission charged. The University of Alaska Matanuska Valley Experimental Station headquarters is located on East Fireweed Avenue past the Visitor's Center. Farm researchers are developing quick growing plant varieties for the north's short growing season.

BOOKSTORES:

The Book Cache is located in Pioneer Square at the corner of the Glenn and Palmer-Wasilla Highways.

FAIRS:

The Alaska State Fairgrounds in Palmer is located at Mile 40.2 Glenn Highway. The annual fair is held during the eleven days preceding Labor Day.

PUBLIC RECREATION:

The Mat-Su Swimming Pool is located in the Palmer High School, on West Arctic Avenue. Phone: 376-4222.

ROAD INFORMATION: GLENN HIGHWAY

SECTION 2: MILE 54.4 (MOOSE CREEK CAMPGROUND) - MILE 106.8 (CARIBOU CREEK)

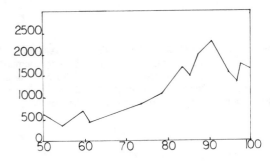

ROAD CONDITIONS/TERRAIN:

This portion of the highway is hilly with considerable gains and losses in elevation. The road is paved and winding with little or no shoulder. The lowest point in this section is 380 feet at Mile 54.4. The highest point is 2,300 feet at Mile 90.4.

JUNCTIONS:

Mile 60.8. Jonesville Road leads 1.5 miles to a gravel road, which leads three miles to Seventeen Mile Lake.

WATER:

Mile 54.6, Moose Creek Campground. Spring water here. Mile 66.4, King River. Mile 77.7, Chickaloon River. Mile 87.5, spring water, left side Glennallen-bound. Mile 88.8, Puritan Creek. Mile 91.3, Cascade Creek. Mile 96.5, Hicks Creek. Mile 106.7, Caribou Creek.

CAMPING:

Mile 76. King Mountain State Recreation Site has 22 campsites and a shelter. Mile 83.3. Bonnie Lake State Recreation Site has nine campsites. Mile 101, Matanuska Glacier State Recreation Site has 12 campsites, a trail and a three day limit. Camping is also possible at Mile 60.8, Seventeen Mile Lake, off Jonesville Road and at Mile 66.4, King River.

FOOD/LODGING:

Mile 60.8. The Jonesville Bakery contains a cafe, laundromat and showers for $2.00. Mile 61. Sutton (pop. 340) was founded in 1918 as a siding and station on the Matanuska branch of the Alaska Railroad. After area coal mines closed, the town became a highway service community. Mile 76.2. King Mountain Lodge, owned by Rick and Mary Podobnik, has a cafe, bar, liquor store, and showers for $2.00. Mile 76.3. The Chickaloon General Store has limited groceries. Mile 96.4. The Hicks Creek Lodge is owned by B.J. Tanner, who bakes and cooks whatever strikes her fancy. Camping is free, showers are $2.00. Mile 102. Glacier Park Resort, owned by John Kimbell who homesteaded the land in 1966, is a private campground and lodge at the foot of the Matanuska Glacier. It is roughly one mile from the highway to the lodge, and an additional two miles, by permit ($5.00), to the glacier. It costs $2.50 per person to camp at the Glacier. Mile 102.2. The Long Rifle Lodge, owned by Eugene and Frances "Lynne" Whitmill, has a cafe, and serves ice cream and homemade cinnamon rolls. Laundry facilities are available: showers cost $1.50.

ROADSIDE SIGHTS:

There are several good views of the Matanuska Glacier between Miles 99 and 108. The Glacier is roughly 27 miles long and 4 miles wide.

ROAD INFORMATION: GLENN HIGHWAY
SECTION 3: MILE 106.8 (CARIBOU CREEK) - MILE 159.8 (LAKE LOUISE JCT.)

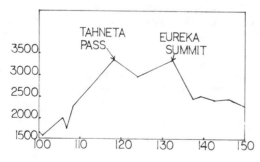

ROAD CONDITIONS/TERRAIN:

The highway climbs 1,540 feet to Tahneta Pass (elevation 3,335 feet/ 1,022 meters) then drops about 400 feet before climbing over Eureka Summit (elevation 3,330 feet/1,013 meters). The highway then descends to Mendeltna Creek at elevation 2,180 feet/665 meters, and after climbs roughly 300 feet. The road is paved, the shoulder narrow. The average July temperature at Eureka Lodge, near Eureka Summit, is 51° F. The average July rainfall is 2.7 inches.

JUNCTIONS:

Mile 159.8. Lake Louise Road, a 17.2 mile gravel road, leads north to the Lake Louise State Recreation Area.

WATER:

Mile 137.6, Little Nelchina River. Mile 147.2, Cache Creek. Mile 152.6, Mendeltna River.

CAMPING/PICNIC AREAS/TRAILS:

Mile 137.4. Little Nelchina State Recreation Site has 11 campsites and a trail. Mile 152.5. Mendeltna River Rest Area has picnic tables and outhouses. Mile 159.8. Lake Louise State Recreation Area, located at Mile 17.2, Lake Louise Road, has 46 campsites and a shelter.

The following trails are all part of the Chickaloon-Knik-Nelchina Trail System. Though extensive, parts of the trail system travel through muddy low lying muskeg areas, making summer riding difficult. Mile 116.5. Squaw Creek Trail leads 3.5 miles to Squaw Creek, 13 miles to Alfred Creek and 15 miles to Sheep Creek. Mile 118.5. Blueberry Hill Trail leads 8 miles to Goober Lake, 11 miles to the Nelchina River and 16 miles to the Nelchina River Trailhead. Mile 123.3. Belanger Pass Trail leads 3 miles to Belanger Pass, 6.5 miles to Alfred Creek and 8 miles to Albert Creek. Mile 126.4. Nelchina River Trail leads 1.5 miles to Eureka Creek, 8 miles to Goober Lake and 9 miles to the Nelchina River. Mile 130.3. Old Man Creek Trail leads 2 miles to Old Man Creek, 9 miles to Crooked Creek and 14 miles to the abandoned mining camp of Nelchina.

FOOD/LODGING:

Mile 113.5. Sheep Mountain Lodge has a cafe with homemade baked goods, a bar, liquor store, hot tub and showers. Mile 128.1. Eureka Lodge, owned by Tom and Mary Ann Berkley, was first opened in 1942. There's a cafe, and showers cost $2.00. Mile 143.2. Nelchina Lodge, owned by Henry Johnson, has a cafe and a bar. Mile 152.8. Kamping Resorts of Alaska is owned by Mr. and Mrs. Atkins. The cafe serves 15 varieties of pancakes and homemade pizza. There's a bar, campground ($5.00) and the Museum of Alaska's Drunken Forest. The outdoor museum has diamond willow burls, rocks, seashells, mammoth bones and some pioneer artifacts. Unfortunately there is no accompanying interpretive information.

Mile 159.8. The Lake Louise Junction Store, owned by Jim and Hala Bates, carries a limited supply of groceries and has a sauna and showers. Arabic and French are spoken here.

ROADSIDE SIGHTS:

Miles 112-117, views of 6,300 foot/1,921 meter Sheep Mountain. Miles 118-121, the highway passes through 3,355 foot/1,022 meter Tahneta Pass. Miles 122-134. Good views of Gunsight Mountain, elevation 6,585 feet/ 2,008 meters. Mile 132.3,

Eureka Summit (elevation 3,322 feet/1,013 meters.). On a clear day, there are excellent views of the Wrangell, Chugach and Talkeetna Mountains. Watch for caribou and other wildlife while riding through the open alpine country.

Road Information: Glenn Highway

Section 4: Mile 159.8 (Lake Louise Jct.) - Mile 189 (Jct. Richardson Highway)

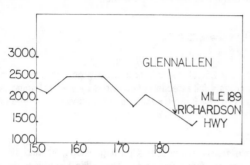

Road Conditions/Terrain:

There are rolling hills to Mile 166, with a slight rise in elevation. It is then down to Glennallen, with an elevation drop of about 1,000 feet. The road is paved, and the shoulder widens near Glennallen.

Junctions:

Mile 189. At the Glennallen Junction, the Glenn Highway joins the Richardson Highway (Alaska Route 4). If traveling to Valdez, turn right (south) on the Richardson Highway. If traveling to Tok, turn left (north) and ride 14 miles to the Tok Cutoff; if traveling to Fairbanks or the Denali Highway, continue north on the Richardson Highway.

Water:

Mile 162, Tex Smith Lake. Access to the lake is possible via an Alaska Department of Fish and Game right-of-way across private property. Mile 172.5, Tonsina Creek. Mile 186, Moose Creek.

Camping/Trails:

Mile 172.5. Tonsina Creek State Recreation Site has 10 campsites and a trail. Mile 169.5. A trail leads one mile to Mae West Lake. Mile 165.8. A trail leads from turnout, roughly two miles to Lost Cabin Lake. Mile 173.5, BLM trail leads to a "mud volcano." About 100 feet in diameter by four feet high, the volcano was caused by hot water pushing up from beneath the earth's surface.

Food/Lodging:

No services until Glennallen.

Glennallen

BACKGROUND

The town of Glennallen (pop. 499) borders the highway from about Mile 182 to Mile 189, with most of the town's businesses between Miles 187 and 188. The name Glennallen is derived from the combined last names of Capt. Edwin F. Glenn and Lt. Henry Allen, U.S. Army. Both men lead early explorations in the Copper River Region. Because of Glennallen's location at the junction of two major Alaska highways, it is primarily a service center. The average July temperature in Glennallen is 56° F, the average July rainfall is 1.7 inches.

MEDICAL SERVICES:

Mile 186.6, Faith Hospital. Phone: 822-3203.

GROCERIES:

Mile 186.9. Pardners Cracker Barrel, the oldest operating general store between Valdez and Anchorage, carries a full selection of groceries as well as fishing tackle, sewing supplies and gifts. Mile 187.8. Park's Place is a full service supermarket with fresh produce.

BICYCLE/OUTDOOR STORES:

Glennallen has no bicycle stores. Glennallen Sporting Goods, at Mile 182 sells fishing tackle, Coleman stoves, fuel and used books. Mike Langelen, the store owner since 1963, claims he has the best water in the basin.

LODGING/CAMPING:

There are numerous hotels and lodges, but no hostels in Glennallen.

EATING ESTABLISHMENTS:

Last Frontier Pizza, on Post Office Road, has a weekday all you can eat lunch special between 11 a.m. and 2 p.m.

POST OFFICE:

The Glennallen Post Office is located on Post Office Road. Zip Code: 99588.

LAUNDRY:

Park's Place Laundromat is located next to Park's Place Supermarket. No showers available.

The Palmer Muskox Farm and The Fairbanks Large Animal Research Station

Hilary Zahnley, a tourguide at the Palmer Muskox farm, unlatched a gate, and walked into a field. On the opposite side of a fence, a handful of tourists watched as she tried to coerce an old muskox, one with a large horn boss, to come closer to the fence. The animal, about the size of a pony, kept a safe distance as she walked behind it. The tourists, losing interest, took pictures of one another next to Little Etuk, a smaller, less impressive, but friendlier yearling.

When Hilary returned, she told the individuals who clustered around her that the current herd of 109 animals subsisted mainly on grass hay, and the more aggresive males were castrated. When a small child asked her about the red and white tags that hung from the animal's rounded ears, she explained to her that they were for identification purposes.

The early evening scene was a fairly typical one at the Palmer Muskox Farm. From late May until mid-September, 17 daily half hour tours are given by Hilary or other farm workers. The farm is a popular tourist attraction. In 1988 it was estimated that over 20,000 people had visited the Palmer Farm, netting over $60,000.

Back in the barn, the tourists lingered and looked at an interpretive display on the white barn walls. Beneath photos was printed information on the history, former workers, quiviut co-op, and muskox birthing process. As Hilary explained, while visitor education is a function of the Palmer farm, quiviut production is equally, if not more important. In the spring, when the muskox shed their fine winter undercoat or quiviut, they are individually herded into squeeze chutes, and combed out. A single muskox might carry ten pounds of the very expensive wool. After the quiviut is collected, it's sent to the more than 200 plus members of the Oomingmak's Producer's Co-op who live in more than a dozen arctic villages along the Bering Sea. The members knit the fleece into garments, which are sold in the Oomingmak Co-operative shop in Anchorage.

Like Palmer, the Fairbanks facility, called the Large Animal Research Station (LARS), welcomes visitors and provides seasonal tours. Outside the gates there is a viewing platform from which the animals can be observed. Inside the gates a sign indicates where visitors should wait for the twice daily, Tuesday - Saturday tours to begin. To the right of the sign is a canvas tent, where tee-shirts and raw quiviut are sold. (Unlike the Palmer quiviut, which is sold to a cooperative, the Fairbanks quiviut is sold raw to spinners and weavers who process it themselves.)

However, LARS is more research oriented than its Glenn Highway counterpart, and so it is set up differently. Instead of being ear tagged, a few female members of the Fairbanks muskox herd, (which numbers 25) have the white saddle areas of their backs spray painted green or red. Beside the two central pastures are two tall green observation towers. There's also a small white barn on the premises. Inside are squeeze shoots and pens, but there are no photographs on the walls.

According to Bill Hauer, the manager of the Large Animal Research Station, the facility is run by the University of Alaska Institute of Arctic Biology. Said Bill, the main focus of ongoing research is the affects of nutrition on the reproductive ability of muskox cows.

LARS also has one reindeer herd (which numbers seven) on the premises as well as two caribou herds. The Delta caribou herd has seven, and the Porcupine herd, 10 animals. The two herds, from separate geographical areas, are used for comparative reproductive studies.

Another ongoing project involves both the reindeer and the caribou. Hopefully researchers will answer questions about the general effects of intermingling herds. The results of this study will be important to Seward Peninsula herders, who need to know if Northwest Alaska caribou-reindeer hybrids are capable of reproduction.

Observations have been an integral part of the reproductive studies. Hence, the marked animals and the towers. LARS staff, UAF graduate students, and Project Earthwatch volunteers have put in many hours in the towers, monitoring the eating, sleeping, playing, nursing and reproductive behavior of both muskox and caribou. Researchers such as Dr. Kathy Parker, who is now working on a similiar project in Wrangell, write papers based on gathered research information.

During the past two summers, Earthwatch volunteers have helped with general farm maintenace, quiviut combing, and urine sample collecting. And UAF graduate student Pam Groves, who helped domesticate some of the Palmer muskox, has done observations and additional work at the Large Animal Research Station. She is now drawing upon her acquired skills in her current research project. In March 1988, she and Dr. Bob White, who supervises University Research, accompanied two muskox, Tanya and Spike (renamed Tanana and Koyuk) to China. Groves remained after White left, to study Takin. This animal, a relative of muskox, is found in Central China and Burma. In December 1988, she returned to Fairbanks, and is now writing her Master's thesis on her findings.

According to Bill, the Alaska Department of Fish and Game has also taken advantage of the research facility. For the past three or four years, tracking collars have been tested on the Fairbanks muskox and caribou. Later, when the collars are attached to their wild counterparts, the researchers are able to study their behavior patterns.

Although research is the primary activity at LARS, tours are still considered important. Not only do tours provide revenue to run the farm, but they also educate people. "We encourage visitors—we like people to know what's going on around here," Bill said.

ANCHORAGE

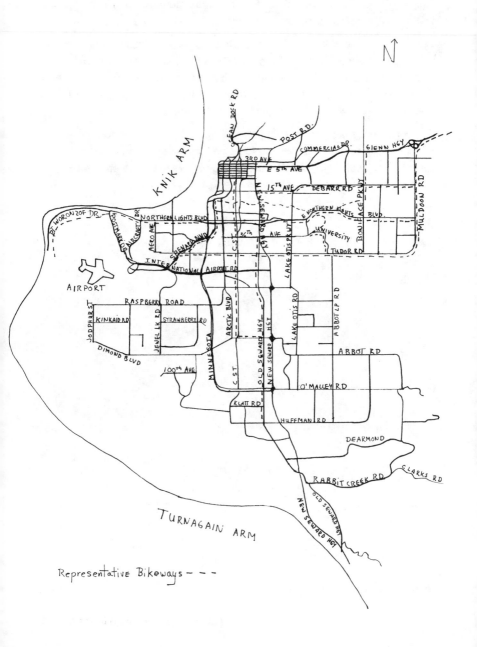

Representative Bikeways – – –

CHAPTER 27: ANCHORAGE

BACKGROUND

In 1914 Congress approved the construction of a railroad to link an Alaskan ocean port with Interior river shipping routes. The Cook Inlet anchorage at the mouth of Ship Creek was chosen as the construction camp and headquarters for the Alaskan Engineering Commission. Shortly after the construction camp was up, the bluff south of the creek was cleared and surveyed. The intersection of Fourth and C Streets eventually became the Anchorage core business district. The federal government named the town Anchorage when a post office was established in 1915. Anchorage was incorporated in 1920.

Anchorage's growth in the past fifty years has been sporadic. In 1917 the Alaska Railroad headquarters were transferred from Seward to Anchorage. The colonization of the Matanuska Valley in the 1930's gave the area economy another boost. Later, in the 1940's, Fort Richardson and Elmendorf Air Force Base were built. After the 1964 Good Friday Earthquake, construction began anew. In the last twenty years, oil discoveries in the Cook Inlet, the development of North Slope Oil fields and the Alaska Pipeline have caused urban growth spurts.

Today the primary area employers are the state, federal and local governments, the military, and the oil, tourism, service and transportation industries. Approximately one half of the state's population live within the city limits. Anchorage's population is approximately 235,000. The economy has slowed in recent years as a result of the softening of the international oil market.

There are numerous civic, cultural, and entertainment opportunities in Anchorage , and the city has 152 parks encompassing 13,200 acres.

Over the past twenty years Anchorage has developed an extensive bike path network. The 135 miles of trails and roadside paths (known as the Anchorage Bikeway Network) have been designed to accommodate multiple recreation use. Incorporated into the bikeway system are tunnels or culverts, and pullouts. The tunnels allow bicyclists and other users to go under roads and railroads. The pullouts, which are used by area trail users as rest stops and pull over areas, also offer nice views.

It costs the city $1,500 a mile per year to maintain the bikeway system. This includes snow removal, weekly inspection and cleaning, repair work, brush removal and winter maintenance. In 1982, the city, realizing that high crime results in decreased use of bicycle trails, developed the Park Ranger program. The Park Rangers provide formal law enforcement for Anchorage parks and trails. The use of Park Rangers improved trail safety and made bike paths seem like a welcome addition to Anchorage area neighborhoods.

Although Anchorage is close to the sea, the climate is drier than one might expect. Protected from excess Pacific moisture by the Kenai Mountains to the south, Anchorage's average annual precipitation is 14 inches. The July average temperature is 58° F, and the July average rainfall is 2 inches. The prevailing winds are from the north.

VISITORS INFORMATION

VISITOR'S CENTER:

The Anchorage Log Cabin Visitor Information Center, located at Fourth Avenue and F Street, is open from 8:30 a.m. to 6 p.m. daily. The center has information on lodging, eating establishments, walking and sight-seeing tours, the performing arts, area parks, adventure opportunities, and a free booklet with many maps; area bikeways and bike trails are marked. Foreign language specialists provide emergency translations. Phone: 274-3531. Bikes are available for use for a deposit. For additional information contact: Anchorage Convention and Visitor's Bureau, 201 East Third Avenue, Anchorage, AK 99501. The All About Anchorage Line (ACVB) has recorded visitor information. Phone: 276-3200.

AIRPORT:

The Anchorage International Airport, approximately seven miles from downtown, on International Airport Road, has two staffed Visitor's Centers. The first is on the lower level for passengers arriving on domestic flights, the second is in the customs secured area of the international terminal. The airport services about 35 Alaskan, domestic and international airlines. Anchorage is the air crossroads of the world.

PUBLIC LIBRARY:

The Z.J. Loussacc Public Library has packets containing maps, tour and visitor information which may circulate. The $37 million facility has an extensive Alaskana section, paintings by noted Alaskan artists Eustace Ziegler and Sydney Laurence, a gift shop, and occasional live entertainment. The library is located on West Sixth Street. Hours: noon to 8 p.m. Monday through Thursday, 10 a.m. to 6 p.m. Friday and Saturday, and noon to 6 p.m. Sunday. Phone: 264-4481.

STATE PARKS:

Information on the Chugach and other Alaska State Parks is available at the Chugach State Park Office, 2601 Commercial Drive. Phone: 279-3413. Friends of Chugach State Park sponsor a series of guest naturalist programs at various points in the park. Phone: 762-2451 or 345-5014.

FOREST SERVICE INFORMATION:

The Chugach National Forest Anchorage District Office is located at Huffman Business Park, Building C, 12050 Industry Way, Anchorage, AK 99515-3512. Phone: 345-5700.

NATIONAL PARK SERVICE:

The NPS Information Center has information on Alaska National Parks, including Lake Clark National Park and Preserve whose headquarters are in Anchorage. Telephone: 271-4243.

MAP INFORMATION:

Topographic maps can be purchased at the USGS office in the Federal Building on Second Avenue. Maps are also available for examination at the University of Alaska library.

Cooperative Extension Service:

The CES office has brochures on wild and edible plants and berries, preparing fish and game, gardening and sourdough cooking. The office is located at 2221 East Northern Lights Boulevard, Suite 240. Phone: 279-5589.

TRAVELLER'S NEEDS

Medical Services:

The area emergency number is 911. Humana Hospital is located at 2801 DeBarr Road. Phone: 276-1131. Providence Hospital is located at 3200 Providence Drive. Phone: 562-2221. For dental emergencies phone: 279-9144.

Groceries:

There are numerous supermarkets and grocery stores throughout Anchorage. Carrs Supermarket is near downtown at 1340 Gambell Street. Muldoon Foodland is located near the Centennial Campground, about half a mile from the Glenn Highway on Muldoon Road. Another Carrs Supermarket is located in the Seward and Dimond Shopping Center at 900 Dimond Blvd.

Bicycling/Outdoor Stores:

Anchorage has at least six bicycle stores and many outdoor stores. R&R Bicycle is located at 908 W. Northern Lights Boulevard. The mechanics do most repairs, including building and truing wheels. R&R stocks Shimano, Suntour, and some Campagnelo components, as well as standard touring equipment. The store is a short distance from local trails, and the staff will provide local trail information. R&R owners are Chuck and Fran Morton; the shop manager is Joe Yates. Hours: 10 a.m. to 7 p.m. Monday through Friday, 9 a.m. to 6 p.m. Saturday, and noon to 5 p.m. Sunday. Phone: 561-5246.

The Schwinn Shop across the street from R&R Bicycles at 1035 W. Northern Lights Boulevard carry Schwinn, Suntour and Shimano parts, top of the line mountain and road bicycles and touring equipment. Hours: 10 a.m. to 7 p.m. weekdays, 10 a.m. to 6 p.m. Saturday, 11 a.m. to 5 p.m. Sunday. Phone: 272-5219. The shop owner is Mike Shupe.

Arirang Bicycle is a full service shop which does repairs. Arirang is located at 929 E. 81st Avenue (Old Seward Highway). Hours: 10 a.m. to 7 p.m. weekdays, 10 a.m. to 6 p.m. Saturday, and 11 a.m. to 6 p.m. Sunday. Phone: 522-1451.

REI has a complete line of bicycle touring gear and componentry and has a staffed repair shop. Stoves, sleeping bags, clothing, and other backpacking gear is sold. The store has an excellent selection of bicycle repair and touring books. REI is located at 2710 Spenard Road, near R&R Bicycle and the Schwinn Shop. Phone: 272-4565.

Barney's Sports Chalet carries quality outdoor equipment including Eureka, Jansport, and Sierra Design Tents and MSR and Svea stoves. Local trail information provided. Barney's is located next to R&R Bicycle at 906 W. Northern Lights Boulevard. Phone: 561-5242. Gary King Sports, one of Alaska's largest sporting goods stores, sells bikes. They are located at 202 East Northern Lights Blvd. (272-5401) and 300 East Dimond Blvd. (522-3003).

Bikes can be rented at America Rents, 3600 Arctic Blvd. (563-3600); Big Boy Toys, 6511 Brayton Drive (349-1425); Mountain Bikers of Alaska, 12701 Reya Drive (345-3960); and Engle Expeditions, 5521 Windflower Circle (563-0706).

BICYCLE TOURS:

Engle Expeditions offers Alaska bicycle tours. Write: Box 90375, Anchorage, AK 99509. Phone: 563-0706 or (800)462-BIKE. Tours are also offered by Copper River Adventures (333-9746).

LODGING/CAMPING:

The three story AYH Youth Hostel has 72 beds, cooking facilities, showers, laundry facilities, a common area, and dining areas. Hostellers must do a daily chore. The nightly fee is $10.00 for members and $15.00 for non-members. Bicycle storage is available. A bulletin board has local restaurant, transportation, for sale, and employment information. Check-in time is from 5 to 10:45 p.m. There is an 11 p.m. curfew and hostellers must be out by 9 a.m. The houseparent is Beth Velkovitz. The hostel is located at 700 H Street, between 7th and 8th streets, across from the ARCO Building. Phone: 276-3635.

The Dogpatch Hostel, a private hostel owned and managed by Stephon and Linda George, is located at 212 East 6th between Barrow and Cordova Streets. Although this hostel is frequented more by local transients than travellers, the George's are very responsible houseparents. The Dogpatch Hostel has full kitchen, and laundry facilities and a garden. There's a strict 11 p.m. curfew and no drugs or alcohol are allowed in the house. The nightly fee is $5.00. Two private rooms are available for a slightly higher fee. Payment must be made in advance. Stephon also runs a private taxi service, The Dogpatch Dispatch.

There are many hotels, motels and bed and breakfast establishments in and around Anchorage. Check at the Visitor's Information Center for more information.

The Centennial Park Campground, at Muldoon Road and the Glenn Highway is city run and has 89 campsites. The campsites, in a wooded area, are close together. The nightly fee is $10.00 for Alaska residents and $12.00 for non-residents. Free showers for campers, but there are no hot or cold controls. Firewood must be purchased and there is a seven day stay limit.

The Lion's Camper Park, located at Boniface Parkway and DeBarr Road has 60 campsites, 10 for tents only. The nightly site fee is $12.00.

POST OFFICE:

The Anchorage Post Office (downtown branch) is located on the lower level of Post Office Mall, on Fourth Avenue. Phone: 266-3340. Zip Code: 99510.

LAUNDRY/SHOWERS:

The Maytag Home Style Laundry has both do it yourself and drop off service. The laundromat is located at Olympic Center at the corner of 36th Avenue and Arctic Boulevard. Hours: 8 a.m. to 8 p.m. Monday through Friday, 9 a.m. to 4 p.m. Saturday and Sunday. In addition, there are about 12 other laundromats in the city. Check the *Yellow Pages*.

ALTERNATIVE TRANSPORTATION:

The Alaska Railroad is located at 411 West First Avenue. Phone 265-2494, or after 5 p.m. 265-2686. For information on the Whittier Shuttle, phone: 265-2607. See Introduction for more information.

Alaska Denali Transit has passenger van service from Anchorage to Haines and offers connections to Denali National Park, Talkeetna, and Fairbanks. For information write: Box 4557, Anchorage, AK 99510. Phone: 273-3234. The city owned People Mover Bus Line provides free transportation within the downtown area.

ENTERTAINMENT AND RECREATION

TRAILS:

Anchorage has roughly 135 miles of paved bikeways. The bikeways parallel many of the major traffic arteries and trails pass through Anchorage's Green Belt area. The Visitor's Center has maps.

MUSEUMS/HISTORICAL SITES:

The Anchorage Museum of History and Art, at Seventh Avenue and A Street, is run by the Municipality of Anchorage. Permanent exhibits in the Alaska Gallery include historical displays of traditional Native tools and clothing, the Alaska Pipeline, and the 1964 Alaska Earthquake. An average of 30 special exhibits are presented each year, along with more than 300 public programs. Hours: 10 a.m. to 6 p.m. Monday through Saturday, 1 to 5 p.m. Sunday. Admission: $2.00.

The Imaginarium, the world's northernmost science discovery center, has hands-on displays and exhibits on Alaska wildlife, marine biology, geology, and physics. The Imaginarium is located at 725 West Fifth Avenue, across from the Westmark Hotel between H and G Streets. Hours: 11 a.m. to 7 p.m. Monday, 9 a.m. to 9 p.m. Tuesday though Saturday, and Noon to 6 p.m. Sunday. Admission: $4.00.

The Alaska Heritage Library-Museum has Native artifacts, artwork, books, photographs and original paintings on display. The museum is located in the National Bank of Alaska Headquarters at 301 West Northern Lights Boulevard. Hours: Noon to 4 p.m. weekdays. Phone: 265-2834.

Aviation memorabilia and rare photographs from more than 100 aviation pioneers are on display at the Alaska Aviation Heritage Museum, located at 4721 Aircraft Drive, Lake Hood. Phone: 248-5325.

The Fort Richardson Alaskan Fish and Wildlife Center includes a display of over 250 mounted Alaskan sportfish, mammals, and birds. Hours: 9 a.m. to 5 p.m. Monday through Friday, 10 a.m. to 4 p.m. Saturday, and noon to 4 p.m. Sunday. Phone: 863-8228 for directions.

Elmendorf Air Force Base also has a wildlife museum. Hours: 10 a.m. to 5 p.m. Monday through Friday, 10 a.m. to 4 p.m. Saturday. Enter from Elmendorf's Boniface gate. Phone: 552-2282 for directions.

The Oscar Anderson House, the city's first wood frame house, now on the *National Register of Historic Places*, is located at the north corner of Elderberry Park, at the west end of Fifth Avenue. Hours: 1 to 4 p.m. daily and 7 to 9 p.m. Monday through Friday. Phone: 274-2336.

The downtown Performing Arts Complex opened in December, 1988 and is reputed to be one of the finest (and most expensive) fine arts facilities in the U.S.

EATING/DRINKING ESTABLISHMENTS:

Over 350 eating establishments in Anchorage serve a wide range of foods. The Downtown Deli, at 1007 W. Third Avenue has good breakfasts and serves sandwiches, burgers, and salads. Prices are moderate. Hours: 7 a.m. to 10 p.m. Monday through Saturday, and 9 a.m. to 4 p.m. Sunday.

The Greek Corner serves Greek and Italian food, and comes highly recommended by the Anchorage AYH staff. The Greek Corner is located at 302 Fireweed Lane. Hours: 11 a.m. to 11 p.m. Monday through Friday, 4 p.m. to 11 p.m. Saturday and Sunday. Phone: 563-2820.

BOOKSTORES:

Cyranos Crepes and Books is located at 413 D Street. The bookstore sells Alaskana, classics, best sellers, fantasies, and autobiographies. Cyranos will order books and conducts out of print book searches. Hours: 10 a.m. to 11 p.m. daily. Adjacent to the bookstore is a small cafe where espresso, crepes and salads are served. The Book Cache, Alaska's largest book chain, has several outlets in Anchorage. In addition to general trade books, some of the stores have excellent Alaskana collections.B. Dalton, Waldenbooks and the Alaska Natural History Association have bookstores in Anchorage.

GIFT SHOPS:

The Fish Stop has lox and smoked salmon to go or they will take your order and ship express mail direct from the processor. The Fish Stop is located at 733 W. 4th Avenue, Suite 617. Phone: 279-5056. The Fish Exchange, run by Seafoods of Alaska, sells lox, kippered, and canned salmon, as well as salmon jerky. The Fish Exchange is located at 800 Ocean Dock Road. Phone: 278-3474.

At Alaska Heritage Arts, paintings, prints, carved stone and ivory, baskets, and masks are designed and made by Alaska Natives. The shop is located at 400 D Street, Club 25 Building. Hours: 10-6 p.m. Monday through Saturday, Noon to 5 p.m. Sunday. Phone: 278-4787.

The Oomingmak Muskox Producer's Cooperative sells garments hand knitted in traditional patterns by Alaska Native villagers. The cooperative is located at 604 H Street. Hours: 10 a.m. to 5 p.m. Monday through Saturday.

MOVIES/PLAYS:

The Alaska Native Summer Performance Series productions are held throughout the day at the Anchorage Museum of History and Art, at 121 West Seventh Avenue. Admission: $2.00.

The Alaska Renaissance Festival is a post -medieval fair featuring numerous craft and fair booths, minstrels and jousting tournaments. The Festival is held the second week in June at Tudor Center. Phone: 276-8161. Admission: $2.00. The Basically Bach Festival is held in mid-June. The festival features a series of four concerts featuring the music of Johann Sebastian Bach and his contemporaries. Phone: 276-2465.

Anchorage has many theatres and offers a wide variety of cultural and sports events. Check a local paper or speak with someone at the Visitor's Center.

PUBLIC RECREATION:

The Anchorage Municipal Parks & Recreation Department at 620 W. 10th Avenue, Third floor, maintains 59 tennis courts, 40 ballfields, 20 community schools, three community centers and 121 miles of trails. The Parks office also has scheduling and price information on public pools. The public is encouraged to use Alaska's only 50-meter pool. Phone: 264-4474.

A listing of state-wide footraces and triathelons is available at R&R Bicycle or write: Box 22-1166, Anchorage, AK 99522. There is usually a summer solstice marathon in June.

The Alaska Zoo is located at Mile 2, O'Malley Road, Anchorage. Hours: 9 a.m. to 6 p.m. daily. Admission is $4.00. Phone: 346-3242.

The Anchorage Municipal Greenhouse in Russian Jack Springs Park has an exhibition house, annual flower displays and a wildflower garden. The 38 acre park has bicycle and walking trails, tennis courts, picnic facilities, a chalet and a snack bar. Hours: 8 a.m. to 3 p.m. Monday through Friday, and 8 a.m. to 2 p.m. Saturday and Sunday. Free admission. Phone: 333-8610.

Earthquake Park, located on Knik Arm, at the west end of Northern Lights Boulevard, has a small visual display on the 1964 Good Friday Earthquake. On the grounds are mounds, that before the earthquake was a small subdivision.

The Chester Creek Greenbelt Park stretches from Westchester Lagoon to Goose Lake. The greenbelt has an extensive number of public parks and a paved bike trail. The greenbelt is easily accessible; Spenard Road leads to Westchester Lagoon and E Street to the Valley of the Moon Park.

ENVIRONMENTAL ISSUES:

The Alaska Center for the Environment is a non-profit environmental advocacy and educational organization dedicated to the conservation of Alaska's natural resources. They have material relating to environmental issues and their office is located at 700 H Street, Room 4, in the same building as the Anchorage Youth Hostel. Phone: 274-3621.

Kenai Peninsula

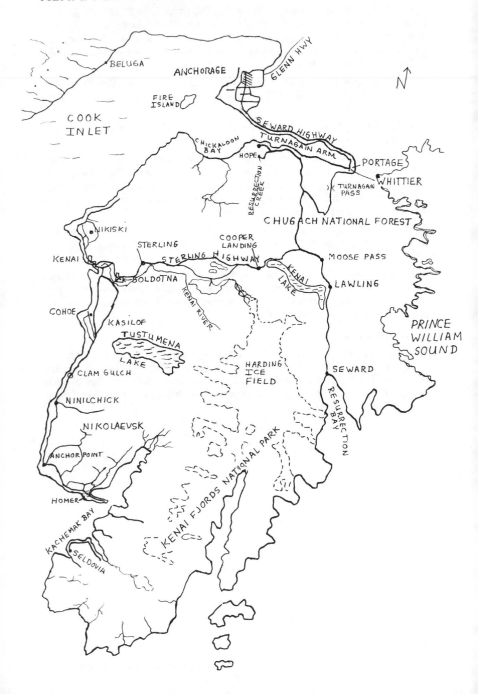

V: Kenai Peninsula

Old Cabin, Hope

CHAPTER 28: THE SEWARD HIGHWAY

BACKGROUND

The 125 mile Seward Highway (Alaska Routes 1 and 9) connect Seward and Anchorage. The highway leads first along the Turnagain Arm of the Cook Inlet, then crosses the Kenai Peninsula and the Chugach National Forest. The ecological terrain along the highway varies. The windy maritime environment of the Turnagain Arm first gives way to the alpine slopes of Turnagain Pass. The road then crosses numerous hills and follows creeks, rivers, and lakes to the lush coastal town of Seward.

For a ways, the highway parallels Turnagain Arm. The long, narrow body of water was named by Captain James Cook in 1778 because when he reached the end of what he thought was a river, he had to "turnagain". Along the Turnagain Arm are flat, sandy areas. These tidal flats, because of quicksand, are extremely dangerous. At least one Anchorage resident was trapped and drowned during the summer of 1988.

The Turnagain Arm winds usually originate from the Portage Glacier, so cyclists heading to Portage from Anchorage may encounter headwinds.

The state mileposts on the Seward Highway begin in Seward and end in Anchorage. Because most cyclists riding the Seward Highway start in Anchorage, road information is given from Anchorage to Seward, and is described using the actual mileposts.

A word of caution: the traffic along the Seward Highway, especially on weekends, is often heavy. Portions of the road are also narrow and winding.

If you are taking the ferry between Whittier, or the Kenai Peninsula and Valdez, we suggest, because of strong southerly winds, riding from Valdez, north.

ROAD INFORMATION: SEWARD HIGHWAY

SECTION 1: MILE 127 (GAMBLE ST./15TH AVE.)-MILE 79 (PORTAGE GLACIER ROAD)

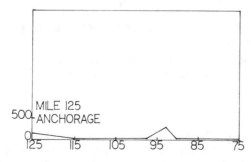

Road Conditions/Terrain:

For the first 12 miles, cyclists must ride on the Old Seward Highway. If riding from downtown and wishing to ride one of the Anchorage bikeways, follow C Street south to Dimond Boulevard. Turn left (east) on Dimond Boulevard. The Dimond Boulevard bikeway leads to the Old Seward Highway, and to a bikeway between Old Seward Highway and New Seward Highway.

Follow either the Old Seward or the bikeway about one and one half miles to O'Malley Road. About two and a half miles from O'Malley Road, the bikeway parallels Old Seward Highway. Follow the Old Seward Highway for three more miles, to the end of the New Seward Highway.

After leaving Anchorage, the Seward Highway parallels the Turnagain Arm, has a wide shoulder and is fairly flat to Mile 97.3. At this point the road becomes winding, narrow and dangerous, and gains and loses about 250 feet to Mile 91.7, where the road again has a wide shoulder and the terrain is level.

Junctions:

Mile 125, Tudor Road. Cyclists traveling north on the Seward Highway and wishing to by-pass Anchorage and connect with the Glenn Highway, turn east (right) on Tudor Road. Tudor Road leads east to Muldoon Road, which leads north to intersect with the Glenn Highway at Mile 4.5. The bypass route is part of the Anchorage Bikeway System. Mile 118.1, Old Seward Highway crosses the New Seward Highway. Mile 114.1, the Old Seward Highway joins the New Seward Highway. This is the end of the New Seward Highway.

Mile 90, Girdwood Junction. Paved Alyeska Boulevard leads 3.2 miles to Alyeska Ski Resort, an AYH hostel, and a few shops. Mile 80.3, Portage Train Station. The 12 mile, 35 minute Whittier Shuttle connects Portage to the town and ferry port of Whittier. In 1988, a one way passage cost $7.50, no reservations required. For more information on the State's Ferry and Railroad Systems, see the Introduction. Mile 79, Portage Glacier Access Road leads 5.5 miles to the Begich-Boggs USFS Visitor's Center.

Water:

Mile 111.8, McHugh Creek. Mile 103, Indian Creek. Mile 101.6, Bird Creek. Mile 90.6, Virgin Creek. Mile 89.8, Glacier Creek. Mile 84.1, Peterson Creek. Mile 80.7, Twenty Mile River. Mile 79.4, Portage Creek.

Camping:

Mile 101.2. Bird Creek Campground, a part of Chugach State Park, has 25 campsites, a trail and a shelter.

There are three USFS campgrounds along the Portage Glacier Access Road. Mile 2.9. Beaver Pond Campground has seven campsites, Mile 3.7. Black Bear Campground has 12 campsites. Mile 4.1. Williwaw Campground has 36 campsites and a nature trail.

Food/Lodging:

For the first ten miles the highway travels through the Anchorage Business District. Mile 103.7. Indian House has a restaurant, bar and rooms. Mile 102.9. Mary Lou's Bar and Liquor Store, owned by Mary Lou Redmond was opened in 1951. Following the 1964 Good Friday Earthquake, the store was moved from the devastated town of Portage, to its present location. Mile 101. B.J. Grocery and Liquor Store sells a limited supply of groceries. The store was opened by Bill Johnston in 1981. Mile 90, Girdwood Station. Grocery store, a donut shop and a laundromat with showers for $3.00. There are many establishments along Alyeska Boulevard east of Girdwood Junction including the Alaska Candle Factory at Mile 0.5. George and Ida Dailey sell homemade candles made from North Slope crude oil and seal oil.

The Alyeska AYH Hostel is located near the Alyeska Ski Resort. Ride two miles from the Girdwood Junction on Alyeska Boulevard to Timberline Drive. Turn right on Timberline Drive and proceed 0.2 miles to Alpina. The hostel is 0.4 miles down Alpina on the right. Look for signs. The six-bed hostel has a sauna but no running water or electricity. If houseparent Walter E. Morgan isn't around, registration and payment is by the honor system. The nightly fee is $8.00.

ROADSIDE SIGHTS:

Mile 115.2, Potter Section House State Historic Site. The Potter Section House was built in 1929 and presently houses historical and interpretive displays, including a railroad diarama built by Max Corey of Palmer. Between Miles 115 and 90.3, the highway travels through Chugach State Park. Mile 110.5, Beluga Point. Interpretive signs explain the bore tides.

Mile 90. At Mile 0.3 Alyeska Boulevard is the Chugach National Forest office, which has trail, campground and public use cabin information. Hours: 8 a.m. to 4:30 p.m. Monday through Saturday. At the end of Alyeska Boulevard is the Alyeska Ski Resort. There are eating establishments and gift shops in the immediate area.

Mile 81, interpretive signs on the Twenty Mile River wildlife. Mile 79. At the Portage Glacier Access Road's end is the Begich-Boggs U.S. Forest Service Visitor's Center, which has interpretive displays, a movie and an excellent view of the glacier.

ROAD INFORMATION: SEWARD HIGHWAY

SECTION 2: MILE 79 (PORTAGE GLACIER ROAD)-MILE 37 (TERN LAKE JCT.)

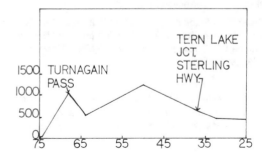

ROAD CONDITIONS/TERRAIN:

For the first four miles, the road is flat. At Ingram Creek, Mile 75.5, the highway climbs to 1,050 feet/320 meter Turnagain Pass at Mile 68. From the pass, the road drops 500 feet to Mile 64.8, then climbs to 1,210 feet at Mile 50. From here, the road is rolling, but drops to Tern Lake Junction (elevation 650 feet). The road has a wide shoulder to Mile 65, where it narrows to about one foot. At Mile 57, a wide shoulder begins.

JUNCTIONS:

Mile 56.7, junction with the Hope Highway. This road leads 17 miles to the town of Hope (pop. 224). Mile 37, Tern Lake Junction. Junction with the Sterling Highway, leading to the western Kenai Peninsula and ending at the town of Homer.

WATER:

Mile 78.2, Placer River. The Alaska Railroad leaves the roadside and follows the Placer River to Upper Trail Lake. Mile 75.5, Ingram Creek. Miles 73.5-71, the road crosses numerous small unnamed streams. Mile 67.9, Lyon Creek. Mile 65.6, Bertha Creek. Mile 65, Spokane Creek. Mile 63.3, Granite Creek. Mile 62, East Fork Six Mile Creek. Mile 61, Silver Tip Creek. Mile 57.6, Dry Gulch Creek. Mile 57.1, Canyon Creek. Mile 48, Fresno Creek. Mile 46, Colorado Creek. Mile 45.7, Summit Lake. Mile 42.6, Summit Creek. Mile 42.2, Quartz Creek. Mile 38.6, Jerome Lake. Mile 37, Tern Lake.

CAMPING/TRAILS:

Mile 65.6. Bertha Creek USFS Campground has 18 campsites, is located 0.5 miles from the highway and has a campground host. Mile 62.9, Granite Creek USFS Campground has 12 campsites. Mile 56.7. At the end of the 17 mile Hope Highway is the USFS Porcupine Campground, which has 24 campsites. Mile 37. Tern Lake USFS Campground has 33 campsites and is located just beyond the junction on the Sterling Highway.

Mile 62.9. Also at the Granite Creek Campground, is the trailhead to the 23 mile, fairly level Johnson Pass Trail. The trail, which follows much of the route of the old Iditarod Trail, meets the Seward Highway at Mile 31.7. Mile 56.7. At Mile 16 of the Hope Highway is the Resurrection Pass Trail. The 33 mile trail climbs over 2,600 foot/793 meter Resurrection Pass, then drops to Mile 53 of the Sterling Highway. This is said to be a good mountain bike trail. From the Sterling Highway, it is possible to travel the Russian Lakes and Resurrection River Trails to Seward.

Mile 39.5, the Devil's Creek Trail leads over 2,400 foot/732 meter Devil's Pass, to connect with the Resurrection Pass Trail. For information on area USFS trails, or public use cabins, stop at the USFS Ranger Station at 0.3 Mile Alyeska Boulevard, or at the Seward USFS Ranger Station.

FOOD/LODGING:

Mile 56.7. At the town of Hope, Mile 17 of the Hope Highway, are two small grocery stores, a cafe, a laundromat, showers and the Hope Post Office. Zip Code: 99605. Mile 45.8. Summit Lake Lodge, owned by Marty and June Arnoldy, has a cafe and showers.

ROADSIDE SIGHTS:

Mile 68.2, 1,050 foot/320 meter Turnagain Pass. There are state rest areas with outhouses on both sides of the highway. Mile 56.7. There is an active historical society and small museum presently located next to the Hope Post Office. Anne Miller, the town postmaster, knows a great deal about the history of Hope.

ROAD INFORMATION: SEWARD HIGHWAY
SECTION 3: MILE 37 (TERN LAKE JCT.) - MILE 0 (SEWARD)

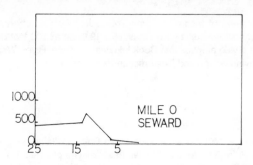

ROAD CONDITIONS/TERRAIN:

At the junction, the road narrows and descends to Upper Trail Lake. The road parallels Trail and Kenai Lakes, and is fairly level to Snow River at Mile 13.7. From the Snow River, the road climbs 200 feet to Mile 12.9, then descends about 700 feet to Seward. At Mile 10.3, the highway widens to its end.

JUNCTIONS:

Mile 3.7. Exit Glacier Spur Road leads nine miles (gravel) to the Exit Glacier Ranger Station and to a short trail which leads to the glacier.

WATER:

Mile 32.1, Moose Creek. Miles 32-25, highway passes Upper and Lower Trail Lakes. Mile 25.6, Trail River. Mile 25, Falls Creek. Mile 24.3, Fish Creek. Mile 23.1, Ptarmigan Creek. Miles 23-17, road parallels Kenai Lake. Mile 19.5, Victor Creek. Mile 17.7, Center Channel Snow River. Mile 17.2, South Fork Snow River. Mile 8.1, Grouse Creek. Mile 6.6, Bear Creek. Mile 3, Resurrection River.

CAMPING/TRAILS:

Mile 24.2. Trail River USFS Campground is 1.5 miles from the highway and has 63 campsites. Mile 23.1. USFS Ptarmigan Creek Campground has 18 campsites. Mile 17.2. USFS Primrose Campground is one mile from the highway and has 10 campsites.

FOOD/LODGING:

Mile 29.5, Moose Pass. Moose Pass (pop. 145) contains the Estes Brothers General Grocery Store, a gift shop, cafe and post office. Zip Code: 99631. The town began as a construction camp along the Alaska Railroad. Moose Pass holds an annual Summer Solstice celebration on the weekend closest to June 21st. Mile 19.7. IRBI Knives, finely crafted handmade knives are made by Irvin and Virgil Campbell.

Mile 18. Snow River AYH Home Hostel has 14 beds. Houseparents Dennis and Robin Helminski adhere strictly to AYH rules. The nightly fee for members is $8.00. Mile

6.8. At Sam's Custom Sewing, repairs can be made to zippers or damaged gear. Phone: 224-3431. Mile 0, Seward.

ROADSIDE SIGHTS:

Mile 32.4. Alaska Department of Fish and Game Trail Lakes Fish Hatchery. Mile 29.5. Water wheel and grindstone built by Ed Estes. Mile 12.9. Small 700 foot divide. Water to the north of this divide empties into Cook Inlet via the Kenai River. Water to the south empties into Blying Sound and Resurrection Bay near Seward.

SEWARD

BACKGROUND

The town of Seward (pop. 2,279) began in 1903 when Frank Ballaine bought the homestead of Mary Lowell for $4,000 and 37 town lots. Ballaine planned to build a railroad from Resurrection Bay to the rich coal reserves of the Matanuska Valley and Healy. The Central Railroad, as it was called, went bankrupt and was taken over by the Alaska Northern Company. In 1911, the company declared bankruptcy, and the partially built railroad was acquired by the U.S. Government. In 1923 the railroad was complete, and Seward and Fairbanks were connected.

The Alaska Railroad, requiring additional space, offered to buy land in and around Seward. However, the owners of the land and railroad officials were unable to agree on a price. For this reason, the railroad's headquarters were moved to its present location in Anchorage.

During the construction of the railroad, Seward became a boom town and was considered by many to be a lawless place. Prostitution was "firmly established" and the town, claimed long time resident John Paulsteiner in his book *Seward Alaska: The Sinful Town on Resurrection Bay*, (1975) was run by the "Dirty Dozen" from around 1911 to the late 1940's. Gang members were rumored to have prevented others from securing bank loans and controlled the city council. When prohibition was passed, the new law "was almost entirely ignored by Sewardites."

After construction of the railroad, Seward became a stable supply center and fishing port. But when the Second World War began, Seward became the center of military operations for the North Pacific. But unlike many other places, Seward's economy stabilized following World War II.

The town was severely damaged by the 1964 Good Friday Earthquake. The disaster claimed thirteen lives, cleared the harbor of all boats and cut Seward off from the rest of the world. Subsequent tidal waves broke the Standard Oil pipelines which set every waterfront building and dock on fire. Since the earthquake, a new railroad dock has been built, but the tracks leading from Mile 1 into town haven't been replaced.

Today Seward has a fishing fleet, a cannery, a Ferry Terminal, a sawmill, and state prison. The Silver Salmon Derby, held in June, attracts thousands of fishing enthusiasts.

The average July temperature in Seward is 56° F. The average July rainfall is 2.8 inches.

VISITORS INFORMATION

VISITOR'S CENTER:

The Seward Information Cache is located in a historic railroad car on the corner of Third Avenue and Jefferson Street. The center has information on lodging and area activities. Hours: 9 a.m. to 5 p.m. For information write: Box 749, Seward, AK 99664. Phone: 224-3094.

FERRY TERMINAL:

The Seward Ferry Terminal is located on the south end of town at Fourth and Railway Avenues. The MV *Tustumena* makes scheduled trips along the Kenai Peninsula, the Aleutian Chain and Norton Sound. The terminal is open when the ferry is in port. Phone: 224-5485.

FOREST SERVICE INFORMATION:

The Seward District Office of the Chugach National Forest is at 334 Fourth Avenue. The office has information on public use rental cabins and trails. The office is open Monday thru Saturday, 8 a.m. to noon and 12:30 to 5 p.m. Write: Box 390, Seward, AK 99664. Phone: 224-3374.

NATIONAL PARK SERVICE:

The Kenai Fjords National Park contains much of the Harding Icefield and the fjords to the south and west of Resurrection Bay. The Park Visitor's Center is located on south Harbor Street near the Harbor Master's Office, and is open from 8 a.m. to 5 p.m. Write: Superintendent, Kenai Fjords National Park, Box 1727, Seward, AK 99664.

TRAVELLER'S NEEDS

MEDICAL SERVICES:

Seward General Hospital is located on First Avenue. Phone: 224-5205. For emergencies phone: 911.

GROCERIES:

Seward Foodmart Supermarket is at Mile 2 Seward Highway. Hours: 8 a.m. to 10 p.m. daily.

BICYCLE/OUTDOOR STORES:

Seward has no bicycle shops.

LODGING/CAMPING:

Seward has no hostels. There are several hotels in Seward; check the Information Cache for price information. Camping is permitted on the beach in designated areas off Jefferson Street. The nightly fee is $4.50. Forest Acres Municipal Campground, located at Mile 2.5 Seward Highway, has running water, and is more sheltered then the city's waterfront campground.

Post Office:

The Seward Post Office is located on Madison Street. Zip Code: 99664.

Laundry/Showers:

Seward Laundry and Dry Cleaners, Fourth Avenue and B Street near the Small Boat Harbor, has showers and drop-off laundry service. Coin operated showers (.75 for five minutes) are available at the Harbor Master's Office near the Small Boat Harbor.

Alternative Transportation:

The Alaska Railroad presently offers thrice weekly service between Seward and Anchorage. See Introduction for more information on the Alaska Railroad.

Entertainment and Recreation

Trails:

The Two Lakes Trail begins on Second Avenue behind the Alaska Vocational Technical Center and goes through Two Lakes Park. The Mount Marathon Trail, which begins on Lowell Street, leads to the top of 3,022 foot/921 meter Mount Marathon. The trail begins on Lowell Street.

Museums/Historical Sites:

The Seward Museum is located in the City Hall basement on the corner of Adams Street and Fifth Avenue. The museum has shipping and railroad artifacts, and exhibits on the Iditarod Trail and the 1964 Good Friday Earthquake. The start of the Iditarod Trail is marked by a metal dog sled on the waterfront near the Ferry Office.

The Seward walking tour begins at the Information Cache at Third Street and Jefferson Avenue and includes short histories on the town's historic structures.

Book Stores:

The Book House at 328 Third Avenue is owned by Dan and Sue Greer and sells used books. Phone: 224-8708.

Movies/Plays:

The University of Alaska Seward Marine Center is open Monday through Saturday and shows educational movies and marine slides. The center has fixed and live marine displays, and is located in the K.M. Rae Building at 125 Third Avenue. The "Quake Story" is shown daily at the Frontier Restaurant. Admission: $3.50. Phone: 224-3040.

Side Trips:

Many charter operators in Seward offer a variety of excursions into the Kenai Fjords National Park.

Public Recreation:

Each year on the Fourth of July Seward holds the nation's second oldest foot race. The Mount Marathon Race is three and a half miles long. The first race was run in 1915.

Caine's Head State Recreation Area is located six miles south of Seward and four miles south of Tonsina Point. Fort McGilvary, an abandoned World War II Army encampment, is set in a rainforest. It is possible to visit the area only when the tide is out.

Ed Estes showing his hydroelectric plant to tourists,
Moose Pass

CHAPTER 29: THE STERLING HIGHWAY

BACKGROUND

The 173 mile Sterling Highway (Alaska Route 1) begins at Tern Lake Junction, at Mile 37 Seward Highway and ends at Homer. The salmon fishing on the Kenai Peninsula is reputed to be the best in the world, and so in the summer months, thousands of fishing enthusiasts migrate to the area. For this reason, travellers and locals alike aren't asked, "Where are you from?" but, "where are the fish?"

When the fish are in, the river and stream banks are lined with anglers. These areas, because of noise, litter and lack of privacy, aren't the best for camping. However, the people-watching here is good, and if you're lucky, someone may part with a freshly caught dolly varden or salmon.

The Sterling Highway, narrow, winding, and paved, can accommodate a moderate traffic load. However, because of the large influx of people in June and July, it is a dangerous road to ride.

All along the highway from Cooper Landing to the end of the Homer Spit, are numerous eating and lodging establishments, suggesting that locals are eager to cash in on what in recent years has become "salmon mania." There are numerous public campgrounds off the Sterling Highway, but when the salmon are running, finding a campsite can be difficult.

The scenery along the Sterling varies. The road from Clam Gulch to Homer parallels Cook Inlet, and although the beach isn't always visible, it's easily accessible via sideroads. The town of Ninilchik, located a short ways off the Sterling Highway, isn't as touristed or as developed as Soldotna, Kenai, or Homer. At the end of the Sterling Highway is the town of Homer. The road leading into Homer is heavily travelled, and narrow, but the roadside offers excellent views of Cook Inlet and the distant mountains.

ROAD INFORMATION: STERLING HIGHWAY

SECTION 1: MILE 37 (TERN LAKE JCT.) - MILE 83.5 (SWANSON RIVER ROAD)

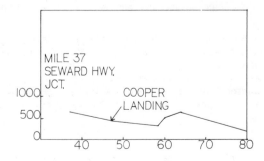

ROAD CONDITIONS/TERRAIN:

The Sterling Highway begins at Mile 37, Seward Highway, that is 37 miles from Seward. (Mileposts show the distance from Seward.) The road has a narrow shoulder, and loses elevation to Mile 58, where the shoulder widens, then climbs to Mile 64. From Mile 64, the road descends to Moose River at Mile 82, then climbs to Mile 83.5. At Mile 80, the shoulder narrows.

JUNCTIONS:

Mile 37, Tern Lake Junction. Beginning of the Sterling Highway at Mile 37 of the Seward Highway. At the junction, two roads form a Y. The northern fork of the Y is at Mile 37.7, Seward Highway; the southern fork is at Mile 37. Mile 45. Quartz Creek Road leads to two U.S. Forest Service Campgrounds. Mile 57.9. Skilak Loop Road (gravel) leads to Skilak Lake and is approximately twenty miles long, rejoining the Sterling Highway at Mile 75.4. Mile 83.5. Swanson River Road (gravel) leads north (right) 18 miles to Swanson River. Scout Lake Loop Road leads south (left) and in seven miles rejoins the Sterling Highway at Mile 85.

WATER:

Mile 37, Tern Lake. Mile 39, Daves Creek. Mile 41, Quartz Creek. Mile 44.2, small creek. Mile 47.8, Kenai River. Mile 50.5, Cooper Creek. Mile 53, Kenai River. Mile 58, Kenai National Wildlife Refuge Information Cabin. (Water Pump) Mile 82.1, Moose River.

CAMPING/TRAILS:

Mile 37.3, Tern Lake USFS Campground has 33 campsites. Mile 44.9. Crescent Creek and Quartz Creek USFS Campgrounds are both located on Quartz Creek Road. Quartz Creek Campground, 0.3 miles from the highway, has 46 campsites. Crescent Creek Campground, three miles from the highway has 13 campsites. Mile 50.5. Cooper Creek USFS Campground has 27 campsites. The campground occupies land along the Kenai River on one side of the highway and along Cooper Creek on the other. Campsites 7-9 on the Cooper Creek side are for tents.

Mile 52.8. Russian River USFS Campground has 83 campsites and is located two miles from the highway. This campground has five different camping sections and is a popular fishing spot. Mile 57.9. There are four U.S. Fish and Wildlife Service (F&WS) Campgrounds along the Skilak Lake Loop Road. Mile 59.8, Jean Lake F&WS Campground has three campsites. Mile 68.5. Kelly Lake and Peterson Lake F&WS Campground (3 campsites each) are about 0.5 miles from the highway. Mile 70.8. Watson Lake F&WS Campground has three campsites and is roughly 0.5 miles from the highway.

Mile 79. Bings Landing State Recreation Site has 37 campsites. Mile 81. Izaak Walton State Recreation Site has 38 campsites. Mile 83.5. Along Swanson River Road are three campgrounds managed by the F&WS. Dolly Varden Lake Campground (Mile 15) has 12 campsites; Rainbow Lake Campground (Mile 16) has four campsites; and Swanson River Campground (Mile 18) has eight campsites. Mile 53, Resurrection Pass Trailhead. The trail leads 38 miles over Resurrection Pass to the town of Hope.

FOOD/LODGING:

Mile 44.7. Sunrise Inn, owned by Dwight and Evelyn Masheimer, has a small cafe and a store with limited groceries. Mile 48.1. Cooper Landing Grocery sells limited groceries and some fresh produce. The store, owned by Howard and Marion Percefull, is open from 9 a.m. to 8 p.m. Monday through Thursday, 8 a.m. to 10 p.m. Friday and Saturday, and 9 a.m. to 9 p.m. on Sunday.

Mile 48. Cooper's Landing Restaurant, owned by Jim and Eula Mae Eltinge, serves homemade soups, stews and pies. On the restaurant wall is a recipe for "Road Kill Surprize." Hours: 6 a.m. to midnight. Mile 48.4. The Shrew's Nest, owned by Larry and Joyce Olsen, sells film, rope, bungi-cords, books, some hardware and other miscellaneous items. Mile 81. Bing Brown's Sportsmen's Service has rooms, canned goods, a laundromat and coin-op showers.

SIDE TRIPS:

Mile 50. The Alaska Rivers Company offers float trips on the Kenai and other Alaskan rivers. Local residents Gary and Carol Galbraith will transport bicycles for customers. Write: Box 827, Cooper Landing, AK 99572. Phone: 595-1226.

ROADSIDE SIGHTS:

Mile 37. Tern Lake interpretive sign explains the migratory patterns of Arctic Terns. Mile 45.6, interpretive sign and observation point for Dall sheep and mountain goats. Mile 50.5. The Charlie Hubbard Mining Museum is open daily except Wednesday and offers gold panning in nearby Cooper Creek.

Mile 54.7. Highway leaves the Chugach National Forest and enters the approximately two million acre Kenai National Wildlife Refuge. The Refuge was established in 1941 by President Roosevelt as the Kenai National Moose Range. Mile 55, Kenai-Russian Rivers USFS Recreation Area. A ferry crosses the river. Telescopes on the near side are for viewing fishing enthusiasts, mountain goats and Dall sheep. Mile 82. Seafoods from Alaska Inc. sells fresh, smoked or canned fish. Tours and free samples available.

ROAD INFORMATION: STERLING HIGHWAY

SECTION 2: MILE 83.5 (SWANSON RIVER ROAD) - MILE 135 (NINILCHIK)

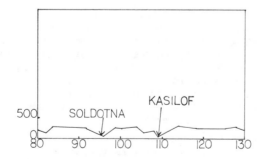

ROAD CONDITIONS/TERRAIN:

The road is mostly level to Mile 91.8, then descends to the town of Soldotna and the Kenai River at Mile 96. After crossing the Kenai, the road climbs close to 200 feet to Mile 98.9, then rolls to Mile 104, where it begins to descend to Kasilof at Mile 109.

From Kasilof, the road climbs roughly 250 feet to Mile 114, then stays approximately level in elevation to Mile 128, where it descends to Ninilchik at Mile 135. In Soldotna at Mile 92, the road becomes four laned and has a wide shoulder. At Mile 96, the road becomes two lanes but retains a wide shoulder to Kasilof.

JUNCTIONS:

Mile 85.7. Road leads a short distance to the Sterling Post Office. Zip Code: 99472. Mile 94.2. Kenai Spur Road leaves the Sterling Highway in downtown Soldotna, and leads 11 miles to the town of Kenai on Cook Inlet. Kenai may also be reached via the Kalifonski Beach Road, a loop road which intersects the Sterling Highway at Mile 96, the north junction, roughly 9.5 miles from Kenai and Mile 108.8, the south junction, roughly 20 miles from Kenai. The Kenai Spur Road and the Kalifonski Beach Road are paved and flat.

Mile 111.5. North junction of the Cohoe Loop Road east (right) and Johnson Lake Road west (left). The 13 mile Cohoe Loop Road leads 6.5 miles to the mouth of the Kasilof River on Cook Inlet, then returns to the Sterling Highway at Mile 114.4. Mile 135. Road leads to the Old Village of Ninilchik and to Ninilchik Beach.

WATER:

Mile 95.9, Kenai River. Mile 109.6, Kasilof River. Mile 135, Ninilchik River.

CAMPING:

Mile 85. Scout Lake State Recreation Site, located near the highway has eight campsites, a shelter and a trail. Less crowded than other nearby campgrounds. Mile 95. Soldotna has two municipal campgrounds. Mile 109.5. Kasilof River State Recreation Site has 16 campsites. Mile 110. Johnson Lake State Recreation Area has 43 campsites and a shelter. Mile 117. Clam Gulch State Recreation Area; beach-front camping and a shelter.

Mile 135, Ninilchik State Recreation Area with three campgrounds. The first, just north of the Ninilchik River, has 35 campsites and a shelter. The second overlooks Cook Inlet and the Ninilchik village and has 12 campsites. The third is a beach-front camping area.

FOOD/LODGING:

Mile 88.3. Longmere Lake Grocery and Liquor Store carries limited groceries and is owned by John Cho. Miles 94-96, highway passes through Soldotna. Mile 109. Kasilof (pop. 643) was settled by the Russians in 1786. The Kasilof Grocery, owned by Don and Kary Rivers, carries limited groceries and some produce, but, says the cashier, no bananas. The store is next to the Kasilof Post Office (Zip Code: 99610). Hours: 7 a.m. to 11 p.m. daily. Mile 109.4. Kasilof River View Restaurant, owned by Jim and Joanne Browning, has an extensive menu.

Mile 118.2. Clamshell Lodge has a laundromat, cafe and showers for $3.00. Mile 118.3. Iditastop sells canned goods, and has local clamming information and rents clamming shovels. Mile 132. The North Bar, owned by Daryl Shaw, offers horseback riding, and live music on Friday and Saturday nights.

NINILCHIK

BACKGROUND

Mile 135. Ninilchik (pop. 450) was settled by employees of the Russian American Company in the early 1800's. The small village, which hosts the Kenai Peninsula State Fair, has many old log cabins and a historic Russian Orthodox Church. The Old Village of Ninilchik lies off the highway at the end of Village Road. Newer businesses line the highway and occupy land a short ways east of the highway.

MEDICAL SERVICES:

The Ninilchik Clinic is located on Kingsley Road, west (right) of the highway. Phone: 567-3412 or 911.

VISITOR'S CENTER:

The Ninilchik Visitor's Center is located in the library at Mile 135.5.

GROCERIES:

Mile 135.8. Ninilchik has two grocery stores. Both sell limited groceries, fresh produce and fishing tackle. Ninilchik General Store, owned by Duane Garratana, opened in 1988. T.J. Grocery, owned by John and Tammy Stass, opened in 1977. The Ninilchik Village Cache, in the Old Village, sells homemade ice cream, cinnamon rolls, snacks and gifts.

LODGING/CAMPING:

Mile 135.8. The Inlet View Cafe and Liquor Store has cabins. Among many interesting statements coming from the afternoon patrons was "No one with a conscience can be a Republican."

For camping information, see Road Information.

LAUNDRY/SHOWERS:

Rub-A-Dub Laundromat is on the corner of Kingsley and Oilwell Roads west (left) of the highway. Laundry and shower facilities are available at Hylen's Camper Park at the junction of the Sterling Highway and Kingsley Road.

POST OFFICE:

The Ninilchik Post Office is located on Kingsley Road. Zip Code: 99639.

MUSEUMS/HISTORICAL SITES:

The Ninilchik Russian Orthodox Church (Transfiguration of Our Lord Church) was built in the late 1800's and sits on a bluff overlooking the Old Village and Cook Inlet. For a closer look at the church, follow the trail behind the store in the Old Ninilchik Village.

SOLDOTNA

BACKGROUND

Soldotna (pop. 3,818) was established in the early 1940's at the junction of the Sterling Highway and Kenai Spur Road. The town was named after Soldotna Creek, a tributary of the Kenai River. The word Soldotna is believed to be derived from either the Russian word "soldat" meaning soldier or from an Indian word "tseldatna," meaning either stream fork or a type of herb.

The average July temperature in Soldotna is 56° F, the average July rainfall is 1.6 inches.

VISITORS INFORMATION

VISITOR'S CENTER:

The Soldotna Visitor's Center is located at Mile 96, on the opposite side of the Kenai River from downtown Soldotna. The center has area maps and information on fishing, lodging and special events such as the Progress Days Celebration, held the last weekend in July. Write: Box 236, Soldotna, AK 99669.

U.S. FISH AND WILDLIFE SERVICE:

The Kenai National Wildlife Refuge Visitor Center and Headquarters is located about a mile from the highway on Ski Hill Road, just past the Kenai River Bridge. The center has displays, a slide show, movies and a staffed information desk.

TRAVELLER'S NEEDS

MEDICAL SERVICES:

Central Peninsula Hospital is located on Hospital Street. Follow the Kenai Spur Road to Corral Street. Turn west (left) on Corral Street and ride to Hospital Street. Phone: 262-4404 or 911.

GROCERIES:

Soldotna has a roadside supermarket, as well as numerous convenience stores.

BICYCLING/OUTDOOR STORES:

Randy's Yamaha, owned by Randy Anderson, is located on the Kenai Spur Road, about 0.5 miles from the Sterling Highway. The shop does repair work, and sells Shimano, Schwinn and Suntour components. Hours: 10 a.m. to 5:30 p.m. Monday through Friday, 10 a.m. to 3 p.m. Saturday.

LODGING/CAMPING:

The Soldotna AYH Youth Hostel, situated in a suburban ranch-style house, has 16 bunks with separate male/female sleeping areas. The hostel has a full kitchen. The nightly fee is $10.25. The hostel is located at 444 West Riverside Avenue. Phone: 262-4369. To reach the hostel, follow the Kenai Spur Road a short ways to Redoubt Avenue. Follow Redoubt Avenue west (left) to south Sterling Street. Follow Sterling Street south (left) to where it ends on Riverview Avenue. Turn west (right) on Riverview Avenue. The hostel is a short distance on the right. For information about area hotels and lodges, check the Visitor's Center.

Soldotna has two municipal campgrounds. Swiftwater Campground is located to the southeast (left) about 0.5 miles from the highway at approximately Mile 94, or just after the road becomes four laned. Centennial Park Campground is located off Kalifonski Beach Road on the other side of the Kenai River Bridge.

POST OFFICE:

The Soldotna Post Office is located off the Kenai Spur Road. Zip Code: 99669.

LAUNDRY/SHOWERS:

North Village Laundry located at Mile 95.2, just before the Kenai River, has showers for $3.00. Hot Tubs and saunas are available at Tubs 'n Fun, owned by Bob Boynton. It is located in the mall near the Kenai Spur Road. Phone: 262-3114.

ALTERNATIVE TRANSPORTATION:

The Soldotna airport is located off Funny River Road.

ENTERTAINMENT AND RECREATION

MUSEUMS/HISTORICAL SITES:

Soldotna has no museum. There are plans to build one near the Visitor's Center.

BOOKSTORES:

The Book Cache is located on the Sterling Highway.

SIDE TRIPS:

The Soldotna Visitor's Center has information on area flightseeing, canoeing, and fly-in fishing.

KENAI

BACKGROUND

Kenai (pop. 6,518), the largest community on the Kenai Peninsula, is located at the mouth of the Kenai River on Cook Inlet. Originally the site of an Indian fishing village, Kenai was settled by the Russian American Company in 1791. The Russians named their trading post St. Nicholas Redoubt. In 1869, the U.S. Army built Fort Kenay, and named it after local Indians. In 1899, a post office was established, and Kenai became the official town name.

Commercial fishing has always been a major economic activity in Kenai. In 1957, oil was discovered in Cook Inlet, and since, petroleum development has contributed greatly to the area's economy.

The average July temperature in Kenai is 54° F. The average July rainfall is 2 inches.

VISITORS INFORMATION

VISITOR'S CENTER:

The Kenai Visitor's Center is located in "Moose Meat" John Heldburg's log cabin on the corner of the Kenai Spur Road and Main Street. "Moose Meat" John got his name because he was generous with his game. Run by the Chamber of Commerce, the Visitor's Center has information on area businesses and activities. Write: Kenai Chamber of Commerce, Box 497 Kenai, AK 99611. Phone: 283-7989.

TRAVELLER'S NEEDS

MEDICAL SERVICES:

For emergencies phone: 262-4404 or 911.

GROCERIES:

Carrs Supermarket is located in the Kenai Mall on the Kenai Spur Road.

BICYCLING/OUTDOOR STORES:

Fred Braun Sporting Goods sells mountain bikes, carries Shimano and Suntour components and does repairs. The store sells sporting goods, white gas and Coleman Stoves. Hours: 9 a.m. to 8 p.m. Monday through Friday, 9 a.m. to 7 p.m. Saturday, and 10 a.m. to 5 p.m. Sunday.Phone: 283-4648.

LODGING/CAMPING:

Kenai presently has no hostel. Information on area lodges and hotels is available at the Kenai Visitor's Center. The City of Kenai Municipal Campground is located behind the National Guard Armory on Forest Drive off the Kenai Spur Road at the west end of town. North of Kenai on the Kenai Spur Road is Bernice Lake State Recreation Site at Mile 23 (11 campsites). At Miles 36 and 39, are two campgrounds in the Captain Cook State Recreation Area.

POST OFFICE:

The Kenai Post Office is located on Caviar Street off the Kenai Spur Road. Zip Code: 99611.

LAUNDRY/SHOWERS:

Kenai Wash and Dry, located on the Kenai Spur Road in downtown Kenai, is open 7 a.m. to midnight and has showers.

ALTERNATIVE TRANSPORTATION:

The Kenai Airport is located on Airport Drive.

ENTERTAINMENT AND RECREATION

MUSEUMS/HISTORICAL SITES:

The Fort Kenay Museum has Russian and pioneer artifacts, an old knitting machine and a few renovated log cabins built by early settlers. The city-run museum is open Monday through Saturday from 10 a.m. to 5 p.m. and is located on the corner of Mission and Overland Avenue, a short distance from the Visitor's Center.

Across the street from the Fort Kenay Museum is the Holy Assumption Russian Orthodox Church. Built around the turn of the century, it is the oldest Russian Orthodox Church in Alaska. The church was designated a National Historic Landmark in 1971. For a small donation, a resident priest provides tours.

At the corner of Mission Street and Main Street is the Beluga Whale Lookout. Mount Iliamna (elevation 10,016 feet/3,054 meters) and Mount Redoubt (elevation 10,197 feet/3,109 meters), both active volcanos, are across the Inlet in Lake Clark National Park and Preserve.

BOOKSTORES:

The Book Cache is located in the Kenai Mall.

SIDE TRIPS:

Check at the Kenai Visitor's Center for information on fishing guides and charter operators.

Public Recreation:

The Kenai Recreation Center has showers for $1.00. The use of the racquetball courts or sauna costs $4.00. Hours: 6 a.m. to 10 p.m. Monday through Saturday and 1 to 10 p.m. Sunday. Kenai has a 18 hole golf course which is located off the Kenai Spur Road. Phone: 283-7500.

ROAD INFORMATION: STERLING HIGHWAY

SECTION 3: MILE 135 (NINILCHIK)-MILE 173 (HOMER)

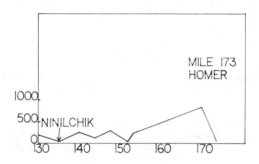

ROAD CONDITIONS/TERRAIN:

From Ninilchik the road climbs 200 feet to Mile 140, then descends to Happy Creek at Mile 143.9. The road then climbs 200 feet to Mile 147.5, before dropping 250 feet to Starski Creek at Mile 151.8. From Starski Creek the road climbs 770 feet to Mile 169.5, then descends into Homer. The road has a narrow shoulder.

JUNCTIONS:

Mile 157, turnoff for Old Sterling Highway. Gravel road parallels the New Sterling Highway on the Inlet side to Mile 165, where it rejoins the highway.

WATER:

Mile 136.6, Deep Creek. Mile 143.9, Happy Valley Creek. Mile 150.7, Starski Creek. Mile 161, Anchor River.

CAMPING:

Mile 138. Deep Creek State Recreation Area has beach camping with no designated campsites. Good clamming during low tide. Mile 151.8. Starski State Recreation Site has 30 sites and is situated on a bluff overlooking Cook Inlet. The campsite at the rear of the campground on the bluff has a good shelter. Mile 157. Anchor River State Recreation Area has 38 campsites and is on the beach. Mile 161.5. Anchor River State Recreation site is located on the banks of the Anchor River, and has walk-in tent sites.

FOOD/LODGING:

Mile 145.2. Happy Valley has a grocery and liquor store, rooms, cafe and a bar. Mile 153.2. Shortstop Camper Park has coin operated showers, a laundromat and sells some groceries and snacks.

Mile 156.3. Anchor Point (pop. 327) is the farthest west point on North America's connected highway system. Anchor Point has a post office (Zip Code: 99556), motel, tackle shop, liquor store, cafe and grocery store. The Waterhole Motel and Cafe has a laundromat and showers. Mile 173, Homer.

ROADSIDE SIGHTS:

Mile 142.5. Rest area with scenic view of Cook Inlet and 10,016 foot /3,054 meter Mount Iliamna. Mile 145.2, Free Museum/ Happy Valley Rodeo Grounds. (The Fourth of July rodeo site.) Mile 148.5, interpretive sign on Mount Redoubt and Mount Iliamna.

HOMER

BACKGROUND

A study of the history of Homer (pop. 4,020) is a study of the history of the Homer Spit, a narrow strip of land that extends from the town of Homer itself, nearly four miles into Kachemak Bay.

Homer was founded in 1898 when Homer Pennock and his Alaska Gold Mining Company brought a crew of 50 men to the area. Despite the lack of nearby fresh water, the town at the end of the Spit grew. For the first ten years, the town's economy was supported by a nearby coal mine at Bluff Point.

In 1907, an act of Congress closed the coal mine. By this time, fishing and other resource industries had been established. In 1939 the Civilian Conservation Corps built a town dock on the spit. The dock was destroyed by ice in the winter of 1947, but this prompted the community to establish a tax system to support a new dock.

During the 1964 Good Friday Earthquake, the spit dropped six feet, and most of the local buildings were destroyed. Since then, millions of dollars have gone into rebuilding and paving the road and supporting the banks against high tides and rough seas.

Today the spit is a business area, a playground for tourists and a seasonal home for cannery workers. On the waterfront are boat charters, restaurants, bars, the Ferry Terminal and a small boat harbor.

As midsummer approaches, the recreational vehicles accumulate and the beachside cannery tenting area takes on a more cluttered appearance as the workers collect and add driftwood, crates and other beach memorabilia to their summer homes. But after Labor Day, the businesses close down, the RVer's go home, and the tent city is disbanded. Human activity on the spit diminishes, but the year round residents, including artists, writers and musicians, continue to enjoy the very scenic area.

VISITORS INFORMATION

VISITOR'S CENTER:

The Pratt Museum, located on Bartlett Street and Pioneer Avenue, has information on lodging, area businesses and sport fishing. Write: Homer Convention and Visitor's Bureau, Box 2706, Homer, AK 99603. Phone: 235-7875.

FERRY TERMINAL:

The Homer Ferry Terminal is located at the end of the Homer Spit and is open when the M/V *Tustamena* is in port. The *Tustamena* runs between Homer and Kodiak Island, Seward, Valdez, and the Aleutian Chain. Phone: 235-8449. A small wooden vessel, the *Danny J.*, connects Homer to other local communities. Phone: 235-8449.

TRAVELLERS NEED'S

MEDICAL SERVICES:

South Peninsula Hospital is located past the Pratt Museum on Bartlett Street and Bayview Avenue. Phone: 235-8101 or 911.

GROCERIES:

Kachemak Food Cache, a full service supermarket, is located on the corner of Pioneer Avenue and Lake Street. Hours: 8 a.m. to 10 p.m. Monday through Saturday. Closed Sundays.

Ribbons Gourmet Fudge, owned by Joyce Turkington and Nancy Sejelstad, sells 17 varieties of homemade fudge and is located on Pioneer Avenue.

Homer Natural Foods at Pioneer Avenue and Bartlett Street, sells teas, bulk food, fresh produce, milk, cheese, and fertile eggs. The store is owned by Ray Hodge. Hours: 8 a.m. to 8 p.m. Monday through Saturday and 10 a.m. to 6 p.m. Sunday.

BICYCLING/OUTDOOR STORES:

Quiet Sports on Pioneer Avenue is owned by Dan Del Missier and sells top of the line backpacking equipment, including Colemen, Svea, and MSR Stoves. The shop also sells mountain bikes, carries Shimano and Suntour components and repairs bikes. Area topographic maps are available. Phone: 235-8620.

LODGING/CAMPING:

Homer has no youth hostel. There are numerous hotels, lodges and bed and breakfasts. The City of Homer operates two campgrounds. Camping is permitted on the beach in several locations on the Homer Spit. The spit tends to be windy, and has no picnic tables or water. Homer's other campground is on a hill above town. To reach the campground, follow Bartlett Street past the Pratt Museum to Fairview Avenue. Turn left (west) and follow Fairview Avenue to Campground Lane. The campground is just up the hill. A $4.00 nightly site fee is charged at each campground.

POST OFFICE:

The Homer Post Office is located on the Homer Bypass near Lake Street. Zip Code: 99603.

LAUNDRY/SHOWERS:

The Washerboard Laundromat on the road to the Homer Spit is large, clean and has showers for $2.25.

ALTERNATIVE TRANSPORTATION:

The Homer Airport is located between Beluga Lake and the Homer Spit.

ENTERTAINMENT AND RECREATION

TRAILS:

Quiet Sports on Pioneer Avenue has information on area trails.

MUSEUMS/HISTORICAL SITES:

The Pratt Museum, at 3779 Bartlett Street, is one of the most impressive public small town museums in Alaska. The museum houses Native and pioneer artifacts, as well as an art gallery, a marine exhibit including two marine aquariums, and an outdoor botanical garden with native plants. Hours: 10 a.m. to 5 p.m. daily.

EATING/DRINKING ESTABLISHMENTS:

Fresh Sourdough Express Bakery and Cafe serves breakfast to 11 a.m. and sells delicious baked goods. The bakery offers all you can eat salmon and halibut, and has vegetarian food on the menu. Sourdough Express is owned by Donna Goodman. Hours: 6 a.m. to 10 p.m. daily.

The Salty Dawg Bar, first opened in 1957, is made from two of Homer's oldest cabins. The rustic bar with sawdust on the floor, is located at the end of the Homer Spit and is popular with fishing enthusiasts, commerical fishermen, and tourists.

BOOKSTORES:

The Bookstore, in Lakeside Mall on Lake Street, sells classics, Alaskana, and Native books. Owned by Lee and Joy Post, the store has been open for "13 or 14 years."

The Book Exchange, open Monday through Saturday from noon to 6 p.m., sells used books.

MOVIES/PLAYS:

The Homer Family Theater, on the corner of Main Street and Pioneer Avenue, is open nightly. Phone: 235-6728.

SIDE TRIPS:

Kachemak Bay State Park is a 250,000 acre park across the bay from Homer. The Kachemak Bay Ferry leaves the Homer Spit daily for Halibut Cove. (For current schedule check the Pratt Museum Visitor Center).

Halibut Cove has a State Park Ranger Station as well as a network of trails and campsites. The M.V. *Tustumena* runs from Homer to Kodiak twice weekly. Kodiak Island is Alaska's largest island, and has nearly 100 miles of roads. The town of Kodiak is the largest town on the island, (pop. 6,175) and commercial fishing is the main industry. There is no bicycle store on Kodiak, but there are full visitor facilities.

The town's average July temperature is 54° F. The average July rainfall is 3.7 inches.

Public Recreation:

The Homer High School Swimming Pool is open for lap and family swims. Phone: 235-7416 for current schedule.

VI: THE NATIONAL PARKS ROADS

CHAPTER 30: DENALI NATIONAL PARK AND PRESERVE

BACKGROUND

Denali National Park and Preserve was established through the efforts of naturalist Charles Sheldon who was determined to preserve the wilderness he called Denali. As chairman of the Boone and Crockett Club, he spearheaded a political struggle that included the efforts of many, including Judge James Wickersham. In 1917 Congress approved a bill that Sheldon personally delivered for signature to Woodrow Wilson, and Mount McKinley National Park was established.

Today the Park is enjoyed by backpackers, bicyclists, and tourists alike. The Park has only one main road, which extends 86.4 miles from the Park entrance at Mile 237.3 Parks Highway to Wonder Lake. The road actually continues an additional 6.5 miles to privately owned Kantishna Lodge in the Preserve. The first 12 miles are paved, and the rest of the road has a hard packed dirt surface. The Park has implemented the use of shuttle buses, which run daily from Riley Creek Information Center to Eielson Visitor Center and on to Wonder Lake. The round trip to Eielson Visitor Center takes 8 hours; to Wonder Lake, approximately 11 hours.

The buses make regularly scheduled stops along the road for wildlife viewing. Park users may get on or off the buses in almost any given area. However, this is discouraged in the Sable Pass due to the large numbers of bears.

Bicycles may be placed on shuttle buses and removed at any given point in the Park, providing the buses aren't full. According to Park Ranger Jane Anderson, the Park's position on bicycle use has not yet been firmly established. It is possible that in the near future bicycle use may be outlawed or that buses may be fitted with bike racks.

For those who wish to camp off the road, it is best to leave bicycles at Morino Park Campground or Park Headquarters since there are no "official" places for bikes. Said Anderson, Morino Campground may have bicycle racks in the near future.

The Morino, Savage River, Sanctuary, Igloo, and Wonder Lake Campgrounds are the best roadside camping areas. Morino, located near the park entrance, is free. This somewhat open camping area is a good place to meet other campers, and is seldom full. Information on space availability at the campgrounds is available at the Park Visitor Center. It is not possible to reserve campsites.

Morino and all the campgrounds have bear-proof food storage lockers and garbage containers. However, Morino does not have water. Water can be obtained at McKinley Mercantile, or in the Denali Park Hotel bathrooms.

A free backcountry use permit for overnight camping must be obtained and then returned when the trip is complete. Permits are issued in the summer at Riley Creek Information Center. A stove is recommended for backpacking. All garbage must be packed out.

The park contains a great deal of wildlife, including wolf, caribou, moose, and bear populations. There have been no bear fatalities at Denali. From 1972-1980, the number of bear encounters has increased three to five fold. During the same period the number of visitors has increased ten-fold. In the early 1970's there were about 50,000 visitors annually; In 1988 it is estimated there were over 500,000 visitors.

The Visitor's Center sells books, maps, and brochures as well as *The Denali Road Guide*, (Alaska Natural History Association, 1986) which has information on plants and wildlife and area geology. The park newspaper, *Denali Alpenglow*, has Park and area business information. Naturalist activities and schedules are listed in the *Alpenglow* as well as on campground and hotel bulletin boards, and at the Park offices.

The weather in Denali Park is unpredictable in May, early June, and in mid-September, and may delay the opening and closing of park roads and facilities. Phone: 683-2686 for information.

The average July temperature at the park entrance is 54° F. The average rainfall is 2.8 inches.

ROAD INFORMATION: DENALI PARK ROAD

SECTION 1: MILE 0 (JCT. OF THE PARK ROAD WITH THE PARKS HIGHWAY)- MILE 46 (POLYCHROME PASS)

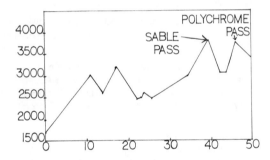

ROAD CONDITIONS/TERRAIN:

The first 14.8 miles of the road is paved, and the first 10.3 miles has a 1,300 foot climb. The road continues to be hilly and quite rolling with a good climb to 3,800 foot/1,189 meter Sable Pass at Mile 39.1. From Sable Pass the road descends nearly 800 feet to the East Fork Toklat River, then climbs 660 feet to Polychrome Pass at Mile 46.

JUNCTIONS:

Mile 0.2. Entrance to Riley Creek Campground and old Visitor's Center. Mile 0.6, new Visitor's Center and shuttle bus staging area. Mile 1.5, Denali Park Railroad Station and access road to Denali Park Hotel. Mile 1.7, Morino Campground entrance. Mile 3.4, Park Headquarters. Mile 12.7, Savage River checkpoint. Visitors must show fee receipt to venture beyond this point.

WATER:

Mile 3.3, Rock Creek. Mile 7, small creek. Mile 14.8, Savage River. Mile 16.9, small creek. Mile 20.3, small creek. Mile 21.1, Hogan Creek. Mile 22.7, Sanctuary River. A water pump is just across the river. Mile 26.3, small creek. Mile 31.4, Teklanika River. Mile 34.1, Igloo Creek. A water pump is near the ranger cabin. Mile 35.9, small creek. Mile 43.4, East Fork Toklat River.

CAMPING:

Mile 0.2. Riley Creek Campground has 102 campsites with a nightly site fee of $8.00. Mile 1.7. Morino Campground is a large area with scattered picnic tables for tent camping only. Camping is free, and highly recommended. Mile 12.9. Savage River Campground has 29 campsites. Mile 22.9. Sanctuary Campground has seven campsites, all good for tenting. Mile 29.1. Teklanika Campground has 50 campsites, only a few are good for tenters. Mile 34.1. Igloo Creek Campground has seven campsites for tents only. This is a nice campground. Make reservations and pay fees at the Visitor's Center.

FOOD/LODGING:

Mile 1.4. McKinley Mercantile sells limited groceries, some fresh produce and beer. Prices are high. Showers cost $2.00. Mile 1.5. The Denali Park Hotel has a gift shop, an auditorium, a cafeteria and a dining room. For information or reservations for area hotels and lodges write: Central Reservations, Box 200984, Anchorage, AK 99520. Phone: 274-5366.

ROADSIDE SIGHTS:

Mile 3.4, Park Headquarters. Twice daily sled dog demonstrations. Mile 7. The road leaves the lower elevation tiaga forest and enters the hardier tundra region. Tiaga, a Russian word meaning land of little sticks, is a forest which contains black and white spruce, birch, aspen, and alder. Tundra, another Russian word, has come to mean flora and fauna of any open treeless, arctic region area. Lower elevation tundra, because of moist conditions, tends to be shrubby and contains scrub birch, willow, and grasses and sedges. With elevation increases, the conditions become harsher and the tundra becomes correspondingly less scrubby, lower, and more fragile.

Mile 11.7, interpretive sign and road view of Mount McKinley. Mile 17.3, last view of Mount McKinley for the next 20 miles. Miles 38.3-42.9. Land on both sides of the road is protected grizzly bear habitat and is closed to access. Mile 39.1, Sable Pass (3,900 feet/1,189 meter). The Sable Pass area supports a large population of grizzly bears. The Toklat grizzly bears, common to Denali National Park, subsist on a low meat diet and are about one third smaller in size than their fish eating cousins who inhabit other regions in the state.

Mile 43. View of the East Fork Ranger Station. One of the two area cabins housed famed naturalist Adolf Murie who studied the park's wolves. The cabin is now used by researchers. Mile 45.9. Polychrome Pass, 3,700 feet/1,128 meters, so named for the multi-colored landscape. There is a bus stop rest area with outhouses.

ROAD INFORMATION: DENALI PARK ROAD
SECTION 2: MILE 46 (POLYCHROME PASS)-MILE 86 (WONDER LAKE)

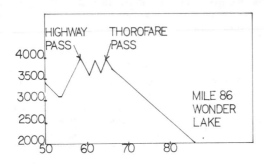

ROAD CONDITIONS/TERRAIN:

From Polychrome Pass, the road drops 600 feet to the Toklat River. From the Toklat River, the road climbs 890 feet to Highway Pass, and is rolling with gains and losses of 300 feet to Thoroughfare Pass. After Thoroughfare Pass, the road is mostly downhill and there is an elevation loss of about 2,000 feet to Wonder Lake.

JUNCTIONS:

Mile 84.6, road to Wonder Lake Campground. The road (north) leads to the Kantishna Mining District.

WATER:

Mile 50.1, small creek. Mile 53.2, Toklat River. Mile 56.6, small creek. Mile 60.6, Stony Creek. Mile 63.1, small creek. Mile 66. The Eielson Visitor Center has running water. Mile 86, Wonder Lake Campground.

CAMPING:

Mile 86. Wonder Lake has 20 campsites (tent camping only). The NPS plans to expand it to 30 campsites. Wonder Lake is 28 miles from Mount McKinley.

FOOD/LODGING:

None

ROADSIDE SIGHTS:

Mile 53.1, two commemorative plaques. The first commemorates Harry Karstens, the Park's first superintendent and second person to stand on the summit of Mount McKinley. The second plaque commemorates Charles Sheldon, who was the first person to study the Denali region, when he wintered on the Toklat River in 1907-08.

Mile 58.3, Highway Pass. At 3,980 feet/1,213 meters, this is the highest point on the Denali Park Road. Mile 60.6. North, down the canyon of Stony Creek, is Bergh Lake. The lake was formed in the summer of 1953 after a landslide blocked Stony Creek. Mile 61.9, Stony Hill Overlook. Mile 64.5, Thorofare Pass (3,950 feet/1,204 meters.)

Mile 66, Eielson Visitor Center. Information on park wildlife and geology, as well as books. Mount McKinley is 33 miles away.

The average July temperature at the Visitor Center is 50° F. The average July rainfall is 5.6 inches. Mile 67.3. Muldrow Glacier, the largest glacier in Denali National Park, is visible for several miles.

Nabesna and McCarthy Roads

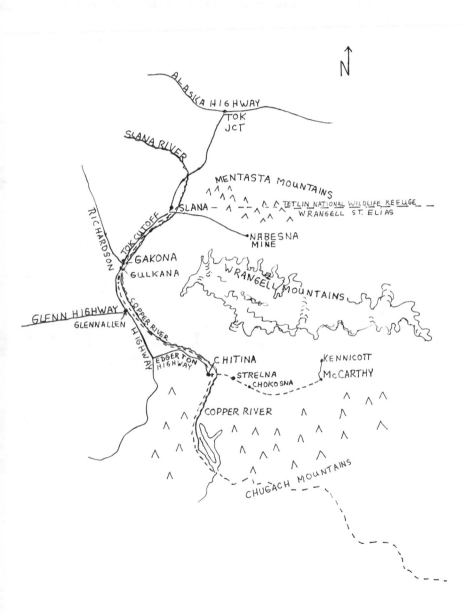

Chapter 31: Wrangell-St. Elias National Park and Preserve

Background

At 12.5 million acres, Wrangell-St. Elias National Park and Preserve is six times larger than Yellowstone, and by far the Nation's largest National Park. The Park borders Canada's Kluane National Park, the two of them comprising the world's largest (19 million acres) non-polar icefield and highest collection of peaks in North America. In October, 1979, the two adjoining National Parks were designated a World Heritage Site by the United Nations and have been labelled "North America's Mountain Kingdom."

Though vast and seemingly impenetrable, the Park is the site of many early mining operations including the Kennicott Copper Mine and the Nabesna Gold Mine, which were once large scale operations.

Care should be taken not to trespass on privately owned property. Some Park areas such as mines, Native claims or homesteads are privately owned. For information write: Superintendent, Wrangell-St. Elias NP/P, Box 29, Glennallen, AK 99588. Phone: 822-5234.

Nabesna Road

Background

The Nabesna Road, built in the early 1900's, was originally a trail leading to the Nabesna Mining area. During World War II it was used as a military road to Reeve's Field on the Nabesna River. The mine closed during World War II, and was never reopened but the road continued to be used.

Although almost completely in the Wrangell-St. Elias NP/P, the state maintained road is in bad shape. Most tourists that aren't turned around by the road's rough surface are halted by a handful of stream crossings which begin at Mile 29.4.

The lack of tourist traffic has hindered Nabesna roadside businesses. There has been a decline in the number of hunters since the formation of the Park and Preserve. Many hunters mistakenly believe that hunting is no longer allowed in the Preserve. In the future, the demand for easier access into the Park will result in road improvements which should indirectly help area lodges.

For the time being, the road's lack of traffic makes it an excellent cycling road for mountain bikers. The road may, however, be difficult for individuals riding touring bicycles with narrow tires.

ROAD INFORMATION: NABESNA ROAD
SECTION 1: MILE 0 (MILE 60, TOK CUTOFF) - MILE 46 (NABESNA MINE)

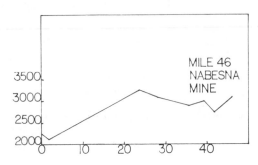

ROAD CONDITIONS/TERRAIN:

Within the first 1.7 miles, the road drops 100 feet, then has occasional rollers, but travels upwards climbing 1,100 feet to Mile 23.8. The road becomes increasingly more rolling, but loses about 500 feet by Mile 41.8. From here, it is about a 400 foot climb to the Nabesna Mine. The road is paved for the first 1.5 miles, then gravel for the remainder. Trail Creek, at Mile 29.4, and Lost Creek at Mile 31.2 may, depending upon rainfall, cross the road. Be prepared to get wet. From Trail Creek the road becomes rougher and is less trafficked. Road maintenance ends at Mile 42. The road from Mile 42 is rough, torn up ground, and seldom travelled.

WATER:

Mile 1.7, Slana River. Mile 6.2, Rufus Creek. Mile 12.1, Caribou Creek. Mile 18.6, Caribou Creek. Mile 21.5, Rock Creek. Mile 22.2, Rock Lake. Mile 22.8, Long Lake. Mile 29.4, Trail Creek (rises quickly, may cross road). Mile 31.2, Lost Creek. Mile 32.1, Chalk Creek. Mile 33.8, Radiator Creek. Mile 35.8, Jack Creek. Mile 43, Jacksina Creek.

CAMPING/TRAILS:

There are no official campgrounds along this road. Camping is possible along any one of the above mentioned creeks, though check to make sure it is not private property.

Mile 9.1, Batzulneta's Trailhead. Mile 11.2, Suslot Lake Trailhead # 1. Mile 12.4, Copper Lake Trailhead. Mile 24.5, Tanda Lake Trailhead. Mile 29.4, Trail Creek Trailhead. Mile 31.2, Lost Creek Trailhead. Mile 41, Reeve's Field and Nabesna River Trailhead.

FOOD/LODGING:

Mile 2. Dave's Country Store sells some groceries. Area trail information available. Mile 25.5. Silvertip Lodge, open since 1960, is owned by Tom Bertrand. The lodge provides flightseeing trips and fly-in fishing to tent camps or cabins. Breakfast, lunch, and some dinners are served, but meals are mostly for clients. Mile 28.5. Sportsmen's Paradise Lodge, owned by Dick and Lucille Frederick, has been open since 1969. The lodge has a bar which serves sandwiches. Showers cost $3.00. Cabins available for $25, include the use of shower facilities. A boat on a lake is also for rent. Mile 42. Devil's Mountain Lodge is primarily a hunting lodge, and offers no services until fall.

ROADSIDE SIGHTS:

Mile 0.2. The Wrangell-St. Elias National Park and Preserve Slana Ranger Station is on the right side of the road. The staff has current information on road conditions, as well as detailed area maps.

The further one rides on this road, the more spectacular the scenery, with the last 15 miles being the best. Miles 2.7-4. The road forms the Parks and Preserve boundary. Mile 4, Wrangell-St. Elias NP/P boundary. Land to the south of the road is in the Park, and land to the north of the road is in the Preserve.

Mile 25, watershed divide. Water before the divide drains into the Gulf of Alaska via the Copper River. Water beyond the divide drains into the Bering Sea via the Nabesna, Tanana, and Yukon Rivers. Mile 28.5. End of northern Park boundary, Preserve on both sides of the road. Mile 42, end of the state maintained road. The Nabesna Mine is about five miles beyond. Owner Kirk Stanley, or a caretaker should be on the property. Check in with him and get permission before exploring. Firearms are prohibited.

The average July temperature in Nabesna is 52F. The average rainfall is 3.2 inches.

CHAPTER 32: THE EDGERTON HIGHWAY

BACKGROUND

Named for Major Glenn Edgerton of the Alaska Road Commission, the Edgerton Highway (Alaska Route 10) leads 33 miles to the town of Chitina and the beginning of the 61 mile McCarthy Road. The scenic road travels through farming country up the Copper River Valley, where there are excellent views of the Copper River.

ROAD INFORMATION: EDGERTON HIGHWAY

SECTION 1: MILE 0 (MILE 82.6, RICHARDSON HIGHWAY)-MILE 33 (CHITINA)

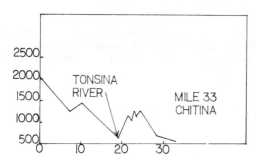

ROAD CONDITIONS/TERRAIN:

There are a few rollers, but for the most part, the road drops 1,390 feet to the Tonsina River at Mile 19.2. From the Tonsina River, there is a hard 500 foot climb to Mile 21.6. From Mile 21.6 the road is rolling to Mile 24.5, where it begins a 700 foot descent to Chitina. The road is paved, with a medium to narrow shoulder.

JUNCTIONS:

Mile 7.3. Old Edgerton Loop Road (gravel) leads eight miles to Mile 91, Richardson Highway.

WATER:

Mile 7.2, Willow Creek. Mile 19.2, Tonsina River. Mile 23.5, Liberty Creek. Mile 28.7, Five Mile Creek. Mile 30, Three Mile Lake. Mile 31, Two Mile Lake. Mile 32, One Mile Lake.

CAMPING:

Mile 23.5. Liberty Falls State Recreation Site has eight campsites and a trail.

FOOD/LODGING:

Mile 7.2. Kenny Lake Mercantile, a small grocery store, has limited groceries. Hours: 9 a.m. to 9 p.m. daily. Mile 33. Chitina.

CHITINA

BACKGROUND

Chitina (pop. 40) was established in about 1908 as a railroad and mining supply town on the Copper River and Northwestern Railroad. The town is at or near the site of an Athabaskan village on the banks of the Copper River. Although the Copper River has a very high silt content, it supports one of the state's largest salmon runs. When the salmon are in, they are collected with fishwheels. Many local residents provide boat transportation for subsistence fish gatherers, who catch their winter supply with dipnets.

VISITOR'S CENTER:

The Wrangell-St. Elias NP/P Chitina Ranger Station is located in Chitina. Park information, as well as information on the current condition of the McCarthy Road is available. Write: Box 110, Chitina, AK 99566. Phone: 823-2005.

LODGING/CAMPING:

The Copper Nugget has rooms and a cafe serving breakfast, lunch and dinner. A Department of Transportation campground is located on the opposite side of the river from town, at the beginning of the McCarthy Road. This campground may be windy and dusty.

POST OFFICE:

The Chitina Post Office was established in 1910. Zip Code: 99566.

McCARTHY ROAD

BACKGROUND

The rich copper deposits of the Kennicott were first discovered by the Copper River Indians. During the turn of the century, prospectors began staking claims along the east side of the Kennicott Glacier. One group of prospectors sold an interest in their claim "The Bonanza," to a young mining engineer named Stephen Birch. Birch then persuaded some very influential people, including the House of Morgan and the Guggenheims, to buy out the remaining claims, thus forming the Alaska Syndicate, and later, the Kennecott Copper Corporation. (Notice that the corporation name has a different spelling.)

Were it not for the mine's extremely rich ore, most likely it would have remained undeveloped. Most copper mines in the Lower 48 have an average yield of about two percent copper. The veins of the Kennicott Mine yielded an average of 12.7 percent, and occasionally as much as 70 percent of the valuable element.

To transport the ore out of its remote setting, the 23 million dollar Copper River and Northwestern Railway was built by Michael J. Heney, the same contractor who constructed the White Pass and Yukon Railroad. The railroad was in operation from 1911 until 1938 when the high grade ore veins were depleted.

The mining company town of Kennicott, consisted of a power plant, hospital, dormitories, dairy, school, a tennis court, and housed over 600 people. The town buildings, painted the corporate colors of red with white trim, are still standing, but are badly in need of renovation. Kennicott was listed on the the *National Register of*

Historic Places in 1976, and there is talk locally of the National Park Service acquiring the land and restoring privately owned buildings.

The state is considering upgrading the McCarthy Road and constructing a bridge over the Kennicott River, thus replacing the two hand operated trams. According to McCarthy Lodge owner Betty Hickling, the many residents and business owners would like to see a foot bridge built across the river. She added, the residents aren't necessarily against road upgrading, but don't want to see the road paved.

The two trams span two branches of the Kennicott River. In recent years many items, including the McCarthy Lodge refrigerator have been transported by tram across the river. The trams are technically state maintained, but the locals do much of the maintenance work.

There are hooks on the sides of both trams, so bicycles can be "hung" on the carriers. We suggest that cyclists bungi or tie their bicycles to the trams, and if concerned about the paint job, wrap a cloth around the top tube. A pair of gloves will prevent rope burns. Lastly, if you're pulling yourself across, and someone on the other side appears to help, be careful: hands can easily be pulled into the pulleys.

The McCarthy road sees more RV and car traffic than the Nabesna Road. Despite the traffic, it is still an excellent bike ride.

ROAD INFORMATION: MCCARTHY ROAD

SECTION 1: MILE 0 (EAST END OF COPPER RIVER BRIDGE)-MILE 61 (KENNICOTT RIVER)

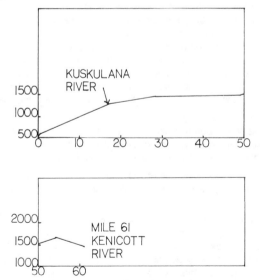

ROAD CONDITIONS/TERRAIN:

The road follows the old railroad bed and has only a few steep hills. There is a short steep climb at the beginning of the road, and a few river crossings where old railroad trestles are no longer functional. From the Copper River (elevation 500 feet) the road climbs gradually to Mile 54 (elevation 1,650 feet). The road then drops 200 feet to the Kennicott River.

JUNCTIONS:

Mile 13.5. Access road leads 3.5 miles to backcountry trailheads: Nugget Creek Trail, Dixie Pass Trail, and Katsina Trail.

WATER:

Mile 0, Copper River. Mile 13.9, Strelna Creek. Mile 17, Kuskulana River. The 525 foot span bridge was built in 1910, and is 238 feet above the river. Mile 28, Chokosna Creek. Mile 28.5, Gilahina River. Mile 27.9, small pond. Miles 31.1, 40.5, small creeks. Mile 41.6, Crystal Creek. Mile 41.7, Crystal Lake. Mile 44, Lakina River. Miles 45.6 to 48.2, road parallels Long Lake. Mile 53.6, West Fork Tractor Creek. Mile 54.5, East Fork Tractor Creek. Mile 57.2, Swift Creek. Mile 61, Kennicott River.

CAMPING:

With the exception of the Kuskulana River, which is inaccessible, camping is possible at all of the above mentioned creeks and rivers. Some land around Crystal and Long Lakes is privately owned.

FOOD/LODGING:

Mile 11. Nelson's Lakeside Camping is a privately owned campground situated on the banks of Sculpin Lake. The nightly site fee is $5.00. Soda, candy, and rental rowboats are available. Mile 61. McCarthy is about a quarter of a mile distant from the far side of the Kennicott River. Kennicott is about five miles north of McCarthy. There are two ways to get to Kennicott. The standard way is to follow the old railway grade. This road has a hard packed dirt surface, and leads gradually uphill to Kennicott. A less used route is the old wagon road, a rough and slightly overgrown trail that begins about 0.2 miles from the museum, across from Tony Zac's house, and leads past an old cemetery and emerges at Kennicott next to the old school. About 0.6 miles up the old wagon road, is a road leading to the foot of the Kennicott Glacier.

McCarthy has more services than Kennicott. In the old McCarthy railroad depot is the McCarthy-Kennicott Historical Museum which includes historic mine and railroad construction photographs as well as pioneer and mining artifacts.

Unlike the company town, McCarthy allowed alcohol, prostitution, and gambling. When miners had a chance, which wasn't often, they hiked to McCarthy for entertainment.

Only a handful of people live year round in McCarthy. Most own tourist related establishments. C.J.'s Wrangell Mountain Country Store sells limited groceries and fresh fruit and is open daily except Tuesdays from 9 a.m. to 6 p.m. The McCarthy Lodge, owned by Gary and Betty Hickling, provides rooms in the historic Ma Johnson Hotel, built in 1916, and has a cheaper bunkhouse hostel. The lodge also has a cafe and saloon, showers for $5.00, and a sauna. For information, write: McCarthy Lodge, McCarthy, AK 99588 or contact Doug and Nan Ogden. Phone: 333-5402 or 373-6909.

St. Elias Alpine Guides, located in the old Mother Lode Powerhouse, (on the *National Register of Historic Places*) provides bread and breakfast accommodations, raft trips, and glacier treks. They specialize in leading first ascents in the Wrangell and St. Elias Mountains. For information contact: St. Elias Alpine Guides, Box 111241, Anchorage, AK 99511. Phone: 277-6867.

Up in Kennicott is the Kennicott Glacier Lodge. Traditionally, this hotel has catered more to the "upper crust" than the McCarthy Hotel, and this still holds true today. The lodge was reopened by Richard Kirkwood in 1987.

Author on tram crossing Kennicott River

VII: THE ARCTIC CIRCLE RIDES

DEMPSTER HIGHWAY

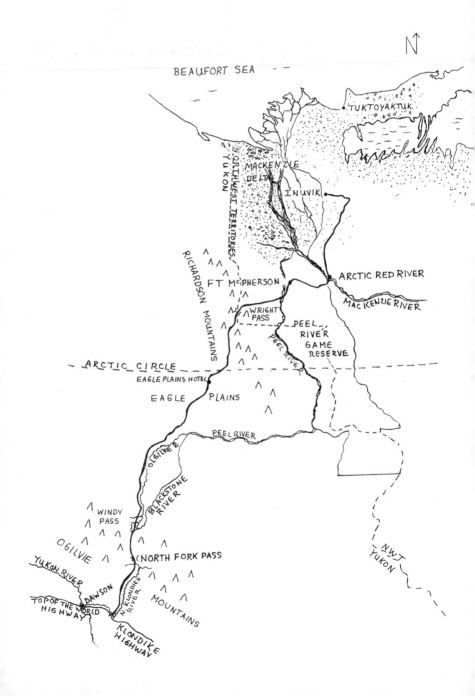

CHAPTER 33: THE DEMPSTER HIGHWAY

BACKGROUND

The 736 kilometer Dempster Highway (Yukon Route 5 and Northwest Territories Route 8) is one of the best northern bicycling roads. However, like Alaska's Dalton Highway, a gravel road surface, hills, unpredictable weather, mosquitoes, and limited food stores and water stops make cycling difficult. For these reasons, only those who are in good shape and have prepared properly should ride the Dempster. This highway shouldn't be rushed. The Dempster is surrounded by some of the most unusual wildlife and scenery in North America.

Summer weather along the Dempster can be erratic. In the Yukon, the southern Ogilvie Mountains form a major weather barrier and the Richardson Mountains is known as a high wind area. In the NWT region east of the Richardsons, the weather is milder. The July average temperature is 52°F, and the average June-August rainfall is six inches. The Southern Ogilvies receive the most rain. The driest region in the Yukon portion is the Eagle Plains area, where there is no water for 60 miles before the Eagle Plains Hotel. From mid to late May most of the snow is gone at the highway levels, and from June to mid-August snowfall is rare, except at high elevations. Heavy snowfall begins again in September.

The mosquito season is from mid-June to early August, and peaks in mid-July. Mosquitoes are problematic north of the Ogilvies along the Dempster and can even be found on high mountain ridges.

The Dempster Highway was named after RCMP Corporal W.J.D. Dempster who for 37 years travelled much of the current highway route by dog team.The highway's construction began in 1959 in an effort to reach oil and gas reserves in the Eagle Plains, and was inspired by Prime Minister John Diefenbaker's "Road to Resources" program. Highway construction ended when oil reserves were found to be less than originally thought. In the early 1970's, when oil deposits were found in the Beaufort Sea, work resumed on the Dempster. The highway now runs from the Klondike River, just south of Dawson City, to Inuvik, 100 kilometers south of the Beaufort Sea.

Since the Dempster Highway has no sideroads and ends in Inuvik, cyclists may ride up to Inuvik, turn around and bicycle back. Or they may fly, hitchhike or arrange to be met at either end of the highway. Of this single directional approach, it is our opinion, and that of other cyclists we met, that it is easier to ride north than south. If there's only time for a short trip, the first 200 kilometers of the Dempster is the most scenic.

There are two excellent resource guides on the Dempster Highway. *Along the Dempster* by Walter Lanz (Oak House Publishing, 1985) has excellent photographs and trail information, particularly on the Ogilvie regions.

Ornithologist and botanist Robert Frisch's book *Birds by the Dempster Highway*, (Morriss Publishing Company, 1987) is another fine publication. As Frish explains, numerous migratory birds spend the summer and raise their young along the Dempster. Frisch's book, a supplement to other guides, lists and describes the birds that inhabit the various zones. In 1985, Frisch died of natural causes while riding his bicycle in the lower Northfork Valley. He is buried alongside the road in the Tombstone Pass area. His book may be purchased in Whitehorse, or at the Tombstone Campground Interpretive Center, Km 73, Dempster Highway.

Scientists have divided the Dempster Highway into seven eco-regions. Frish, in his book, has subdivided these seven regions into fourteen ecological zones. The zones and regions, each with their own unique ecological and geological character, are described below, and given before the Dempster Highway Road Information sections.

REGION I: THE TITINA TRENCH AND SOUTH FORK OF THE OGILVIE MOUNTAINS

REGION DISTANCE: KM 0-KM 73

The Tintina Trench is a rift valley and forms the northern boundary of the Boreal Zone.

ZONE I: TINTINA TRENCH AND LOWER NORTH KLONDIKE RIVER VALLEY

ZONE DISTANCE: KM 0-KM 50. HIGHWAY ELEVATION: 457-884 METERS

The Dempster runs north up the valley, through Boreal forest (a northern forest of large, tall trees) spruce, aspen, birch, and cottonwood, and muskeg (a swamp containing scraggly black spruce, scrub birch varieties, and sphagnum moss). Along the river in Zone 1 are willow and alder stands, as well as white spruce and cottonwood.

ZONE II: UPPER NORTH KLONDIKE RIVER VALLEY

ZONE DISTANCE: KM 50-KM 73. HIGHWAY ELEVATION: 884-1036 METERS

The highway reaches the timberline zone at around Km 68. The zone is mostly montane spruce forest with willows, cottonwood and alder near the streams and aspens on the bluffs.

REGION 2: SOUTHERN OGILVIE MOUNTAINS

REGION DISTANCE: KM 73-KM 132

The Ogilvie Mountains form the southern border of the subarctic in this area of the Yukon. The region is almost completely above treeline.

ZONE III: NORTH FORK PASS

ZONE DISTANCE: KM 73-KM 87. HIGHWAY ELEVATION: 1036-1311 METERS

The North Fork Pass forms the Continental Divide between the Yukon and Mackenzie River systems. The Yukon River drains into the Bering Sea, and the Mackenzie River empties into the Arctic Ocean. Much of the roadside terrain is shrubby tundra (scrub birch and willow) and tussock tundra (a thick tuft of twigs, grass, and sedges). At elevations of 1372 meters, and higher is alpine tundra.

ZONE IV: BLACKSTONE UPLANDS

ZONE DISTANCE: KM 87-KM 132. HIGHWAY ELEVATION: 914-1036 METERS

The Dempster follows the Blackstone River. The flora is primarily shrubby tussock and tundra, with tree willows along the River. There is a spruce and cottonwood grove between Kms 113 and 116, and a few scattered spruce west of the highway between Kms 120 and 125. There are numerous lakes and ponds, including Moose Lake at Km 105, and Chapman Lake at Km 120.

REGION 3: NORTHERN OGILVIE MOUNTAINS

REGION DISTANCE: KM 132-KM 248

This mountainous region is mainly dolomite-limestone, has extensive talus and stone outcroppings.

ZONE V: NORTHERN OGILVIE MOUNTAINS

ZONE DISTANCE: KM 132-KM 197. HIGHWAY ELEVATION: 609-1006 METERS

Taiga forest, (spindly trees like muskeg, but not quite as swampy) mainly white spruce and cottonwood, and muskeg in the valley bottom. Alpine tundra and tussock tundra are at higher elevations.

ZONE VI: OGILVIE RIVER VALLEY

ZONE DISTANCE: KM 197-KM 248. HIGHWAY ELEVATION: AROUND 609 METERS

The highway is lined mostly by taiga forest (mainly white spruce with cottonwood by the streams). There is no roadside tundra.

REGION 4: EAGLE PLAINS

REGION DISTANCE: KM 248-KM 410

The highway follows the ridgetops (many of which form the Continental Divide) of this rolling, sparsely forested upland.

ZONE VII: EAGLE PLAINS

ZONE DISTANCE: KM 248-KM 410. HIGHWAY ELEVATION: 610-915 METERS

Black spruce taiga thinning northward to black spruce, tamarack and shrubby tundra. White spruce and cottonwood can be found in the lower valleys, especially along the Eagle River. (The Eagle River is part of the Yukon drainage system.)

REGION 5: RICHARDSON MOUNTAINS AND FOOTHILLS

REGION DISTANCE: KM 410-KM 492

The Richardson Mountains, a north running mountain chain of moderate elevation, are considered to be the northernmost portion of the Rocky Mountains.

ZONE VIII: SOUTHERN RICHARDSON MOUNTAINS AND FOOTHILLS

ZONE DISTANCE: KM 410-KM 450. HIGHWAY ELEVATION: 457-762 METERS

The highway skirts the foothills of the Richardson Mountains, travelling through tussock tundra with intermittent spruce woods until the Cornwall River Valley at Km 447.

ZONE IX: NORTHERN RICHARDSON MOUNTAINS

Zone Distance: Km 450-Km 492. Highway Elevation: 457-915 meters

The highway climbs to Wright Pass through alpine tundra and rocky terrain. There are some ponds and lakes on the NWT side of the mountains. Rivers before the pass drain into the Yukon system, those on the NWT side drain into the Mackenzie system.

Region 6: The Peel Plateau

Region Distance: Km 492-Km 541

This large sloping upland region is crossed by many creeks.

Zone X: Peel Plateau.

Zone Distance: Km 410-Km 541. Highway Elevation: 915-610 meters

The terrain is similar to that of Eagle Plains, but not as rolling. The flora is mostly tussock tundra and tiaga. The valleys contain taller spruce, cottonwood, and birch.

Region 7: Peel-Mackenzie Lowlands

Region Distance: Km 541-Km 615

The region is mostly flat, and thinly forested.

Zone XI: Peel River Valley

Zone Distance: Km 541-Km 544. Highway Elevation: 30 meters

The short zone is thickly wooded with white spruce. Closer to the river are tree willows.

Zone XII: Peel River to Mackenzie River

Zone Distance: Km 544-Km 609. Highway elevation: 92 meters

The flora is primarily muskeg and taiga. White spruce and birch are found in less swampy areas. There are many lakes, but few creeks.

Zone XIII: Mackenzie River Valley

Zone Distance: Km 609-Km 615. Highway Elevation: 30 meters

The warm air and good soil are characteristic of the Mackenzie River Valley. Large trees, (white spruce and birch) the size of those in the Tintina Trench area are seen here.

Zone XIV: Mackenzie River to Inuvik

Zone Distance: Km 615-Km 726. Highway Elevation: 92-10 meters

The road terrain is mostly flat, and travels through thin muskeg and taiga made up of black spruce, tamarack, and tussock tundra. There are numerous lakes. Closer to Inuvik there are some hilly areas with birch forests.

Road Information: Dempster Highway

Section 1: Km 0 (Jct. with the Klondike Highway)-Km 82 (North Fork Pass)

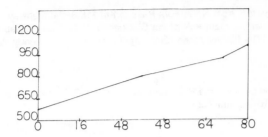

ROAD CONDITIONS/TERRAIN:

Mostly up and rolling, gaining 329 meters to Tombstone Campground at Km 72.5. The road then climbs steeply, gaining 390 meters to North Fork Pass at Km 82.

WATER:

Km 27.5. Bensen Creek. Kms 32.6, 35.1, 39.6, 79.9, unnamed creeks. Km 41.5, Wolf Creek. Kms 68 and 72.5, Klondike River.

CAMPING:

Km 72.5. Tombstone Mountain Yukon Government Campground has 22 campsites and an interpretive center. The campground is located in the last wooded section before the highway climbs above tree level. Camping is also possible along the creeks mentioned under Water, and off the road at approximately Km 36.1.

FOOD/LODGING:

None.

ROADSIDE SIGHTS:

Km 48.3, Klondike Maintenance Camp. Km 72.5, Tombstone Campground Interpretive Centre. Much information on the Dempster Highway and surrounding wildlife. Km 82. North Fork Pass (elevation 1,289 meters/ 4,229 feet) forms the Continental Divide between the Yukon River drainage into the Bering Sea and the Mackenzie drainage into the Arctic Ocean.

ROAD INFORMATION: DEMPSTER HIGHWAY

SECTION 2: KM 82 (NORTH FORK PASS)- KM 155 (WINDY PASS)

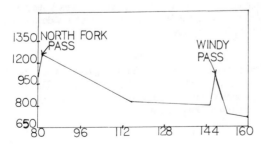

Road Conditions/Terrain:

After dropping 466 meters from North Fork Pass to Km 115.3, the highway follows first the east fork, then the main fork of the Blackstone River, dropping about 25 meters to Km 147.3. The highway then climbs about 200 meters to Windy Pass at Km 155.1.

Water:

Kms 94.5-147.7, road parallels the Blackstone River. Km 117, highway crosses the Blackstone River. Km 128, small creek.

Camping:

There are no formal campgrounds in this section, but camping is possible on the gravel bars of the Blackstone River, especially in the wooded areas.

Food/Lodging:

None.

Roadside Sights:

Km 95.5, Outfitters Cabin. Km 116, interpretive sign on the RCMP.

Road Information: Dempster Highway

Section 3: Km 155 (Windy Pass)-Km 244 (Highway leaves Ogilvie River)

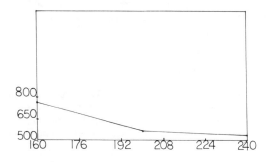

Road Conditions/Terrain:

Windy Pass, as its name suggests, can be windy. After crossing this pass, the highway heads downhill 40 kilometers into the Engineer Creek Valley and to the Ogilvie River. After crossing the Ogilvie River, the road continues downward, and is rolling. The highway loses 488 meters in this section.

Water:

After leaving Windy Pass, the highway first follows Engineer Creek and then the Ogilvie River to the end of this section. Km 173.5, Iron Creek. This water is not palatable. Km 181. Don't drink water from Engineer Creek where Iron Creek enters it. Km 212, Warm Creek. Km 194.5, Ogilvie River.

Camping:

Km 194. Engineer Creek Yukon Government Campground has 23 campsites. Camping is also possible along Engineer Creek and the Ogilvie River.

FOOD/LODGING:

None.

ROADSIDE SIGHTS:

Km 155.1, 1,006 meter/3,300 foot Windy Pass. Km 294.5, Ogilvie River Maintenance Station.

ROAD INFORMATION: DEMPSTER HIGHWAY
SECTION 4: KM 244 (HIGHWAY LEAVES THE OGILVIE RIVER)-KM 325

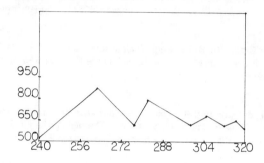

ROAD CONDITIONS/TERRAIN:

The Dempster Highway snakes along the ridgetops of Eagle Plains, except when crossing Big Timber Creek and the Eagle River. The Eagle Plains separate the Ogilvie and Richardson Mountains. The terrain is rolling, with many steep hills. After an initial climb of 363 meters, overall gains and losses in elevation average around 150 meters.

WATER:

None. Stock up on water where the highway leaves the Ogilvie River. If need be, stop an RV for water.

CAMPING:

There are no campgrounds in this section. Camping is possible in one of the many open areas, but no water is available.

FOOD/LODGING:

None.

ROAD INFORMATION: DEMPSTER HIGHWAY
SECTION 5: KM 324-KM 404

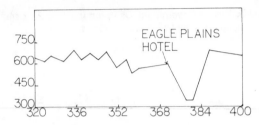

ROAD CONDITIONS/TERRAIN:

The terrain of the first 45 kilometers is the same as the last section, except that there are only elevation differences of about 50 meters. There is a 260 meter drop from the Eagle Plains Hotel to the Eagle River which is followed by a 330 meter rise. The rest of this section is less rolling and more open with little elevation change.

WATER:

Km 351.7, Big Timber Creek. Km 371.5, Eagle Plains Hotel. Km 380.1, Eagle River. The river, from which Eagle Plains is named, flows into the Porcupine River, which empties into the Yukon River.

CAMPING:

Km 371.5. Open-site campground with coin operated showers and firewood is located adjacent to the Eagle Plains Hotel. No shelter. The nightly site fee is $6.00. Camping is also possible at Big Timber Creek and the Eagle River. Eagle River is the nicer of the two areas.

FOOD/LODGING:

Km 371.5. Eagle Plains Hotel has a restaurant (which sells groceries from the kitchen), a bar, and a small expensive store which sells souvenirs and some food (mostly snacks). In the restaurant, a dish of stewed prunes costs $2.50.

POST OFFICE:

There is no official post office, but goods can be mailed to Eagle Plains; this is very expensive.

ROADSIDE SIGHTS:

Km 371.5. Lining the bar walls of the Eagle Plains Hotel is the story of Albert Johnson, the "Mad Trapper of Rat River."

ROAD INFORMATION: DEMPSTER HIGHWAY
SECTION 6: KM 404-KM 484 (NWT KM 18)

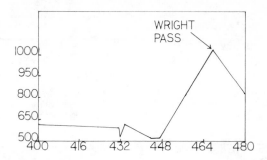

ROAD CONDITIONS/TERRAIN:

Rolling hills become more gradual towards the Cornwall River Valley at Km 447. At Rock River, Km 431.9, there is a steep downhill which is followed by a steep uphill climb. After the Cornwall River Valley, the road climbs 479 meters to Wright Pass at Km 466. From Wright Pass, the road has a few rollers, but descends roughly 250 meters.

After entering the Northwest Territories at Wright Pass, Km 466, new kilometer posts begin, with the border being Km 0. In parentheses at the beginning of each section, kilometer distance from the Northwest Territories border is given. After each subsection, kilometer distance is given from the NWT border.

WATER:

Km 415.1, small creek. Km 431.9, Rock River (dry). Km 447, Cornwall River. Km 479.9 (Km 13.9 NWT), James Creek.

CAMPING:

Km 447. Cornwall River Yukon Government Campground, one of Yukon's newest campgrounds, has 20 campsites, three for tents only. It sits in the bottom of the Cornwall River Valley and is sheltered from the wind. A heavy mosquito area. Camping is also possible at the small creek at Km 415.1, or at the gravel pit just beyond this creek at Km 415.9. Rock River is a good place to camp if the water is flowing.

FOOD/LODGING:

None.

ROADSIDE SIGHTS:

Km 408.9, Arctic Circle. Interpretive signs and picnic table. Often here is the Keeper of the Arctic Circle, who wears a tuxedo and serves champagne. Km 466. Wright Pass, Continental Divide and border between the Yukon and Northwest Territories. Wright Pass is named after Allen A. Wright, who surveyed much of the Dempster Highway route.

ROAD INFORMATION: DEMPSTER HIGHWAY

SECTION 7: KM 484 (NWT KM 18)-KM 564 (NWT KM 98)

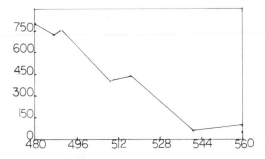

ROAD CONDITIONS/TERRAIN:

Mostly down, but with a few hills to climb. There's a steep climb from Midway Lake at Km 43.7 up to Km 49.8, gaining 150 meters. From the top of the hill, the highway drops 528 meters to the Peel River.

WATER:

From Km 17.6-Km 21.9, the road closely parallels a creek. Km 27, small creek. Km 34.2, road passes lake. Km 42.6, Midway Lake. An annual summer music festival is held here; to the right are a bandstand and bleachers. Km 76.6, Peel River.

CAMPING:

Km 77. Natuiluie NWT Government Campground has 20 campsites and an interpretive center. The Roberts family are the campground hosts. Ken Roberts says they should have a shelter by 1989. Free NWT Certificates and hot chocolate are available. Natuiluie is a Kutchin word meaning "fast flowing water."

FOOD/LODGING:

Km 86.7, Fort McPherson.

FORT MCPHERSON

BACKGROUND

Fort McPherson (pop. 800) is located on the northern part of an isolated hill about one kilometer long and half a kilometer wide. The town is approximately 30 meters above sea level.

According to *Settlements of the NWT*, by the Canadian Advisory Commission, John Franklin named the Peel River after Sir Robert Peel when he returned from his second expedition in the mid 1820's and mistook the Peel River for the MacKenzie River. After he informed the Hudson's Bay Company that the area was rich in furs, the company sent fur trader John Bell to explore the Peel River as far as the Snake River.

The first Hudson's Bay Company post was established on the Peel River in 1840. In 1848 the post was named after the chief trader of the Hudson's Bay Company, Murdoch McPherson.

In 1852, an Indian Village situated on the bank of the Peel River opposite Stony Creek was moved to the present location of Fort McPherson. The early French

Canadian voyageurs called the tribes who lived on the Peel and Porcupine Rivers Loucheux, meaning "Squint Eyed." The Indians who now live in Fort McPherson belong to the Kutchin tribe. The average July temperature is 58° F and the average annual rainfall is 7.4 inches. Prevailing winds are from the north.

MEDICAL SERVICES:

There is a nursing station in Fort McPherson.

GROCERIES:

The Co-op Grocery, The Hudson Bay Co., and the Latitude 67 Cafe and Grocery are all located on Fort McPerson's Main Street.

LODGING/CAMPING:

There are no hostels in Fort McPherson. Latitude 67 Cafe has some rooms.

POST OFFICE:

Postal Code: XOE OJO.

LAUNDRY/SHOWERS:

There's no public laundromat, but the Community Recreation Center has free showers.

MUSEUMS/HISTORICAL SITES:

Buried in Fort McPherson's Anglican Church Cemetery are Inspector Fitzgerald and three other RCMP, who in December of 1910 died while on a routine patrol and mail run between Herschel Island and Dawson City.

GIFT SHOP:

The Fort McPherson Tent and Canvas Factory produces garments, bags, tents, and backpacks. Visitors are welcome.

ROAD INFORMATION: DEMPSTER HIGHWAY

SECTION 8: KM 564 (NWT KM 98)-KM 634 (NWT KM 178, RENGLING RIVER)

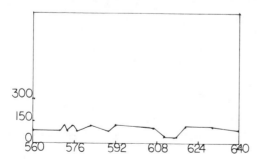

ROAD CONDITIONS/TERRAIN:

Mostly gradual terrain but with three hills, each about a 30 meter climb, before the Mackenzie River. After the river, there is one hill, (a 50 meter climb) coming out of the Mackenzie River Valley. After, the road is mostly flat.

WATER:

Km 108, lake. Km 123.5, Frog Creek. The water is warm because the constant sun warms the many shallow lakes which drain into this creek. Km 143.2. Mackenzie River, the second largest river in North America. Km 178, Rengling River.

CAMPING:

There are no campgrounds in this section. Camping is possible at Km 123.5, Frog Creek, at Km 143.2, the Mackenzie River and Km 178, Rengling River (a popular camping area for cyclists). Those who camp on the right side of the road, where the water flows from, will have to take their bicycles and gear down a steep dirt incline.

FOOD/LODGING:

Km 143.2. The Arctic Red River Village is located at the confluence of the Mackenzie and Arctic Red Rivers, and the site of the ferry crossing. There is a small grocery store with limited hours. Access is by a free ferry. Hoses on board the vessel may be used to wash down muddy bicycles.

ROADSIDE SIGHTS:

Km 143.2, Arctic Red River.

ROAD INFORMATION: DEMPSTER HIGHWAY

SECTION 9: KM 634 (NWT KM 178, RENGLING RIVER)-KM 736 (NWT KM 270, INUVIK)

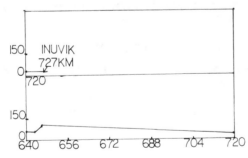

ROAD CONDITIONS/TERRAIN:

Mostly flat and fast, with a few small hills closer to Inuvik. It can be windy here.

WATER:

Km 218.5, Caribou Creek. Km 241.3, Cabin Creek. Km 244.4, Campbell Creek.

CAMPING/PICNIC AREAS:

Km 218.5. Caribou Creek NWT Government Campground has 10 campsites. There is no shelter here; get water from the creek. Km 241.3. Cabin Creek is mostly a fishing spot and boat launch with picnic facilities. Km 244.4. Campbell Creek Picnic Area has six campsites, but no shelter. Km 267.1, Chuk NWT Campground. There is a steep climb to the campground which is located on a ridge overlooking Inuvik. The campground has 38 campsites, showers and a shelter. The site fee is $8.00 per night. Videos are shown in the evenings and there is a staffed information desk.

FOOD/LODGING:

Km 270.1, Inuvik.

INUVIK

BACKGROUND

In the mid 1820's Dr. John Richardson led a party to investigate the Arctic Coast from the Mackenzie Delta to the Coppermine River. Richardson's party discovered numerous communities of Mackenzie Inuit, some with as many as 500-1000 people. Unfortunately, the whaling boom of 1889-1912 brought with it many foreign diseases. Richardson estimated that at the time of his visit, there were between 2,000 and 4,800 Inuit living in this area. In 1911 an RCMP census recorded only 40 Inuit.

Since the original inhabitant's deaths, many Alaskan Inuit and non-Natives have moved into the area. The increasing population, as well as oil and gas exploration in the Beaufort Sea, have resulted in a town with a high percentage of government employees. Before 1950 most of the government administrative offices were located in the village of Aklavik, located within the Mackenzie Delta. Due to flooding and erosion, the government relocated to Inuvik.

Inuvik (pop. 3,100) sits on the east channel of the Mackenzie River, bordering the delta. The site of present day Inuvik was chosen because it did not flood easily, could be serviced with water and sewer facilities, and allowed for the construction of a dock and an airport. Built between 1955 and 1961, the "Place of Man" as Inuvik means in Inuktitut, is the main government center and transportation hub for the Canadian Western Arctic.

Construction in Inuvik has been ongoing. Entering town one observes brightly painted houses, with water and sewer line corridors running between them. In the winter, the corridors keep the pipes from freezing.

Inuvik's average July temperature is 56° F. The average yearly rainfall is 4 inches.

VISITORS INFORMATION

VISITOR'S CENTER:

The Inuvik Visitor's Center is located on the corner of Mackenzie Road and Distributor Street next to a school playground. Free maps and printed material is available. Write: Box 1525, Inuvik, NWT XOE OTO. Phone: 979-3765.

TRAVELLER'S NEEDS

MEDICAL SERVICES:

Inuvik Hospital is located on Mackenzie Road on the way into town. Phone: 979-2955 or 979-2935.

GROCERIES:

Hudson Bay Supermarket is located in town on Mackenzie Road. Corner Store, a convenience store, is located north (right) off Mackenzie Road on Dolphin. Hours: 11 a.m. to 11 p.m.

BICYCLE/OUTDOOR STORES:

RDR Sports is located by the river on Distributor Street. Camping gear and some bicycle parts are available.

LODGING/CAMPING:

The Mackenzie Hotel and the Eskimo Inn, both located on Mackenzie Road, have cafes and cost about $90.00 for a single room. See road notes for information on Chuk NWT Campground. Also, Happy Valley Campground in town has 28 campsites, ten for tents, and is located on Franklin Street in the west end of Inuvik.

POST OFFICE:

The Inuvik Post Office is located on the corner of Mackenzie Road and Distributor Street, across from the Visitor Center. Postal Code: XOE OTO.

LAUNDRY/SHOWERS:

Mat-Laundry and Confections is located on Mackenzie Road. Washers/dryers and drop off service are available. Hours: 10 a.m. to 7 p.m. Monday through Friday, 10 a.m. to 6 p.m. Saturday, and 1 p.m. to 4 p.m. Sunday.

ALTERNATIVE TRANSPORTATION:

Inuvik has a modern airport. Flights are available to many of the local communities and lakes, as well as to Dawson City and Yellowknife. For tourist information, write: Tourism and Industry Association of Northwest Territories, Box 506 , Yellowknife, NWT XIA 2N4.

ENTERTAINMENT AND RECREATION

MUSEUMS/HISTORICAL SITES:

The big round building on Mackenzie Road is the Roman Catholic Igloo Church. Interpretive information about the church and its construction is available inside.

BOOKSTORES:

The Boreal Bookstore, located at 181 Mackenzie Road, has northern and specialty books, area topographic maps, and federal government publications. A mailing list is also available. For information write: Boreal Books, Box 1070, Inuvik, NWT XOE OTO.

SIDE TRIPS:

Inuvik is the jumping off spot for the western Canadian Arctic. The most popular and least expensive trip is to Tuktoyaktuk, located on the Beaufort Sea, about 100 kilometers from Inuvik. Antler Tours Inc., located at 181 Mackenzie Road, next to the Boreal Bookstore, has regularly scheduled tours.

CHAPTER 34: THE DALTON HIGHWAY

BACKGROUND

The 421 mile Dalton Highway, originally known as the North Slope Haul Road, was constructed by the Alyeska Pipeline Service Company (a corporation formed by the Prudhoe Bay oil companies) as a building supply line for the Alaska Pipeline. When constructing the Dalton, the engineers stayed close to the pipeline's planned route. Because of this, the road seems to travel over some irrational terrain.

Dalton Highway construction began in the summer of 1974. In 1978, the highway was turned over to the State of Alaska and was opened to the public as far as the Yukon River. In 1981, the highway was opened as far north as Disaster Creek.

The Dalton runs through a 24 mile-wide corridor administered by the Bureau of Land Management. The corridor begins at the junction of the Elliot Highway and runs through the middle of the North Slope. Hunting with firearms, or using motorized vehicles within the corridor is illegal.

Much of the highway, particularly north of the Disaster Creek checkpoint (Mile 210.9), is not presently up to Alaska Department of Transportation standards. Therefore permits are required for vehicles past this point. And for some reason not fully explained in the present policy, even bicyclists with permits are prohibited beyond the checkpoint.

Aside from some steep hills (with grades as much as 13 percent), the road is suitable for riding. The surface is gravel, and except in recently graded areas, hard packed. The traffic is relatively light in May, when tourist traffic is minimal and road restrictions on the state paved roads leading to the Dalton Highway are in effect.

The Dalton can be difficult to ride in the early spring because of light snow, strong winds and cold temperatures. Those choosing to ride the Dalton at any time should be prepared to deal with steep hills, trucks, and long stretches without grocery stores or lodges. There are usually more semis then regular pickups or cars on this highway. Because truck drivers are in constant radio contact with each other, they're usually aware of cyclists. But for safety reasons, these vehicles should be given the right of way. Semis can usually be heard at the distance: however, a mirror is recommended because strong winds sometimes make it difficult to hear their approach.

When we rode the Dalton, we weren't permitted to ride past the Disaster Creek checkpoint, so information is only given to this point. The Alaska State Legislature could change the laws governing access to the Dalton Highway. For this reason we are including profiles for the entire highway. The highway is divided into four sections of approximately fifty miles. All sections begin and end at easily recognizable locations.

ROAD INFORMATION: DALTON HIGHWAY
SECTION 1: MILE 0 (JCT. AT MILE 72.8, ELLIOT HIGHWAY)-MILE 56 (YUKON RIVER)

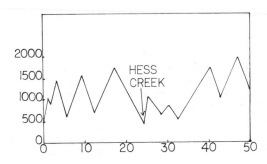

ROAD CONDITIONS/TERRAIN:

This is the toughest portion of the Dalton Highway. There is a series of very steep rolling hills and little level ground. Hill grades vary from eight to 13 percent. Gains and losses in elevation range from 500 to 1,000 feet.

WATER:

Mile 5.5, Lost Creek. Mile 23.5, Hess Creek. Mile 33.6, small, unnamed creek. Mile 42.8, Isom Creek. Mile 56, Yukon River.

CAMPING:

Mile 23.5. Hess Creek, the largest stream before the Yukon River, has two unofficial camping areas. The first is next to the bridge. A better place is off a small road just past the bridge. Mile 56, Yukon River. Unfortunately, the best place to camp on the Yukon is on private property. There is an open place to camp near the bridge, but it is more suitable for an RV.

FOOD/LODGING:

Mile 56. Yukon Ventures Restaurant is owned by Fredi and George Young and the Williams family. Showers are $3.00. The cafe serves large meals and good homemade pie. This is the last service facility before Mile 175, Coldfoot.

ROADSIDE SIGHTS:

Mile 33.6. A large white cross marks the spot of trucker Charles E. Kelly's 1982 fatal accident.

ROAD INFORMATION: DALTON HIGHWAY
SECTION 2: MILE 56 (YUKON RIVER)-MILE 105.6 (KANUTI RIVER)

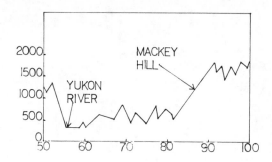

ROAD CONDITIONS/TERRAIN:

After leaving the Yukon, the road is gradually upward for about five miles, but becomes increasingly hillier with tough 200 foot climbs at Mile 72.6, Sand Hill, Mile 75, Rollercoaster Hill, (a very steep 250 foot descent followed by a very steep 200 foot ascent) and Mile 87.2, Mackey Hill (a 1,300 foot climb named for Dick Mackey, owner of Coldfoot Services.) The hills are separated by some steep rollers which end after a steep 400-foot climb to the top of Finger Mountain Summit, Mile 101.4.

WATER:

Mile 79, No Name Creek. Mile 105.6, Kanuti River. Unnamed creeks at Miles 59.7, 63.7, 91.1, 101.1.

CAMPING:

Camping is possible at Mile 79, No Name Creek, Mile 105.6, Kanuti River and the unnamed creeks at Miles 91.1 and 101.1.

FOOD/LODGING:

None.

ROADSIDE SIGHTS:

Mile 63.5, Department of Transportation maintenance station. Mile 70.4, view of Ray River and Fort Hamlin Hills to the west. Mile 72.6, Sand Hill. Mile 75, Rollercoaster Hill. Mile 87.2, Mackey Hill. Mile 101.4. Finger Mountain Summit; outhouses and an excellent view.

ROAD INFORMATION: DALTON HIGHWAY
SECTION 3: MILE 105.6 (KANUTI RIVER)-MILE 155 (SOUTH FORK KOYUKUK RIVER)

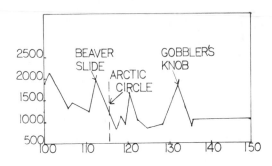

ROAD CONDITIONS/TERRAIN:

This section is more open, with much of it above or around tree level. Rolling hills separate the ascents and descents of Mile 112.2, Beaver Slide; a 1,100 foot drop (slippery when wet), Mile 119.5, Alder Mountain Summit; a 700 foot climb followed by a 600 foot drop, and Mile 132, Gobbler's Knob Summit; a 900 foot climb followed by a 900 foot drop.

WATER:

Mile 114, Fish Creek. Mile 124.5, South Fork Bonanza Creek. Mile 125.5, North Fork Bonanza Creek. Mile 135, Prospect Creek. Mile 140.2, Jim River #1. Mile 141.1, Jim River #2. Mile 141.8, Douglas Creek. Mile 144.2, Jim River #3. Mile 155.1, South Fork Koyukuk River. Miles 128.7 and 153.3, unnamed creeks.

CAMPING:

Mile 114, Fish Creek. Mile 124.5, South Fork Bonanza Creek (nicest). Miles 140.2 and 144.2, Jim River # 1 and # 3 and the small creek at Mile 155.3.

FOOD/LODGING:

None.

ROADSIDE SIGHTS:

Mile 112.2, Top of Beaver Slide. Mile 115.2, Arctic Circle. Mile 119.5, 1,668 foot/509 meter Alder Mountain Summit. Mile 132, 1,806 foot/ 551 meter Gobbler Knob Summit (named for two turkeys that worked near the summit during the pipeline construction). Mile 138, Jim River State Maintenance station.

Road Information: Dalton Highway

Section 4: Mile 155 (South Fork Koyukuk River)-Mile 210.9 (Disaster Creek Checkpoint)

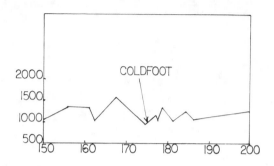

Road Conditions/Terrain:

As the highway makes its way toward the Brooks Range, rolling hills with overall elevation gains and losses of about 200 feet are separated by long gradual inclines. There is an overall gain in elevation of 200 feet in this section. Cyclists are not permitted beyond the Disaster Creek checkpoint.

Water:

Mile 175.1, Slate Creek. Mile 178.7, Marion Creek. Mile 185.3, Minnie Creek. Mile 186.7, Middle Fork Koyukuk River #1. Mile 188.7, Hammond River. Mile 189.1, Middle Fork Koyukuk River #2. Mile 195.2, Gold Creek. Mile 206, Middle Fork Koyukuk River #3. Mile 209, Dietrich River.

Camping:

Camping is possible at Mile 178.7, Marion Creek; Mile 185.3, Minnie Creek; and Mile 206, Middle Fork Koyukuk River #3, an "official" camping spot complete with an outhouse.

Food/Lodging:

Mile 175. Coldfoot Service has a restaurant, a 24 hour cafe, a hotel (Arctic Acres) a post office (Zip Code CPO Fairbanks, 99701) and sells groceries from the kitchen. Owner Dick Mackey opened his establishment for truck drivers and other travellers using this road. Also in Coldfoot is Gates of the Arctic National Park and Preserve Visitor's Center. For more information, write: Superintendent, Gates of the Arctic NP/P, Box 74680, Fairbanks, AK 99707.

The average July temperature in Coldfoot is 58° F. The average July rainfall is 2.6 inches.

DALTON HIGHWAY

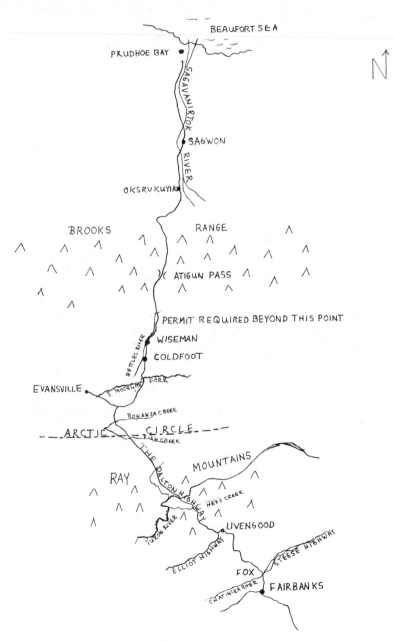

Doing the Dalton

I was wedged in the rear of Pete's Scout between two mountain bikes, eight panniers, a tent and two sleeping bags. Our plan was to bicycle approximately 300 miles from Dietrich Camp on the Haul Road back to Fairbanks.

Once past the road to Livengood, I looked out the window. The gravel was thick, the shoulder narrow. Egg-sized rocks, sent flying by the truck's tires, bounced through the air. For as far as I could see there were hills. I wondered if I could do this ride in a week. We had about eight day's food. If we ran low on supplies, or if my knees gave out, we'd have to hitchhike back to Fairbanks. I pushed this idea out of my mind.

That night our neighbor Roger dropped us off at Mile 210 by the Dietrich River. As he drove off, I wished we'd bicycled up and were getting a lift back. In my estimation, a little terrain information was more unnerving than none at all.

The next morning, as we stood by the Koyukuk River bridge, we heard a semi. As "The Mud Musher" blasted past us, Pete took its photo. It was the first of many trucks which, in the next few days, left us choking in a thick cloud of grey dust. It was 37 easy downhill miles to Coldfoot, our first major stop. But nervous about the truck traffic, we constantly looked back over our shoulders. After a while we were attuned to their low rumble, which at the distance sounded like thunder. Since the Coldfoot Cafe was the only restaurant we'd encounter for the next hundred miles, Pete and I lingered. As he talked to the postmistress about mailing particulars, I ate apple pie and studied the diner's decor. On a bulletin board a business card with a mule's head on it read, "Drygulch Maynard, National Champion Halter Jack 1985." The people who'd left this card were from Idaho. I wondered what they were doing here, and if they'd brought Maynard with them to Coldfoot.

On the far wall, on pegs, were the cups of dozens of truckers, including "J," "Trapper," and "Dutch." Sitting at a table beneath them was Jed, a Koyukuk Yukon School District teacher. He was showing two of his young students how to diagram sentences.

When a trucker at an adjacent table asked me what I was doing in Coldfoot, I told him Pete and I were bicycling the Haul Road. Taking a bite out of his tuna sandwich, the thin, bushy bearded man shook his head. "Those hills out there are steep. I don't see why anyone would want to bicycle over them." I replied that they'd be easy for me because I was in good shape. But I wasn't convinced of this myself. I hadn't been doing much riding lately. And when Alyeska originally put in the Dalton Highway, they had not circumvented any of the major passes. What was left was a road with numerous tough climbs, that would be difficult for anyone.

By the afternoon of the second day I'd finally figured out that the truck traffic was the heaviest during late morning and early evening, when we were off the road. I wondered if the trucks were on any particular schedule, and if we'd continue to be on the road when they weren't. After our second lunchbreak at Prospect Creek, I tried to do a little mental algebra. If a truck, travelling at 55 m.p.h. left Fairbanks at 6 a.m., and a bicycle rider, travelling at 10 m.p.h. left Prospect Creek, Mile 135 at 11:30 a.m., at what time and where would they meet? For the rest of the day as I rode, I tried to figure this out. By our next food stop, 10 miles down the road, I'd given up.

On this trip, the terrain, the scenery and our moods were constantly changing. On the morning of the third day I saw a moose by a creek and a number of redpolls, small birds which looked like flying flecks of black pepper. I also noticed the willows were budding. This was a welcome sign after seven months of winter. Pete was also pleased, for he'd found numerous tools, including a tire gauge, an open ended wrench, a screw driver, and a set of pliers. For weight reasons he discarded the last two items.

The last part of this 41 mile day was spent cycling in the rain. Soon our freewheel cogs, chains, derailleurs, and bodies were covered with mud. Going downhill it flew out in big chunks from our tires.

Still, we were in good spirits. We took pictures of one another in front of a sign indicating we were at the Arctic Circle, and then headed downhill to Fish Creek.

Before turning off to camp, we saw that the road ahead went straight up, like a ski slope. I hoped that this was a sideroad that we could bypass and tried hard that night not to think about it. The next day, I started up it slowly, behind Pete. According to a blue and yellow sign at its base, the hill was called Beaverslide. This one, we'd been told, had a 12 percent grade. Even before I was one third of the way up it, my legs and back muscles felt like rubber. I alternately stood and sat as I ground steadily uphill. The stiff headwinds only made riding harder. However, I didn't stop. "If Pete can do this, so can I," I thought, and pushed harder on the pedals. I kept climbing, and at times focused on the small grey rocks ahead of me. In my red sweats and on my heavy mountain bike with its wide handlebars, I felt like a fat woman pushing a lawn mower. When a truck roared by, I turned my head sideways, to avoid the flying rocks. At the top, we rested. Unfortunately, going down Beaverslide was slow because of the strong headwinds. Pete and I rode together to the base of Finger Mountain, where we ate lunch.

Looking at Finger Mountain, it didn't seem as steep as Beaverslide, but it was a longer, more gradual climb. Going up, I decided that each hill had its own personality. Finger Mountain was tenacious, but because of level spots, forgiving. About three quarters of the way up, four caribou carefully picked their way across the rock strewn terrain. This sight, I decided, was worth the climb.

That day we also rode over Rollercoaster, Mackey, and Sand Hill Mountains. In order to remember the hills in between, I named them Sidewinder, Knee Knocker, Grinder, Insidious, Meatball and Killer Hills. On the last day of our trip Pete and I discovered that these hills had also been given similar names by the local truckers.

We ended Friday, May 13th, Pete's birthday, at the Yukon River. According to my cyclometer we'd bicycled 57 miles.

The following day, we were wakened by the sound of rain pelting the tent fly. After eating our oatmeal, Pete suggested that we get a cup of tea at the nearby Yukon Ventures Restaurant. I thought this was a good idea. The sky was a thick grey blanket. We wouldn't be able to outride the storm, but we could, for the moment, avoid dealing with it. Inside, we watched the rain stream down the trailer windows. In bits and pieces we learned from the staff and restaurant regulars what was ahead. As I understood it, the next eight miles or so would be uphill, and wet. Later Pete and I realized we were thinking the same thing: Why not sit the storm out in the diner, eat brownies, and play cribbage all day? But neither of us suggested this because we had 4,000 more miles to ride and not much time to waste. We left at noon and found the people we'd talked to were right. There was a combination snow/rain storm ahead of us. Before we'd even gone five miles, Pete had stopped to put on a dry pair of wool socks, and over his shoes, a pair of plastic bread bags. I added a few more layers. However, within minutes the rain had penetrated wool, pile, nylon, and breadbags.

For a while I sang, then daydreamed. My musings were interrupted by a semi, whose wheels came inches from mine and coated me with mud. The cold slush felt like a slap in the face. I started to yell, but stopped myself. The driver, warm and dry, felt no remorse. I wiped off my glasses, which were covered with mud and ice, but they fogged up again. I thought things couldn't get much worse, but they did. My Suntour front derailleur clogged up with mud and wouldn't shift. Pouring water on them didn't help. Because I didn't feel like wasting time by digging in my panniers for my screw driver, I stopped every few minutes and changed my gearing by hand. Shortly after this, my brakes gave out. I suspected that rim grit and riding with a death grip on the levers down the steep hills were partially the reason for this. Finally when my toes went numb and I felt like I couldn't go any farther, I got off my bicycle and walked. Pete, who was ahead of me, got off his bicycle and waited. When I caught up with him, we both started walking uphill. I'd never walked up a hill before. Somehow, having him accompany me, made me feel better. Moving them also warmed my toes. At the top of the hill we climbed back on our bicycles and continued. After a few more miles, the snow turned first to rain, then to a slight drizzle.

Three miles from where we'd decided to camp, Hess Creek, was a steep downhill. Brakeless, I started to walk. Pete rode back up and after talking about it, we decided to adjust the brakes. I spilled the tools out of their bag, into the mud, picked out the ones I needed, and made the final adjustments. We then headed to camp, started a fire, dried our gear, and cooked dinner.

The next day was better—we were aided by a tail wind and the hills were less severe. At Livengood, Pete and I were treated to Koala sodas by John, the owner of John's Likker Box. Sitting on his front porch, in the sun, we listened as he told us about a fellow a few years back who'd bicycled from Fairbanks to Livengood on an old bicycle with a broken pedal. According to John, he was going to ride to Prudhoe Bay.

"He wasn't wearing a shirt and he'd been eaten alive from head to toe by mosquitoes," John said.

"I wonder how anyone could do anything so stupid," I replied.

On our last day, after forty miles of pedalling, 28 miles from Fox, we came to pavement. On asphalt, even the last long late afternoon grind to the Hilltop Cafe was bearable. But the high point of the day was our late evening ride through the Fairbanks Goldstream Valley. The birch and aspen were in bloom, and the air smelled sweet and clean. I drafted behind Pete and we moved fairly quickly over the gently rolling hills. Behind us was the Dalton Highway. Ahead of us was the Alaska Highway.

RECOMMENDED READING

GENERAL

Biddle, Graham and Mark Butler and Caroline Prendergast. *The Anchorage Book: A Select Guide to Events, Establishments and Entertainment.* Anchorage: Butler, 1984.

Connor, Cathy and Daniel O'Haire. *Road Side Geology of Alaska.* Missoula: Mountain, 1988.

Coutts, R.C. *Yukon: Places and Names.* Sidney, B.C.: Gray's, 1980.

Eppenbach, Sarah. *Touring the Inside Passage.* 3rd ed. Seattle: Pacific Search, 1988.

Freedman, Benedict and Nancy Freedman. *Mrs. Mike: The Story of Katherine Mary Flannigan.* New York: Berkley, 1981.

Frisch, Robert. *Birds by the Dempster Highway.* Rev. ed. Victoria, B.C.: Morriss, 1987.

Heacox, Kim and others. *The Denali Road Guide: A Roadside Natural History of Denali National Park.* Anchorage: Alaska Natural History Association, 1986.

Lanz, Walter. *Along the Dempster: An Outdoor Guide to Canada's Northernmost Highway.* Vancouver, B.C.: Oak House, 1985.

Leslie, Lynn D. *Alaska Climate Summaries: Alaska Climate Center Technical Note Number Three.* Anchorage: University of Alaska AEIDC, 1986.

Lopez, Barry. *Arctic Dreams: Imagination and Desire in a Northern Landscape.* New York: Bantam, 1987.

Lopez, Barry. *Crossing Open Ground.* New York: Macmillan, 1988.

McPhee, John. *Coming into the Country*. New York: Farrar, 1977.

Mowat, Farley. *Never Cry Wolf*. Toronto: Bantam, 1981.

Murie, Margaret E., editor. *The Alaska Bird Sketches of Olaus Murie: With Excerpts From His Field Notes*. Anchorage: Alaska Northwest Publishing, 1979.

Orth, Donald. *Dictionary of Alaska Place Names*. Washington: GPO, 1967.

Piggott, Margaret H. *Discover Southeast Alaska With Pack and Paddle*. Seattle: The Mountaineers, 1974.

Reardon, Jim and others, editors. "Alaska's Salmon Fisheries." *Alaska Geographic* 10:3 (1983).

Schorr, Alan Edward, editor. *Alaska Place Names*. 3rd ed. Juneau: The Denali Press, 1986.

Trelawny, John G. *Wildflowers of the Yukon and Northwestern Canada Including Adjacent Alaska*. Sidney, B.C.: Gray's, 1983.

United States Department of the Interior. *Denali National Park and Preserve/Alaska: General Management Plan, Land Protection Plan, Wilderness Suitability Review*. Washington: GPO, 1986.

NATIVE CULTURE AND HISTORY

Balcom, Mary G. *Ketchikan, Alaska's Totemland*. Chicago: Adams, 1961.

Beck, Horace C. *Classification and Nomenclature of Beads and Pendants*. New York: Shumway, 1973.

Duff, Wilson and others, editors. *Totem Pole Survey of Southeastern Alaska*. Juneau: Alaska State Museum, 1969.

Fitzhugh, William W. and Susan A. Kaplan. *Inua: Spirit World of the Bering Sea Eskimo*. Washington: Smithsonian Institution, 1982.

Garfield, Viola E. *Meet the Totem*. Sitka: Sitka Printing, 1951.

Garfield, Viola E. and Linn A. Forrest. *The Wolf and the Raven*. Seattle: University of Washington Press, 1961.

Holm, Bill. *The Box of Daylight: Northwest Coast Indian Art*. Seattle: University of Washington Press, 1983.

Keithan, Edward L. *Monuments in Cedar.* Seattle: Superior Publishing, 1963.

Lee, Molly. *Baleen Basketry of the North Alaskan Eskimo.* Barrow: North Slope Borough Planning Department, 1983.

MacDowell, Lloyd W. *The Totem Poles of Alaska Indian Mythology.* Seattle: Alaska Steamship Company, 1965.

Rakestraw, Lawrence. *A History of the Forest Service Role in Totem Pole Restoration and Preservation, and an Index of Sources for USFS Work in Reference to Totem Poles 1906-1971.* Washington: GPO, 1971.

Stewart, Hilary. *Looking at Indian Art of the Northwest Coast.* Seattle: University of Washington Press, 1979.

GENERAL HISTORY

Balcom, Mary. *Creek Street.* Chicago: Adams, 1963.

Barry, Mary J. *Seward, Alaska: A History of the Gateway City. Part I: Prehistory to 1914.* 2 vols. Anchorage: Barry, 1986.

Cooley, Richard A. *Fairbanks, Alaska: A Survey of Progress.* Juneau: Alaska Development Board, 1954.

DeArmond, R.N. *Some Names Around Juneau.* Sitka: Sitka Printing, 1957.

DeArmond, R.N. *The Founding of Juneau.* Juneau: Gastineau Channel Centennial Association, 1967.

Descriptive of Fairbanks, Alaska's Golden Heart. Fairbanks: Fairbanks Commercial Club, 1916.

Mathews, Richard. *The Yukon.* New York: Holt, 1968.

Minter, Roy. *White Pass: Gateway to the Klondike.* Fairbanks: University of Alaska Press, 1987.

Moore, Bernard J. *Skagway in Days Primeval.* New York: Vantage, 1968.

Morgan, Murray. *One Man's Goldrush: A Klondike Album.* Seattle: University of Washington Press, 1967.

Paulsteiner, John. *Seward, Alaska: The Sinful Town on Resurrection Bay.* Seward: Privately Printed, 1975.

Phillips, Sr., Walter T. *Roadhouses of the Richardson Highway: The First Quarter Century.* Juneau: Alaska Historical Commission, 1984.

Raymond, Charles W. *Report on the Reconnaisance of the Yukon River.* Washington: GPO, 1871.

Satterfield, Archie. *Chilkoot Pass: The Most Famous Trail in the North.* Anchorage: Alaska Northwest Publishing, 1973.

Smith, Michael E. *Alaska's Historic Roadhouses.* Juneau: Department of Natural Resources, 1974.

United States Department of the Interior. *The Idiarod Trail (Seward-Nome Route) and Other Gold Rush Trails.* Washington: GPO, 1977.

BICYCLING

Bridge, Raymond. *The Sierra Club Guide to Outings on Wheels.* San Francisco: Sierra Club, 1979.

Coello, Dennis. *Touring on Two Wheels: The Bicycle Traveller's Handbook.* New York: Nick Lyons, 1988.

Cole, Terrence, editor. *Wheels on Ice, Bicycling in Alaska 1898-1908.* Anchorage: Alaska Northwest Publishing, 1985.

Forester, John. *Effective Cycling.* Cambridge: MIT Press, 1984.

Sloane, Eugene A. *Complete Book of All-Terrain Bicycles.* New York: Simon, 1985.

INDEX OF PLACE NAMES